Rip-Off!

The scandalous inside story of the
management consulting
money machine

by

David Craig

THE ORIGINAL BOOK COMPANY

The Original Book Company
Studio 8
8 Palace Court
London W2 4HR

E-mail originalbookco@yahoo.co.uk
Website: www.consulting-moneymachine.com

A CIP catalogue record for this book is available from the British Library

ISBN 1-872188-06-0

Printed and bound in Great Britain

A MCKINSEY CONSULTANTS' CELEBRATION SONG*

If you aim to get the best result
And maximum performance you want to see
Then you really should consult
A Management Consultancy
McKinsey management consultants are we
We take all our clients' money
We can earn many a million
Because our clients have no vision.

If Process Redesign is what you will
And you think it'll make a success of all you do
Then rely on us to send you a bill
While we redesign your processes for you.
We are from McKinsey – young, bright and flash
We take mountains of our clients' cash
We win lots of new clients rich and fine
When we go round flogging Process Redesign

If your project is in deep shit
And you see no way out of the mess you're in
Then all you need is to get a "Quick Hit"
And to score an "Early Win"
We are McKinsey's loyal troops
We promise our clients great results
"You've huge improvement opportunities", is what we say
To all our clients – provided they pay.

We've got handouts and we've got flip charts
And dazzling PowerPoint presentations
And we blow clients away
With our brilliant explanations.
We are McKinsey's little lackeys
Telling clients they're in trouble is just one of our strategies
Our language is smart and makes our clients ill-at-ease
It's what we call 'Consultantese'.

The culture at ……. is a real dead weight
But we crush resistance before it grows
We're used to organisations in a dreadful state
Because, of course, we are Pros!
We are McKinsey's real hard core
We are the ones who'll win the war
Now we're going to party and have fun because
Cheers! We've just got our bonuses from Santa Claus!

*Reportedly sung at a McKinsey Consultants' Christmas Party.

CONTENTS

INTRODUCTION

IT'S LIKE ROBBING A BANK, BUT IT'S LEGAL

There's an apocryphal story about the Nineteenth Century American outlaw, Willie Sutton. When finally caught after a long and, until then, successful career as a bank robber, he was questioned about his life. Asked by a journalist why he robbed banks, he gave the famous reply "because that's where the money is". Then when asked why he always used a gun, he answered "because charm and wit alone are usually not enough to get banks to hand over the money". If he were alive today, Willie Sutton probably wouldn't be a criminal – he would be a lawyer, a stockbroker or a management consultant. Why? Because that's where the money is. However, he wouldn't need a gun any more, because now charm and wit are enough to get people to hand over the money.

In almost twenty years working for and competing against some of the world's best and worst management consultancies, I have seen some truly great and high value consulting. I've watched as consultants galvanise organisations by injecting enthusiasm, excitement and teamwork where there was previously just passivity, cynicism and inaction. And I've seen teams of consultants achieve the seemingly impossible by turning round companies that would otherwise be heading blindly towards self destruction. But I've also seen much quite average work and far too much lying, cheating, swindling and totally scandalous and dishonest abuse of our clients' confidence and trust. Throughout this time, I've constantly been amazed and often morally outraged at how a bit of charm and wit dressed up with the appropriately fashionable management psychobabble really **are** enough to get clients to hand over millions and millions of pounds, dollars, euros or whatever of their organisation's money to their favourite management consultants.

Consultants, of course, trumpet the value of their services –

"Consultants create value for organisations through the application of knowledge, techniques and assets to improve performance"[1] and *"We help the world's leading organisations define where they want to go. And we help them get there. We create the future of business together"*.[2] However, critics cast doubt on the value consultants actually bring – *"consultants charge huge fees for translating common sense into grotesque jargon"*.[3] Critics also question the capabilities of the management teams who keep on using them. One leading businessman said that you could always tell how well or badly an organisation was run by the number of consultants it used – the first thing he did, on acquiring a company, was to throw out all the consultants and the management who employed them.

Having seen so much that has impressed, shocked and amazed me, I think it's now time to tell the story of what really can happen when management consultants get into an organisation. There are, of course, occasions when hiring a management consultancy can be the best investment management can make. But much more often, letting consultants into an organisation is equivalent to paying a pack of very hungry wolves a massive amount of money to manage the chicken coop – great for the wolves, but not so good for the chickens.

This book is a warning to anybody who has ever thought of hiring consultants or who may have to work with consultants. There is good and even great management consultancy. But there's so much money in consultancy and it's so incredibly easy to get, that the profession attracts some very very sharp people – people who may not always put their clients' interests first.

This is their story. I hope you enjoy it.

---

1   Management Consultants Association website 2005
2   Website for a leading consultancy
3   The Times 23 November 1996

CHAPTER 1

THE MONEY MACHINE

SOME FACTS AND FIGURES

The worldwide Management Consultancy Industry is estimated to be worth around £60 billion ($100bn) a year[1] – in Britain alone, companies and the government pay over £150 million every week for management consulting services, that is more than £30 million every single working day.

Management consultants can charge out their time for anything from £7,000 per week for the cheapest to over £25,000 a week for an experienced specialist or director. That's from between £300,000 to over a million pounds a year per person.

Management consultancy employs probably around half a million people worldwide and over thirty thousand in Britain. These thousands and thousands of management consultants are paid significantly more than most other members of our society. A junior consultant with little to no working experience will typically earn at least £30,000 a year, a project manager like myself around £150,000 a year, whilst most leaders in management consultancies are multi-millionaires.

Some organisations' largesse towards their management consultants is legendary. They seem to spend millions and millions on management consultants, year in year out – for example, in the U.S., AT&T spent a reported $500 million on consultants over just five years, of which one management consultancy alone took $127 million[2] and in Britain the National Health Service spent a massive £200 million on management consultants in just one year – that's probably enough money to pay for several thousand extra doctors and nurses.[3] And famously Enron, the world's largest bankruptcy, was reported as giving Andersens $52 million in 2000 for auditing and consulting fees[4] and also tens of millions of dollars to the world's leading management consultancy, McKinsey, for more than twenty separate projects over an eighteen year period.[5] Moreover, the chief executive of Enron, Jeffery Skilling, was a former McKinsey partner. Yet, in spite of all its expensive accountancy and consultancy, Enron disappeared into thin air taking billions of dollars of investors' and employees' money with it.

Whether the economy goes up or down, or just gently stagnates, the Management Consultancy Industry has usually kept on growing at about twenty percent a year to the delight and profit of those employed in it. As the Chief Executive Officer of one of the world's largest consultancies enthusiastically proclaimed, when we hit the recession of 2001 and 2002 and more than a million people were quickly thrown out of work – *our organisation does well in times when cost reduction is a priority for our clients. Good companies use tough economic times to renew their commitment to be internally efficient.* [6]

HOW I EARNED £10,000 A WEEK (WITHOUT BREAKING THE LAW)

What I always found most astonishing with management consultancy was the incredible amounts of money our clients would pay us. We could take somebody straight off the street, teach them a few simple tricks in a couple of hours and easily charge them out to our clients for more than £7,000 per week. If a new consultant had any kind of reasonable education, yet no business or working experience whatsoever, they'd fetch at least £8,000 per week. And if they had also worked for a few years in what we called 'a proper job' before becoming a consultant, anywhere from £10,000 to £25,000 per week was normal. That means if you had no experience and no knowledge, we could earn £300,000 a year for your services. If you actually did have a bit of useful stuff on your curriculum vitae, you could be sold for half a million to a million pounds a year.

Yet why is it that clients will happily pay such huge sums of money each week for a management consultant's services? What particular qualities or talents do consultants possess, which make their clients willing to fork out up to half a million pounds a year or more for their assistance? What skills or genius do they have? Why are many of the huge multinationals like Xerox and Shell and Ford and General Motors and Unilever and Roche and Mobil and GSK and AstraZeneca and Dupont and BT and ABN Amro and France Telecom and Deutsche Post and major hospitals and leading government departments in countries all over the world apparently unable to find the skills they need amongst their many hundreds of thousands of employees – each one of whom is often more qualified than the consultants they use and paid enormously less per year than each of their consultants cost for just a few weeks' work?

Are all consultants brilliant? – Unfortunately not. Are they all superb communicators? – If only. Do they all have an arm's length of qualifications from the world's greatest centres of learning? – Not by a long shot. Some consultants are, of course, highly qualified and very talented, but very many are not. I, for example, have a literature degree from a backward university, where anything more modern than the nineteenth century was considered unacceptably avant-garde. My specialties were novels and post-romantic poetry. The only proper job I have ever held in my life was working as an unskilled labourer on building sites during my university summer vacations. I know very little. I am impractical – I cannot change the oil in a car nor put up wallpaper, never mind provide brilliant strategic insights for my long-suffering but generous clients. Yet, in spite of all my shortcomings, not only can I earn over half a million pounds a year for my employer as a management consultant, I can also sell multi-million pound or dollar or euro consulting projects to clients in almost any activity sector in almost any country in the world, provided they just let me and my team through the door.

How is this possible? How can my bosses become extraordinarily rich on the back of my inexpert contribution to the well-being of their clients? Well, that's the subject of this book – to explain the mysterious alchemy that permits a very base material like many of my colleagues and myself to be turned into continuous streams of gold for our very wealthy owners.

Before we launch into some real life stories, which will probably get most of the cited organisations and their directors reaching for their lawyers, it may be interesting to examine the more than very healthy economics of the Management Consulting Money Machine.

We'll look at two things:

1. Fees, glorious fees

How the huge fees they charge, enable top managers in management consultancies to become incredibly rich – certainly much richer than their clients could ever dream of becoming

2. The Seven Deadly Scams

Some of the tricks and scams they use to extract further money from their clients to increase their wealth even more

1. FEES, GLORIOUS FEES

First – fees. Let's take a typical organisation structure in a typical consultancy.

For each Partner, or Director or Vice President or whatever they are called, there are on average fourteen consultants.[7] These would probably consist of about two to three project managers and about ten to twelve consultants. Let's look at how the money comes in.

(Please be patient while I crunch a few numbers.)

We'll assume that there are two project managers. To err on the side of caution, we'll be conservative and say that each of the managers is only billing clients for thirty-three weeks a year at £15,000 per week. So each is only bringing in about £500,000 a year giving a total billing of a million pounds a year. Also we'll work on the basis that each of the twelve consultants is likewise only billed out to clients for thirty-three weeks a year at £10,000 per week generating a healthy £330,000 per year each. This gives a total annual income for the consultants of £3,960,000. So, the area controlled by each partner (or vice president in American consultancies) probably earns just under five million pounds per year in fees. And this does not include any time the partners choose to charge to their clients.

Of course, it's not all pure profit. There are costs to be deducted. Let's look at those now. We'll start with salaries for the troops. For simplicity's sake, we'll assume that each consultant earns £50,000 per year and each manager £200,000 per year. First thing you'll notice is that the salaries of around £1,000,000 don't make that much of a dent in the consultancy's earnings – the area controlled by each partner is still taking in nearly four million pounds a year in profits:

There are also some other costs – some office space, a few secretaries, a pile of computers, some lawyers' fees for frightening off disgruntled former clients and of course a couple of bean-counters to add up all the cash pouring in. The Management Consultants Association reported that there were about three support staff for each consultancy director[7] – their salaries would probably cost less than £100,000 per year. So there's probably about three hundred thousand pounds at most in office space, equipment and indirect staff costs. Thus, after all salaries and costs are deducted from fees, each partner or vice president is earning well over three million pounds a year for the consultancy. And as the partners or vice presidents often *are* the consultancy, they're earning comfortably over three million pounds a year for themselves.

Five to ten years as a partner in a management consultancy pulling that kind of loot is not the worst way to spend one's working life. Directors of consultancies are very, very rich people. This is perhaps one reason why, after assignments are over, we frequently get client employees discreetly contacting us to see if we might be interested in giving them a job – having seen the amount of their employers' money being hoovered up by us consultants, they realise they've been in the wrong game for most of their lives.

For much of my consultancy career I was involved in and frequently responsible for selling large consultancy projects. When we calculated the likely price for projects, we in Sales were often concerned whether our potential clients would accept the embarrassingly inflated amounts we proposed to charge them. However, I was always under strict instructions "never to go below a 75% margin" – that means, we had to sell each consultant's time at a minimum of four times their salary. If a consultant earned say £50,000 a year, I would have to sell their time for a minimum of £200,000 per year and more often for around £300,000 per year. And what was most extraordinary was that for the almost twenty years I worked selling consulting, we and all our many competitors could find sufficient clients willing to pay these fantastic prices. So while many businesses make five, ten or even twenty percent profit margins at best, we were targeting a minimum of three hundred percent for our consultancy – a rather striking and enormous difference from the margins any of our clients would ever make – even after we had been in to supposedly "transform their organisations" and achieve "major improvements in their performance".

2. THE SEVEN DEADLY SCAMS

Unfortunately, consultancy bosses are not only very, very rich, they also seem to have an insatiable appetite for money and are always looking for new, ingenious ways to squeeze more out of their unsuspecting clients to put into their own infinitely deep pockets.

Below are just seven of the tricks I've seen. No doubt there are very many more I haven't yet stumbled upon.

SCAM 1 – TRAVEL REBATES

Although I've observed this scam for about twenty years, it only started to surface publicly towards the end of 2003. In December 2003, one huge international accountancy/consultancy agreed to pay a former client $54.5 million as compensation, when it and two competitors were sued for *"unjustly enriching themselves at the expense of their clients The lawsuit was that for a decade the three firms worked with outside suppliers such as airline firms and travel agencies to obtain rebates of up to 40% on airfare and other costs that were not passed along to clients".*[8]

Moreover, at about the same time the Wall Street Journal wrote that the U.S. Justice Department was accusing a number of accountancies and management consultancies of *"fraudulently padding the travel-related expenses they billed to clients by hundreds of millions of dollars".* The Justice Department had started an investigation *"focusing on whether they have submitted false claims to the Government because they have failed to credit Government contracts with amounts they have received as rebates from travel providers"* [9]

The way this scam works is simple but effective and immensely profitable:

> **Step 1** The consultancy sets up a deal with a travel agent and the main airlines for an end-of-year rebate. The size of this rebate will depend on the amount spent on travel and accommodation during the year. All consultants are instructed to use this particular travel agency and the chosen airline whenever possible.

> **Step 2** The consultancy assures each client that all

consultants will always use the cheapest form of transport possible when working on the client's assignment.

Step 3 The consultancy allows its staff to travel by first class train, often on business class on planes and to stay in the kind of hotels most normal people will never experience, thus spending lots of the client's money on travel.

Step 4 The consultancy invoices the client for the full travel and accommodation costs, which the client contractually must pay.

Step 5 At the end of the year, the consultancy receives a large rebate from the travel agency and the airlines. *None* of this rebate is ever passed back to the clients who have paid for all the travel and accommodation in the first place.

Step 6 The consultancy's bosses share out this little windfall as an extra add-on to their already generous end of year bonuses.

Embarrassingly for some of the defendants, documents already provided to the court show that there were *"complaints by some partners that the practice was unethical"* [10] and in an e-mail, the head of the ethics department *"described the firm's practices as 'a bit greedy'".* [11]

Using a most curious form of logic, the accused admitted to the allegations, but claimed that they had done nothing wrong when cheating their clients, *"The defendants have acknowledged retaining rebates on various travel expenses, for which they had billed clients at their pre-rebate amounts. However, they deny that their conduct was fraudulent, saying that the proceeds offset amounts that would otherwise have been billed to clients. They say they have discontinued this practice."* [8]

However, I worked for one of the companies involved and they have certainly not *"discontinued this practice"*. I have a recent memo telling us to use specific airlines and travel agencies because of the *"considerable"* end-of-year rebates we received. Moreover, as a colleague wrote in an e-mail *"Here's how we do it every time. We state in our contract that we will bill for 'actual' expenses. Then we bill them for your air travel expense. Then we get a kickback on your air ticket. But we don't give the client back the kick-back."*[12]

By the way, the reason why the firm decided to refund $54.5 million to its client had, it claimed, absolutely nothing to do with it being caught red-handed. It was, the consultancy maintained in the court records, *"to permit the operation of ......'s business without further expensive litigation and the distraction and diversion of ....'s personnel with respect to the matters in this action"*.[10]

SCAM 2 – PARTNER BILLING

Most consultancies have a rule that partners must bill some of, or even all of, their time to clients. Many of the partners, with whom I worked, would bill one day a week to each of their projects. Yet often they only actually worked on them one day every two or three months – if at all. So clients end up paying through the nose for consultancy bosses' time in spite of the fact that much of this time may be spent prospecting for new business and/or playing golf on the world's most fashionable courses and very little indeed on the day-to-day running of their lucrative projects. I remember a vice president of one of the largest consultancies telling me of a meeting he had with one of France's most senior business figures. They ended up discussing the CEO of our consultancy; let's call him Tom. The senior business figure laughed when told that Tom was actually our CEO and said "but he can't be – he always plays golf on Mondays". Another of our top directors, Richard, a man on the board of a company employing tens of thousands of employees, was famous for continually boasting to his subordinates about the amount of time he spent getting special services in some of the most exclusive brothels in the world. As he used to say, when explaining why he made such frequent visits to expensive whorehouses, *"good sex means inflicting pain and you wouldn't want to do that to someone you love"*.

So you find that consultancy partners or directors divide their time up amongst their various clients and allocate a certain number of days each month to each client – even when this time is actually not spent working for that client and even if it is, in fact, spent selling to the next bunch of clients, on the golf course or even in a high class brothel. As each partner is probably charging his or her time at up to £25,000 per week, here's at least another one million pounds per year a partner can earn – *in addition* to the more than three million pounds or so pure profit, which the consultants and managers working under the partner are bringing in.

SCAM 3 – CHARGING AND EXPENSING OVERHEAD

Charging for overhead

This next scam may seem quite small, but it can be very rewarding. Normally clients expect the consultancies' extraordinary fees to cover the costs of the management consultancies' own offices and staff. However, in one major consultancy an extra 10% was automatically added to consultancy fees to cover overhead costs. So, if an ordinary consultant was being charged out at say £300,000 a year, clients would also be billed for another £30,000 to pay for administrative overhead. Theoretically, that's enough to pay for at least one full time administrative employee to support each consultant. Yet, according to data from the Management Consultants Association, there is on average one support employee for every four to five consultants.[7] By adding this extra 10%, if you had one to two hundred consultants working from an office, you were probably also charging clients enough money to pay for an extra one to two hundred support staff. But most of these support staff, for which clients were being charged, did not exist. This meant extra profits for the consultancy directors and partners.

To give an example I experienced – the London office of a major international consultancy with about three hundred consultants had about forty to fifty administrative support staff – secretaries, receptionists, human resources, bean counters, marketing support, resource managers, trainers, information centre researchers and document production. Yet, with the 10% add-on, our clients were being charged for the equivalent of about three hundred administrative staff – hence the salaries of up to two hundred and fifty support staff were not being spent, as the staff simply did not exist. Thus this money could be dedicated to the noble cause of further enriching the consultancy directors.

Expensing overhead

However, even though they already charge extra for overhead, to squeeze even more money out of their ingenuous clients, some consultancies have instructed office staff to keep timesheets, where they try to book as much of their time as possible to projects so that it is charged to clients as extra expenses over and above the £30,000 per year already earned by adding the extra 10% to consultant fees. One of the world's largest consultancies even instructed its staff to keep logs of all telephone calls made from the office so that these could also be charged to clients. So clients find themselves paying for administration costs that include photocopying, faxes, stationery, secretaries' time and all sorts of other small but significant items – all making the clients poorer and the consultancy bosses just that delightful little bit richer.

In consultancy, we call this 'double dipping' – being able to charge twice for one thing – very much a case of both having your cake and eating it. Although perhaps this is 'triple dipping' – the margins on consultant fees are already quite sufficient to cover overhead costs, then you charge an extra 10% over and above consultant fees to pay for the same overhead costs and then you have the gall to also expense as much overhead as possible – all in all, a very profitable little process.

SCAM 4 – RELOCATING STAFF

Many management consultancies are international. One advantage of this is that they can move staff to where the business is. For example, if there is a temporary downturn in the U.S.A. and growth in Europe or the Far East, these consultancies can shift experienced staff from the U.S.A. to countries where there is more work. Conversely, if European business dips, they can fly out an army of eager staff to projects in the States. Most consultants would rather spend a few well-paid months on another continent than be fired every time there's a downturn in activity, so there's normally no lack of volunteers for temporary relocation.

Now you might think that consultancies would absorb the costs of relocating their staff. After all, being able to move staff to where they have projects, suits the interests of the management consultancies. Clients would be best served if consultancies had sufficient numbers of experienced staff based locally. After all, why should a client have to pay intercontinental and international flights, relocation costs, school fees, accommodation etc for consultants and their families, just because the consultancy has not been able to recruit and train someone locally to do the job?

To illustrate this, I'll take a real life example from a £2.3 million project I helped sell in Britain to a regional health authority (part of the British National Health Service) for a well-known firm of international management consultants. The practices employed by this particular consultancy were so inventive that, unusually, the project was later subject to a number of official investigations and some quite colourful articles in the press. I say 'unusually' because, in my experience, very few consultancy cock-ups ever see the light of publicity. After all, any management consultancy project is normally a joint effort between the consultants and the organisation's top management who decided to hire them. If the whole thing goes dramatically and impressively belly-up, there are not many management teams who want the world to know that they have made a dreadful and more than expensive mess. Therefore consultancy screw-ups are typically swept quickly and efficiently under the carpet and life goes on. Management consultancies know this and exploit it shamelessly.

At the time, this particular consultancy, which was based in the U.S., was just building up its British operations. We were growing more rapidly than we could hire new people and so when the project was sold to the health authority, there were not enough U.K. based consultants available to staff this assignment. So two to three Americans were put onto the team. The Americans did not have any special skills that could not be found in the U.K. Nor was their background or experience particularly relevant to the assignment – in fact, if my memory serves me correctly, none of them had ever worked on this kind of project before. The consultancy simply had not recruited sufficient U.K. staff at that point, and there was insufficient work for all the American staff in the U.S.

Nevertheless, the health authority paid through the nose for these consultants, using money that might have been better spent looking after patients. First there was the equivalent of £8,000 per week fees for each consultant. Then there was about £300 per week for each consultant's hotel costs. And finally, at least another £50 per day for each consultant's meals, plus a bit more for laundry, dry cleaning, phone bills and entertainment.

Well – almost finally – we nearly forgot the consultants' families. They had no desire to live in the miserable, damp, unfashionable provincial town, where the assignment was based. They wanted to live in London – and not only in London, but in the better parts of London. So there were a few other not inconsiderable items to which the regional health authority made a generous financial contribution. For example, there was up to £200 per week for each consultant to travel to London every weekend to see their families. There was a bucket of money paid out per week for each family's comfortable flat – one in Kensington and the other in Hampstead. A few hundred pounds a week for each family's food and entertainment. The fees for the children's private schools. The taxis used when the bored wives went shopping and, of course, the shopping trips themselves. There were the many afternoon teas taken by the bored wives at the Ritz and the Savoy and the occasional £70 taxi fare when the wives decided it was less troublesome to make a taxi wait than go to the effort of finding another when they had finished shopping or drinking tea. Nevertheless, the client seemed to swallow all this abuse with good grace. It was only when the project manager hired a private plane to return from holiday to attend a meeting, that the auditors finally got wind of the way this particular management consultancy was abusing its client's trust and the press started poking around.

All in all, the regional health authority ended up paying a couple of thousand pounds a week extra for each of these American consultants, purely because the management consultancy did not have enough people available in the U.K. at that time. When the press began to get a little too nosy, our management tried numerous ways of avoiding adverse publicity. At the time, we had just been acquired by a large computer services company and changed our name. When the bad press started to appear, our CEO issued an internal memo that contained the immortal lines:[13]

"You will have noticed in the press recently that A…….. B…….. Consultants (our previous name) has once again been mentioned in connection with the D… Regional Health Authority. The connection between A…..B…….. Consultants (our previous name) and C……. Consulting (our new name) has now been made despite our efforts – successful until very recently – to avoid this"

The gentleman had clearly been hoping that the change of name would enable the previous nasty consultancy to miraculously disappear for ever and for us to re-emerge whiter than white under our wonderful new name. The memo also mentioned and tried to describe as normal business practice things like:

> *"The hire of a private plane"*
> *"Provision of expensive accommodation for executives and their wives"*
> *"Lavish entertainment with fine wines"*

It also, with an unusual degree of honesty, admitted that although around £40 million in financial benefits were promised to this client, little was achieved during the project and once the project was completed *"it is probable that no further benefits emerged"*.

The magazine, Health Service Journal, was not complementary about our contribution to the health of the British taxpayer and also hinted at financial profligacy with money that should have been spent on patients:

"The crisis came to a head last September when the District General Managers (DGMs) were asked to topslice £4.3 million from their budgets for the rest of the year to pay for the reorganisation of regional supplies. Included in the £4.3 million cost, say DGMs, was a bill of £2.3 million from A........ B........ Consultants to help manage the reorganisation, which Regional Health Authority (RHA) officials first claimed would save the region £40 million over the next four years. The RHA has consistently denied A........ B........ Consultants' cost was £2.3 million, but has refused to say what the figure is. The way the A........ B........ Consultants contract was awarded is at the heart of what one DGM describes as a 'financial fiasco'. The claim is that the RHA exercised a lack of financial and management control – a claim backed by the Carver report."[14]

SCAM 5 – FUNDING OVERSEAS EXPANSION

The relocating staff scam is very useful for ensuring that you can both keep your consultants fully occupied even as the workload in different countries changes and make clients pay for the seriously expensive business of you moving your aggressive young consultants around the world.

However, there is a more sophisticated version of this scam, which I've seen a few consultancies successfully perpetrate – getting clients to fully fund the normally very expensive and risky activity of the consultancies' overseas expansion. Most of the cases, I have seen, have been with American consultancies moving into the Asian and European markets.

It goes like this. A management consultancy decides to expand abroad and to set up an office in a country where it doesn't already have an operation. Now it has two choices. Any normal business would have to accept the risk and cost of establishing itself – renting offices and hiring staff, consultants and salesmen and then trying to attack the market. But this is an expensive and dangerous option. After all, what do you do if you don't sell any work in that new market for a while? You'll have huge costs and no income. And consultancy bosses are pretty allergic to giving away any of their cash to anybody apart from themselves.

Fortunately, there is a much cheaper and risk-free way of expanding your management consultancy business to another country. The cheaper way is, of course, to get a client to pay for it. You use some work you've done for a client in one of the countries where you already do business to convince that client, who also has an operation in the country into which you wish to expand, to buy a project from you in your targeted new market. Then, claiming that you want to give the client only consultants already experienced with their particular industry sector and organisation, you staff the project entirely with consultants from your existing operation. You use your presence in the new country to start recruiting locally and to set up a local office. Gradually, you bring your new local consultants on to your project to work alongside your experienced imported consultants and thus the client pays you handsomely for them while you train them. When the first project is completed, you have local trained staff, an office and, if the project has gone well, a positive client reference in that country. So the client ends up paying for you to establish yourself risk-free in that country, to train your staff and to give you that critical first reference you need to sell more consulting to other clients. There are few, if any, other businesses where the normally problematic and costly activity of overseas expansion can be accomplished in such a smooth and secure way.

I saw this conducted most successfully when an American consultancy wanted to break into the Dutch market. At that time Holland was one of the most profitable consulting markets in Europe and the consultancy directors desperately wanted their share of the cake. They already had a project going for a subsidiary of a leading Dutch bank in Britain and used the success of that project to convince the bank to bring the consultancy in to do a major project in their operation in Holland. Claiming they wished to use consultants already familiar with that bank, they staffed the project in Holland almost entirely from their British office. Anyway, although the client didn't know it, at that time we didn't actually have any Dutch consultants we could have used. Some of the consultants on the team did have financial services experience, but many did not. We worked with the client in Holland for over a year which gave us plenty of time to recruit locally, to train up the new consultants at the bank's expense, to repatriate the British consultants and to build the base to sell to more local clients in Holland. Within three years our Dutch operation was our most profitable and it had essentially been set up at no real cost and with absolutely no business risk, thanks to the generosity of one of Holland's leading banks.

SCAM 6 – FLAT RATE EXPENSES

Yet another small but not wholly insignificant little trick. When a project is sold, a management consultancy will often agree with the client that expenses will be around, for example, 10% of fees. So, for every £10,000 paid weekly for each consultant, the consultancy will invoice the client for another £1,000 in expenses. The deal is that at the end of the project there will be a reconciliation between the 10% paid by the client and the actual expenses incurred and the client will be charged more if the expenses exceed the 10% or reimbursed for any difference if they are less than the estimated 10%.

Now, of course, the 10% (or whatever figure is chosen) is usually a huge overestimate as, in spite of some of the horror stories mentioned above, most consultants do not manage to spend £1,000 per week on travel, accommodation, food, booze and entertainment. So this leaves the consultancy two options:

1. Either it can come clean at the end of the project and reimburse the client for the money invoiced, collected but not spent, having gained the interest on this money for many months in the meantime.

2. Or it can be slightly more creative. It can take a bunch of expenses from projects that have got into trouble either because their clients may be less generous with expenses or because more manweeks were used and more expenses generated than expected. It can then pass these over and shove them on to a project where the consultancy has got the client to agree a comfortable level of expenses or where the client is less than assiduous in auditing the expenses charged by the consultancy.

Thus an unsuspecting client can end up covering losses the consultancy has made on other projects for other clients. Very generous indeed of one client to subsidise others.

I remember vividly one project for one of the world's leading manufacturers of military aircraft, missile systems and satellites. Here we had estimated, I think, 12% expenses. So each month the client was paying us our full fees plus this extra 12% to cover our expected level of expenses. But I believe we were actually only running at about 7%. The vice president running the account informed the rest of the consultancy that he had room to soak up expenses both from other projects and from our head office, rather than paying lots of money back to the client. Although I was merely a humble consultant on another project, we had some great dinners at luxurious restaurants and some other more catholic social pleasures at that client's expense.

Very occasionally, clients would audit our expenses and if they found some real horrors, we'd just say there had been an administrative error and refund the minimum necessary to keep the client happy.

SCAM 7 – OVERCHARGING

An old favourite here and one without which any list of management consultancy scams would be incomplete.

Most consultancies have different weekly billing rates depending on the seniority or experience of the consultant. For example, a simple consultant may only cost a mere £7,000 or so a week, a project manager £10,000 to £12,000 and a partner or vice president £15,000 to £25,000 a week.

On the grounds that some consultants might be promoted during a project, the consultancy decides to charge out their services at one level above their actual level for the whole period of the project. During discussions around pricing projects, I've often heard vice presidents and partners saying about an ordinary consultant *"he/she will really be working at a senior consultant level, so we ought to charge them at senior consultant prices"*. However, while they are eager to have clients pay higher fees for that consultant, they too often forget to pay the hard-working consultant at the level for which they are charging them out. It is only well into or even at the end of the assignment that the consultant gets the promotion that the client has being paying for during the preceding six to twelve months.

CONCLUSION

The above are just a few of the little ruses I have observed during my consultancy career. No doubt any reader, who has worked for or come across management consultants, will know of many others – for nobody is as inventive as a management consultancy boss, when thinking of new ways to acquire more loot for himself or herself.

This gives a first flavour of how the money flows in to management consultancies. Perhaps these huge fees and other ways of extracting money from clients would be acceptable if management consultants always delivered enormous value to their clients. Sometimes, of course, they do. But too often consultants are inadequately qualified, their work is of questionable quality and the way they deal with executive teams starts to look more like self-interested manipulation than providing morally defensible business advice.

Now I propose to lead you through the almost twenty years I've spent in all types of consultancy working for almost all types of clients (many, in fact most, of them household names) to show how the whole business sometimes operates and to give some idea of what our clients often get and more importantly don't get for their money. We're going to start where I began my consulting career on projects for some of the most brutal and least capable of the world's management consultancies. Then we'll move on up, as I did, to running major performance improvement programmes for the world's greatest organisations for some of the world's leading consultancies. And finally we'll see how greed, the pressure to sell 'warm bodies', self-interest, sexual promiscuity and the easy availability of huge amounts of money will ultimately corrupt most management consultants, however honourable their intentions may or may not have been when they first entered the Management Consulting Money Machine.

---

1 Management Consultants Association report 2004
2 The Times 6 August 2002
3 Masters of the Universe ITV 1999
4 Business Week Online 28 January 2002
5 Business Week Online 8 July 2002
6 Memorandum to all staff 30 May 2001
7 Management Consultants Association annual report 2003/4
8 Washington Post 27 September 2003
9 Wall Street Journal 26 September 2003
10 TSCPA and Accounting Web 8 March 2004
11 Fraud Updates 30 September 2003 www.trinity.edu
12 E-mail 19 September 2003
13 Confidential memo to all staff 4 May 1993
14 The Health Service Journal (for date: contact author)

CHAPTER 2

THE UNSUBTLE ART
OF COST-CUTTING

WHY THERE'S ALWAYS THIRTY PERCENT OPPORTUNITY FOR IMPROVEMENT

"Seven percent! Seven goddam f........g percent," the American was shaking in fury. He stubbed out one cigarette and lit another. The ashtray was already overflowing with cigarette butts and the desk was littered with ash. "Boy," he pointed threateningly at me as I stood trembling before him, "you goddam stoopid or some'in'. Ah told you thirty f.....g percent! Right? Got that you f..kwit!"

He had another fit of raucous coughing that wracked his whole body. He was probably only about forty-seven or forty-eight years old, but looked as if he was at least sixty. He tried to get control of himself. I looked away as he spat a significant quantity of bodily fluids into a handkerchief, which was a kind of indeterminate greyish brown. He put the handkerchief on the desk in front of him ready for the next serving of yuck produced by his emphysema-ridden body. "Look, boy," his voice became calmer but more threatening, "ah told you thirty motherf.....g percent lost time! Right?"

I nodded meekly – tired, scared and beaten. Tired because it was already three thirty in the morning and I had been working non-stop since eight o'clock the previous morning. Scared – because I didn't want to get fired like so many others who had joined the consultancy at about the same time as I did. Beaten – because I knew I was about to go back to my hotel room and falsify the results of the previous day's studies so that we could more easily sell a productivity improvement project to the client for whom we had just started working. And so, although I had always thought of myself as a reasonably honest person, I found myself distorting data to protect myself. Unfortunately, this would have serious consequences for the employees with whom I had just spent the previous day under the pretence that I was there to help them "work smarter, not harder".

"Now you get the f… outa here," my project manager yelled, "fix this, find the thirty f…..g percent or your ass is grass and ah'm gonna be the f…..g lawn-mower!" Another bout of hawking, coughing and rasping followed. Weakly I turned and headed back down the corridor to my hotel room. "Ah already have one asshole," my boss called out after me, "ah don't need me another."

I'm embarrassed to admit that I then spent the next two hours changing the write-up, so that my study proved conclusively that the department I had been analysing had about thirty two percent too many people. My American project manager would take these results and similar output from the rest of the team to the client's local management group in two days' time. The presentation he would make would be hard and brutal. He would claim that throughout all the areas of the factory, where we had worked, there was on average about thirty percent 'lost time'. This meant that the place could run quite comfortably with about a third less people. The management team then had two choices. Either they could buy a project from us and we would help them to identify who should be fired and ensure an increase in productivity from the remaining usually terrified survivors of the cull. Or they could decide not to use our help to reduce their staff numbers, in which case the American would threaten that he had no option but to report his team's findings to the company's directors and they could decide whether to accept local management's inaction. Usually local management teams bought the project.

Then, the following Monday, we would send in a so-called 'results delivery team' and another 'POPs' (People Off the Payroll) project would begin.

I've worked for a broad range of management consultancies for almost a hundred clients across the world and we and our competitors have found many new and fashionably sophisticated ways of expressing and packaging what we do – productivity improvement, profit improvement, activity based management, lean manufacturing, business process reengineering, enhancing shareholder value, strategic realignment, rightsizing, benchmarking, supply chain optimisation, speed to value, business transformation, overhead value improvement, value engineering, post merger integration, achieving synergies, transformational outsourcing and so on. But all too often, when management consultants enter an organisation, millions of pounds and dollars and euros in fees flow effortlessly into the consultants' pockets and a significant percent of the staff soon find that their services are no longer required and get 'POPped'.

This link between consultants' well-being and people losing their jobs was made delightfully clear when a senior executive of the world's leading management consultancy, McKinsey, said during a television interview explaining how McKinsey worked, *"usually when a consulting firm is known to be coming into a company; let's say McKinsey, it is announced that they are coming in to do a study, there is considerable concern and alarm amongst the people in the company because they expect that probably one of the results will be that people will lose their jobs, because very often that is what is needed."*[1] Another major name in management consulting revealed a similar link between people losing their livelihoods and the prosperity of management consultancy, when it published an article entitled, *"Bring on the recession"* in a consultancy trade journal.[2] A McKinsey consultant remarked in a TV interview when asked about how he felt knowing people would lose their jobs as a result of his work, *"you don't think too much about individuals."* While another McKinsey consultant enthused in a promotional video, *"to be lean is* to *be liberated*".[1] And a manager who had just business-process-reengineered an organisation, reducing staff from 36,000 employees to only 16,000, breezily explained on the same programme that *"we were just getting rid of the rubbish"*.[1]

The first consultancy I ever worked for, an American consultancy, is a legend throughout the management consultancy industry and the guiding father for many consultancies that are in existence today. Some clients used to call us 'The Cowboys' because of our American style and our low level of professionalism. Others called us 'The Butchers' because that best describes the sophistication of our approach and the results of the work we did. Years later, as I worked for other consultancies, I found out that whenever you tried getting into an organisation and you heard that The Butchers had been there within the last five to ten years, you knew it would be really tough to sell in. Generally, people were so scarred by the ghastly experience of working with The Butchers, that it took years before they would trust another management consultant again. The Butchers went through organisations a bit like the Black Death, leaving devastation and misery in their wake – and of course, significantly less people than there had been before their arrival.

At that time, The Butchers seemed to have a very simple business model. They specialized in cost reduction – and those costs were usually people. The Butchers would employ well-known public figures to introduce them to potential clients – when I worked for them many years ago, it was said that in the U.S. a former president and the American Ambassador to the United Nations were both on The Butchers' payroll. While in Britain they used people like the Director of the C.B.I. (Confederation of British Industry) one of the most influential business organisations in the country. In France and Germany and South America and everywhere else they worked, they would likewise pay generous fees to leading figures for introductions which led to sold projects.

Like many management consultancies, The Butchers carried out their work in two main phases. There was a first phase where they studied a client's operation to assess what performance improvements they could make. They would then use their presence at the client's site(s) during this first phase to convince management to hire them for a second phase – a much bigger project to implement the performance improvements that they had ostensibly identified in the first phase. Most management consultancies charge out the first phase – the study – at a reduced price just to try and get through the door at a potential client in the hope that, once they are through the door and are deeply ensconced in the client's organisation, they will find sufficient problems to justify the client paying millions to keep them around to sort out the mess, they claim to have found. They then try to sell a second project, typically up to ten times the size of the original study and typically at twice the cost per manweek of the first discounted study – the 'door opener'. In my later years in consultancy, we would generally do first phases for one hundred to two hundred thousand euros or pounds or dollars with the goal of selling follow-on implementation projects of anywhere between one million to five million pounds, euros or dollars – though we did sometimes manage to sell a few ten and twenty million pound, euro and dollar projects as well.

But The Butchers had an even more aggressive business approach – they were so confident of being able to sell a major consulting project, that they gave away the first study phase, what they called the 'Analysis', free! In the 'Analysis' they would send in a team of six to ten consultants to review the client's operations and identify opportunities for improving results. As The Butchers were paying for the study themselves, they wanted to keep it as short as possible – two weeks. Other consultancies, which actually charge money for the first phase of work, usually take longer – one to two months is fairly common. So you could say that The Butchers staff had to achieve in about two weeks the same amount of work and sales activity that most other consultancies manage in about eight weeks. On a Butchers Analysis fifteen-hour working days were the norm, not the exception. Sometimes, we didn't even have time to go to bed at all. You could say that their staff worked like slaves, but I have the feeling that even slaves don't work that hard.

On a Butchers Analysis the consultants followed a well-practiced and well-documented process. There was no room for inventiveness or individualism. The Butchers needed results quickly. At The Butchers, consultants did things by the book or else they were fired.

The Butchers consultants would:

1. Go to each department of a client's operation and understand what activities took place in that department.

2. Measure how many seconds, minutes or hours it took to complete each activity.

3. Estimate how much of this time was wasted due to inefficiency – what they called 'lost time'.

4. See how many times a day each activity was done.

5. Multiply the number of times each activity was done by the time needed to do it efficiently – that is, by removing the 'lost time'.

6. Use this to calculate how many manhours were actually needed in each department.

7. Compare the number of people required if the department was run without 'lost time' with the number of staff actually employed.

8. Make recommendations about what percent of staff should be fired.

9. Offer the client an expensive project to implement the new management controls, which would allow the place to function more efficiently and thus with significantly less bodies.

For reasons described in the first lines of this chapter, the percent productivity improvement, which the terrorised young consultants identified during the 'Analysis', was usually between 25% and 35%. This meant that The Butchers would claim that they could help the client fire between one in four and one in three client employees. Then The Butchers would sell a project to the client, which promised to strengthen management control, reduce the lost time, improve efficiency and enable the client to reduce their staff costs.

Not exactly a sophisticated way of providing business advice. However, there may be occasions where this method could be defensible because there are some organisations that need this type of service. So, provided The Butchers behaved ethically, one could say they had a valid product offering. But The Butchers were, in my experience, anything but ethical. The Butchers were, it seemed to me, just a brutal but effective money-making machine for a few fabulously rich individuals in America who controlled the company.

LIES, LIES AND EVEN MORE LIES

The Butchers had, in my experience with them, four main ways in which they perverted what they did to ensure they sold projects and made their directors fantastically wealthy at the expense of the clients they worked for and the thousands of client staff, whose lives they devastated.

1. Lying on the Analysis

2. Managing by fear and greed

3. Front-loading the project

4. Only one solution

1. LYING ON THE ANALYSIS

When we did an Analysis for The Butchers, we were instructed that we had to find around thirty percent lost time in every area. There were no exceptions! Each day you would do your studies and each night you would write them up for presentation to the client's management. If you didn't find thirty percent lost time in your studies, the Lead Analyst didn't accept them. If the Lead Analyst didn't accept them, you didn't get to sleep. All studies had to be fully written up before you could start the next day's work. Each time you went to review your work with the Lead Analyst, you were subjected to streams of abuse, blasphemy and humiliation if you had not identified that seemingly magical thirty percent. By three or four o'clock in the morning, you would usually see exhausted consultants falsifying their results just to get a few hours sleep before the next day's work. The scene described at the beginning of this chapter was, as far as I could see, the norm at The Butchers, **not** the exception. I worked mostly on Analyses at The Butchers and time and again, I saw consultants ordered to lie about their results, so that the Lead Analyst could sell the big follow-on project. In factories, administrations, supermarket chains, banks amongst others – the Butchers approach was always the same – conduct the studies, identify about thirty percent lost time (even if it wasn't really there) and then bully the client into buying a project to get rid of the lost time and usually a large number of people.

I remember one new consultant, worried about faking his data, asking the Lead Analyst what would happen if the people in the department he had studied got to see his results and found out he had lied. The Lead Analyst's answer was about as unambiguous as one could wish – *"f—k 'em. Those assholes ain't never going to see nuthin'. Think we're stoopid enough to let that happen? This is for management alone"*. Then the project manager used an expression much favoured by The Butchers leadership, *"now it's time for those management motherf—kers to sh-t or get off the pot."*

This was probably the last mistake this particular consultant made at The Butchers. His first was to turn up for work wearing a brown suit – at The Butchers you always wore dark grey or dark blue suits and you always wore white shirts – not grey, not blue, not striped – only white! Seeing this new consultant arrive for his first day at work, our project manager exclaimed, *"Jesus f—kin' Christ, if you wear brown, you look like sh-t! And who hires sh-t?"* At The Butchers you either had to fit in or get thrown out. This unfortunate individual never quite got the hang of The Butchers' unique culture. He left us a few weeks later, apparently to pursue a career outside management consulting.

Over the years, The Butchers did try to evolve. They bought a number of other consultancies to broaden their service offering. In America, they acquired a Total Quality specialist, B....... Associates. I believe that acquisition was quite successful in that it allowed The Butchers to dress up what they did in a cloak of respectability – namely, Total Quality. In Europe they tried a similar approach and took over a well-known and widely respected human resources consultancy, J.......... However, if I remember correctly, within a year, most of the employees of this consultancy had left in disgust at The Butchers' business approach and the consultancy was declared bankrupt. The Butchers' culture of highway robbery was so deeply entrenched, that it was difficult to change.

Often The Butchers would be on the verge of disappearing from the market, then the economy would start to stagnate, cost-cutting would come back into fashion and The Butchers would suddenly reappear. In one year in the mid nineties, for example, economic growth in the West started to falter, share prices generally tumbled, but The Butchers' share price went the other way and doubled, seemingly defying economic gravity – 'popping' people was clearly back in fashion. And in 2002, when other consultancies were laying off thousands of staff, The Butchers' owners were able to report a 53% increase in turnover and forecast further growth. As the chairman, was quoted saying, *"The operational consulting that R...... Consulting offers to clients continues to be in strong demand."*[3] Moreover, in 2004 I had a meeting with a senior executive at The Butchers. We discussed the 'good old days' and he explained that although they had possibly tried to become more professional, actually very little had changed since I was there almost twenty years earlier.

2. MANAGING BY FEAR AND GREED

Given how awful The Butchers were at that time, you might wonder why anybody would ever work for them. But The Butchers were very smart and were experts at bringing a certain type of person into the company and then controlling them by a well-balanced mixture of fear and greed. Many consultancies seek to recruit from top business schools and leading universities to get the best talent. Some even pay new recruits signing on bonuses of ten to twenty thousand dollars to attract the brightest and the best. In one year, for example, Accenture were offering graduates signing-on bonuses of $15,000.[4] The Butchers had a quite different approach. They hired people who were immediately available and who needed jobs. Talent, education, skills and experience could, of course, be useful at The Butchers, but they were not necessary for you to be offered a job. The Butchers needed cannon fodder, what we called 'billing fodder', and they didn't seem to care too much about the quality or capabilities of their foot soldiers.

When they wanted to recruit, The Butchers put advertisements into middle level newspapers offering exciting careers in the fast-moving and challenging world of 'International Management Consultancy'. In their ads, they just gave a phone number to contact and never mentioned their company name. When you rang the number in the ad, they didn't ask who you were, what your qualifications were, what work experience you had or anything. They just took your name and phone number and told you to attend an interview a couple of days later at a hotel near whatever airport their recruiter would fly into.

In most companies and consultancies, you would normally have to go through two or three rounds of interviews lasting at least an hour each and even do a series of written tests before being offered a job. However, when you applied to work for The Butchers, you had just one interview and that interview usually lasted about ten minutes – sometimes fifteen, but never more. The Butchers' recruiter had a busy schedule. You were asked a few questions about your background and then told how wonderful a career in "international management consulting" would be. Ninety percent of those interviewed were offered a job. Within a year, up to seven out of every ten recruits would have left in disgust or would have been fired. But The Butchers didn't give a damn – they would just hire more billing fodder.

While most organisations have an annual staff turnover of about five to ten percent, at The Butchers staff turnover was up to seventy percent some years. But as they only needed people to go around timing how many minutes clients' staff took to accomplish each activity in their work, The Butchers didn't care too much about recruits' qualities or skills – as The Butchers managers used to joke, all they needed were *'warm bodies'*. Another favourite Butchers saying was: *"we'll take anyone who can walk and chew gum at the same time"*.

The starting salaries paid by Butchers were pitifully low. However, right from the beginning you were told that, once you reached a certain level in the organisation, you became eligible to receive bonuses or *'melons'* as they were referred to, presumably to suggest how big and juicy they were. Nobody ever actually said how large the melons were, but the picture painted was of really considerable lumps of money.

In fact, even the highest performing consultants would generally not reach the melons level till after about two years. So given the fact that up to seven out of ten Butchers employees left within their first year, very few ever got close to anything with even the slightest resemblance to a melon, or any other type of fruit. I believe that the melons must have existed at the project manager level and for the people we called Lead Analysts – those who sold Butchers projects – because they were constantly talking about how much money they had made, how much real estate they had bought and how soon they would be able to chuck it all in and escape from The Butchers. Few Butchers employees could be said to really enjoy their work. The few directors I saw were clearly reasonably wealthy. But I suspect The Butchers was a machine for vacuuming most of the money only up to the very top elite of the organisation and that ninety percent of employees toiled underpaid yet always spurred on by a hope of better times, which were actually never realised. As for my first project manager, S..... D......, I suspect that the stress, chain-smoking and self-abuse put an end to his life in some lonely hotel room long before he had the opportunity to enjoy whatever melons had ever come his way.

3. FRONT-LOADING THE PROJECT

When The Butchers started a project, they knew that the estimated savings potential was often based on analysis by totally inexperienced consultants and frequently, in my experience and according to other consultants I talked to, on something that could be said to vaguely resemble deliberate lies. So the worst thing that they could do would be to rely on project success for their fees. Some projects did deliver the promised savings, some even over-delivered, but many did not. Frequently, The Butchers caused so much disruption and annoyance that they got thrown out before their projects were completed. Often this suited The Butchers – they probably knew the promised savings were not possible and if the project was stopped early and insufficient people were fired, The Butchers could then blame the client's management for incompetence or cowardice or, more usually, both. In all cases The Butchers made sure they got most, if not all, of their money.

If projects were completed The Butchers got paid whether results were achieved or not. This was because they invoiced clients according to how many consulting mandays were used and not according to what results were gained. However, even if projects were stopped early, The Butchers ensured they got almost all their potential fees by applying what we called 'front-loading the project'. This meant that in the first half of any project, The Butchers would put a big team on the project and use up most of the mandays sold. By the time a project was two thirds completed, up to ninety percent of mandays could have been billed. So, even if a project were stopped early, The Butchers would have received almost all the revenue planned for that client.

This 'front-loading' often resulted in grotesque situations where huge consulting teams started projects off. Then only a tiny remnant of the original team was left the almost impossible task of finishing the project, while most of the Butchers staff had been moved off to other assignments. In one steel mill, for example, there were over ten consultants for the first half of the project and only two left for the second half. Yet the most difficult part of any Butchers' project was always the second half – ensuring management had the b——s to fire up to a third of the people and that the place could still more or less run with a significantly reduced number of staff. I remember one of those two consultants telling me how hard they had to work to get the assignment completed.

4. ONLY ONE SOLUTION

They say that when you only have a hammer, then every problem looks like a nail. On the projects I saw, that's pretty much how The Butchers approached their clients' business issues. The Butchers had one product to sell – cost reduction – and almost always people cost reduction. So whatever the situation, The Butchers would try to convince the client that they needed to put in better management control systems to reduce their staff costs – because that was all that The Butchers knew how to do.

One example where this went drastically wrong was when we did a project for a chain of five hundred menswear shops. For a few weeks, we studied how many customers came into each shop during each day. We then set up customer flow diagrams for each shop and based on work-study observations, we concluded how many customers each shop assistant could handle per hour. This then allowed us to calculate how many staff were required in each shop for each hour of each day.

The results showed two things:

- There were currently around thirty percent too many staff in each shop.
- To run the shops at minimum staff cost, it was much better to replace most full-time staff with part-timers – part-time staff were obviously more flexible than full-timers in terms of when they could work and so could be deployed just during busy periods.

After the Butchers project manager had applied enough pressure, client management accepted our recommendations. Loads of full-timers were fired and replaced by part-time staff. What we didn't take into account was that full-time employees were generally people who intended to make a career in that company. They were therefore motivated to achieve the best possible sales results, while many of the part-timers were only looking for the chance to earn a little spending money and didn't have the same level of motivation. Worst of all, the company operated a 'last in – first out' policy. This meant that many of those who were fired were the young trainee shop managers – the most highly motivated group in the company. After the 'successful' completion of our project, where we essentially ripped out many of the best employees, sales collapsed and within just a couple of years that five hundred shop company no longer existed.

Perhaps what is so sad about this whole situation was that the eventual destruction of this company, to which The Butchers so enthusiastically and profitably contributed, was probably quite avoidable. When The Butchers had finished helping management fire about thirty percent of the people who worked in the shops, warehouse and window-dressing team, they convinced the client management to buy another project from them. This new project was aimed at training the remaining staff in the shops to sell more effectively – more of the people coming into the shops should buy something and the number of items sold per customer should also go up. So this project actually did try to achieve something constructive. Unfortunately, by that time, the highly motivated young future shop managers had mostly been 'POPped', morale of the whole organisation was significantly below rock bottom and we were left training a bunch of part-timers who only worked a few hours a week, stayed for only a short time and quite frankly 'didn't give a damn' about the company or its future. And their attitude was quite understandable – they received low wages, little holidays or other benefits and if the company went under, they could always get a part-time job at some other shop.

Had any reasonable consultancy been there, instead of The Butchers and had the company management been worth their fine titles and inflated salaries, our first project with them should have logically been the sales increase project. Because, if we had been able to improve the sales performance of the full-time staff, which had commitment and loyalty to the company and something to lose if their employer collapsed, then all the bloodletting and bankruptcy that eventually followed might have been unnecessary. However, by using The Butchers instead of a more professional consultancy, the company management wasted the window of opportunity to save the organisation.

This was my first ever management consulting project. I later learnt that this was not untypical for a Butchers project and, although I graduated on to work for and compete against some of the world's leading and most sophisticated management consultancies, wherever I worked you could always see practices, which had at least a little in common with the approach and ethics employed by The Butchers.

IMPLEMENTING IMPROVED MANAGEMENT – THE BUTCHERS WAY

Pretty much all Butchers so-called 'performance improvement projects' with which my colleagues and I came into contact, seemed to be extremely similar. The Butchers claimed that they were able to achieve the promised cost savings by *'improving management processes'* and *'enhancing supervisor capability'*. Their constant refrains were *'we'll help your people work smarter, not harder'* and *'we'll help remove all the barriers that prevent your people from fulfilling their potential'*. The Butchers would admit, that unfortunately the increased productivity might mean that a client needed less people. But The Butchers would stress that as consultants their mission was to safeguard the jobs of the majority of workers by strengthening the whole organisation's financial performance

This offering can sound quite seductive to client management teams who often had little understanding of and little control over their own operations. After all, The Butchers professed to be genuinely dedicated to making the working lives of most of the employees more satisfying and more secure. And so, by using stick (*"we've identified thirty percent too many staff"*) and carrot (*"we'll make your workers more productive, more secure and happier"*), The Butchers had over ninety percent success in moving from free Analyses to selling large follow-on implementation projects.

However, in my experience, the reality of making workers happier and more productive as they supposedly *'worked smarter, not harder'* didn't quite live up to the persuasive sales pitch. Essentially, whatever the organisation, The Butchers implemented what they called 'SIS' – this stood for 'Short Interval Scheduling' – basically making sure that supervisors checked on each worker's output against set targets every two hours, day in day out. In fact, they merely resurrected and dressed up a type of Taylorism that had been rejected by any normal company decades before.

Frederick Winslow Taylor (1856-1917) is widely credited as being the father of Scientific Management, which the first Henry Ford so effectively employed at his mass production plants for the Model T. The principles of Scientific Management were that any activity, building a car for example, could be split up into a number of simple repetitive tasks that can be parcelled out to workers so that each worker only completes one simple activity time and time again during their working day. Each activity can then be timed and work standards can be set for each worker. Those who don't achieve the standards can then get trained to improve their productivity or fired, depending on the degree of enlightenment of management and availability of docile labour. Scientific Management marked the move from craftsmanship, where a worker had and used real skills on their job, to mass production, where for most tasks no particular skill was required apart from unthinking obedience.

In their free Analysis, The Butchers consultants would quickly look at what activities were done in each department, time how long each took, see how many times each activity was done per day, week and month and then (fiddling the figures if necessary) calculate that each department could function with about thirty percent less people if lost time was reduced and the employees were more productive. The whole study tended to be more than quick and dirty. Though the 'results' were shown to top management to encourage them to buy a project, they were seldom if ever revealed to operational managers and supervisors, who might have had sufficient knowledge to shoot holes in the consultants' work.

In the implementation project however, The Butchers were much more thorough in their approach and really managed to get the operational managers and supervisors by the b-lls. We would send one to two consultants into each department. They would fill in what was called 'an Area Sequence' – this was a long questionnaire completed with the local manager's help, which described that area in detail:

- Organisation structure

- Number of people

- Skills, experience and salaries of the people

- Activities done with their daily, weekly and monthly volumes

- Quality standards

- Physical layout

- Etc.

Then the consultant would coerce the manager or supervisor into standing with him to accurately measure how many seconds or minutes were required for each work activity to be efficiently completed. Once each activity was timed, the consultant would get the supervisor or manager to sign a form confirming that the time obtained was accurate and reasonable. Then, by simply multiplying the volumes of activity by the time required (as agreed with the client's local supervisor) the consultant could produce a 'Manload' – basically a calculation of how many employees were really needed in that department.

Once the Manload was agreed with the area manager, it was time for what we called 'implementation'. About thirty percent of the people in the area would be removed and the supervisor would be required to complete a 'Daily Schedule Control'. The Daily Schedule Control was usually one piece of A4 paper on which the manager would write up his production or sales plan for the day and then split this into how much had to be achieved by each worker every two hours. Then every two hours, he or she would go round to each employee or work station and assess if the work was proceeding according to plan. If things were on schedule, he or she would just note this on the Daily Schedule Control. If there was some problem, the area manager had to fill in a 'Variance Report'. On this they wrote where the problems were, what production or sales had been lost and what action they had taken to rectify the situation. At the start of each day, the supervisor was expected to meet with their line manager to review the results from the previous day and plan together how they could continuously increase productivity. Each week that manager had to conduct a similar review with their manager and so on all the way up to the top of the organisation. Given this minute level of control that The Butchers instituted, it's hardly surprising that productivity of the staff, which kept their jobs, often soared. But one could dispute whether they really were more satisfied and actually felt more secure.

To give you an idea of how basic and ghastly their approach was in reality, let me describe a piece of a project for which I had responsibility. We were working for the chain of five hundred menswear shops. We had just finished the first part of the project – reducing the number of staff working in the shops and making the workforce cheaper and more flexible by replacing full-time employees with all their associated costs like social security, pensions and holidays by low cost part-timers. In general, this massacre went off quite well and the shop workers failed to organise any effective resistance to management's plans.

Presumably pleased by the way we had managed to get cost savings, the company's management gave The Butchers another two projects. One was improving the effectiveness of the warehouse that shipped clothes to all the five hundred shops – that meant firing up to thirty percent of the people who worked there. The other was increasing the efficiency of the one hundred and twenty five people who travelled round dressing the dummies in the shop windows – that meant reducing the work-force from one hundred and twenty-five to around ninety people, while still carrying out the same workload. This second mini project was mine.

Closely following the instructions of my chain-smoking, blaspheming, sexually and socially inadequate project manager, this is what I did:

1. I made a list of all the shops and how many dummies each had in their windows – there were two types of dummy – full-body and half-body.

2. I sat with the window designers to find out with which clothes each dummy would be dressed for the next major window

change – this was to happen in about four weeks.

3. A window dresser was brought in to head office and asked to dress some dummies with the new season's clothes while I used a stop-watch to time how long it took to put each item of clothing on to the dummy.

4. By adding up the time it took to dress each dummy, I produced what we called the 'Standard Hours', which a window-dresser would earn for doing that dummy.

5. By knowing how many of each type of dummy there were in each shop, I could then calculate the hours required to do the windows in each shop.

6. And, of course, adding up all the hours required across the whole five hundred shops, I could work out how many window-dressers were needed to complete the next season's windows. Miraculously, the number I reached was about eighty people. Then you had to add on another ten people or so to cover for holidays, personal days off and sickness – which gave the magic ninety employees required to get the thirty percent staff savings The Butchers wanted. Gratifyingly for my project manager and critical for my future employment, this happened to coincide with the thirty percent excess staff my project manager had so clairvoyantly predicted.

7. Acting on this highly scientific analysis, the regional managers were instructed to redistribute their window-dressing teams across their shops and fire thirty-five staff.

8. Four weeks after I started my mini-project, the next season's windows were successfully completed by ninety rather than one hundred and twenty five people – after all, this was in the middle

of a recession and so none of the ninety survivors was motivated to kick up a fuss – overwork was better than no work.

9. To make sure that the remaining staff managed to complete their tasks in the times I had calculated as necessary, each day a report was completed showing how many work hours each employee had been paid for and how many 'Standard Hours' they had earned per worked hour. Any employee who fell below a certain efficiency level would get what was euphemistically called 'coaching'. If their performance failed to improve, they would then get fired. Following my intervention, the window-dressers would have their personal work efficiency monitored in this way for the rest of their working lives. This was perhaps acceptable for a machine – but not a particularly pleasant prospect for a human being. Fortunately for the employees, the later bankruptcy of this company also meant the well-deserved disappearance of the awful Management Control Systems that myself and my colleagues at Butchers had introduced.

10. I did not personally feel particularly good about the process I had just conducted – but at least I still had a job.

The Butchers' procedure appeared to me to be the same whether you were working in a bank, shops, factories, mines, steelworks or whatever. And the result was also usually the same – people off the payroll, increased productivity from the petrified survivors and a so-called Management Control System that was reasonably suitable for machines, but way out of order for thinking human beings. At the time, there were many consultancies offering the same types of services as The Butchers and there were many management teams willing to pay generously for these services.

LACK OF PROFESSIONALISM

The Butchers should have been a very efficient selling machine. But the combination of rapacious top management and largely unskilled lower level consultants often gave quite unexpected yet entertaining results.

My next client was a nationwide chain of television, video and electrical goods rental shops. Having just done the project at the chain of menswear shops, I was now considered a 'Retail expert' and made Team Manager on my second assignment for The Butchers. I think The Butchers had earlier done a project to reduce the number of repair and service staff at this client – the 'man in a van' – and wanted to carry out a similar operation in the company's four hundred and fifty or so high street shops. This would, probably, have used the standard Butchers approach of achieving the staff savings by replacing often experienced and knowledgeable full-time staff with yet another army of unskilled and unmotivated part-timers. However, after all the disruption and bad feeling caused in the repair and service operation by the first Butchers project, this client was none too keen to repeat the experience in their shops. Nevertheless, some pushy salesmanship from a Butchers account manager managed to persuade one of the directors to allow us to conduct a preliminary study free of charge in four or five shops to estimate the potential for staff savings. I was sent in with a couple of other consultants to conduct this work. As you can imagine, the account manager left me in no doubt as to the result he expected – in his briefing the magical words "thirty percent lost time" were often mentioned along with a series of very clear threats to my likely future employment at The Butchers were the thirty percent not to materialise.

Dutifully, I arrived at the client's site, sent my small team off to do the necessary studies and settled in to an office, where I tried to imagine what I would do if my two inexperienced consultants failed to find the required thirty percent which would justify the client embarking on a full scale project with us. While my team were doing the studies, my job was to hang around HQ and try to get meetings with all the directors to sound them out on their feelings about buying another big project from us. On about my third day there, I was called in to see one of the directors – not the one who had allowed us to start work. The man was furious, absolutely furious. Before I could introduce myself and exchange a few pleasantries, he launched into an emotional tirade attacking The Butchers and the whole way they went about doing business. This went on for, what seemed to me on only my second consultancy project, an awfully long time. When he had finished, without allowing me to say anything in The Butchers' defence, he evicted me from his office promising that he would do everything within his power to prevent The Butchers ever working for that company again.

Not a very promising start to my first opportunity to try my hand as Team Manager. As I awaited the arrival of my boss and the lashing I knew I would get for "screwing up" his chances of selling a project, I did a little investigation to try and discover why the executive was quite so angry with us. I soon found out that at the end of the previous project, some lowly consultant had forgotten to return confidential project files to our European head office in Brussels. The client's people, finding a couple of boxes of project material had started to look through them and had found our detailed, highly personal assessments of the key client executives. If I remember correctly, one was described as a 'coward' who would do whatever the CEO wanted, another was a 'politician with only his own interests at heart'. There was a 'has-been, who had no real influence' and yet who 'was always voicing his opinions'..... and so on. All in all, not very complimentary stuff. Incidentally, the gentleman who had just given me a right old lambasting was the one the previous team had labelled 'a coward'. Hence his high state of emotional energy on hearing that The Butchers were trying once again to enter his life.

Within a week I found out that the angry man was true to his word. He had talked to his colleagues, shown them the incriminating evidence and we were forced to close the study and withdraw our team – it was fairly clear that the client would not buy another project from us, however huge the potential savings we actually found or claimed to find.

My next assignment at The Butchers was an even greater botch-up. I was sent in again as Team Manager on the Analysis. The place was a factory owned by a massive American engineering company and made sub-assemblies for trains. Appropriately enough, just across the road from the office I was given, there was a slaughterhouse. All day long the screams of the unfortunate pigs meeting their fate and the stench of their offal lying in open skips outside in the summer sun made a life at The Butchers that was already unpleasant, totally unbearable.

We did the Analysis and, of course, managed to identify that if we could remove the 'lost time' by implementing better management controls the factory could run just as well with up to thirty percent fewer employees – the scene described at the beginning of this chapter, where I was forced to falsify the results of my studies, came from this assignment. Although we lied about the results of many of our studies, it must be said that the factory was pretty hopelessly run. As the project manager said when ordering us to fix the answers to show thirty percent room for productivity improvement, *"jus' cos you f.....n' douche-bags can't see the f......n' lost time, don't mean it's not f......n' there!"*

The factory was on the verge of chaos. So the lost time, that we junior consultants couldn't always find, probably really was there. Production planning and control were haphazard and quality a bit of a joke. There were hundreds of work orders out on the production floor many of which should have been completed weeks or even months before. Almost all the orders seemed to be missing parts or just be lost somewhere between different machining operations. To try and sort out the mess, there were over forty people employed as so called 'progress chasers' – they spent all day running around the factory looking for wayward orders and when they found them they would go to the production supervisors and beg them to produce their orders next as they were inevitably hopelessly behind schedule. This resulted in a kind of anarchy where pretty much everything was late and the supervisors, rather than the inappropriately named Production Planning, decided what got made and what would languish incomplete till the end of time. The place was so farcical that the production supervisors used to take bets about how many progress chasers would come running into their offices, with urgent requests to do their work, before the morning tea lady came round with her trolley.

All in all, it was a pretty typical European factory at that time. And like the chain of menswear shops, it presented a wonderful opportunity for an honest and moderately professional consultancy to clean the place up and get it running effectively for everybody's benefit after decades of management neglect and incompetence. However, The Butchers did not have people skilled in production planning, work scheduling, maintenance management, Lean Manufacturing and all the other things that this client and many other Butchers clients so urgently needed. The Butchers only had low-paid consultants who had been trained in one thing – timing how many seconds or minutes each work activity took – and highly pressured project managers, who ruled by fear as a substitute for any real depth of knowledge about how to run an organisation. So, thanks to The Butchers' limited capabilities another great opportunity to do something worthwhile was lost.

Through the usual bullying of the local factory manager, The Butchers managed to get agreement to launch a five to six month implementation project to improve work processes and lay off about one in four employees. I was now faced with the unpleasant realisation that I, as project Team Manager, would be working in one form of slaughterhouse, right beside another form of slaughterhouse for virtually the next half year – I resolved to quit.

Fortunately, Fate intervened to save the factory from the Butchers treatment. On the Monday that we arrived to start the project, the manager of the division to which the factory belonged returned from three weeks holiday and was surprised and displeased to discover that the local factory manager had just decided to give a whole pile of his division's money to a bunch of management consultants – he called the local manager and ordered him to close the project. The local manager, whom we had pushed into buying the project, dutifully informed us

RIP-OFF! – THE MANAGEMENT CONSULTING MONEY MACHINE

that our valuable services were no longer required. This sent shockwaves throughout The Butchers – when our senior management thought they had a huge wad of money heading for their pockets, they tended to be most upset if the money turned round and didn't go their way after all. So, although I couldn't wait to get the h-ll out of there, my project manager was instructed to refuse the client's order to take our team off the client's site and one of Butchers' top directors from the U.S. got on a plane and came over to sort the situation out.

A....., the Butchers director, more commonly known as 'The Gorilla' was a large brute of a man, all thickset body and head, no discernible neck and with more swear words in his vocabulary than normal language. I tried to find out what was going on. My project director, Gareth, explained that the Gorilla was going to deal with the factory manager and save the project. Gareth was feeling pretty confident about the effect the Gorilla would have. "Just wait till the Gorilla gets hold of B............ (the factory manager)" Gareth said, "we'll have our project. The Gorilla's used to situations like this." Then he added in awe of Butchers top management capability, "you'll just see the Gorilla, you won't see the man who trained the Gorilla."

So confident was he about the Gorilla's ability to save the project, that Gareth appeared to have overlooked the fact that the Gorilla might not be delighted with the situation and therefore had apparently decided to warm up a bit on Gareth and I before going to deal with the recalcitrant factory manager. First he dragged Gareth outside and gave him a right going over for causing such a total f—k-up in the first place. Returning ashen white from his session with the Gorilla, Gareth slumped in a chair – a beaten man. Then I was next to benefit from the Gorilla's unique management style. The Gorilla apparently believed that I had given him inaccurate directions as to how to get to the factory. So he felt it necessary to give me a small but exquisitely phrased piece of what he called 'his f....n' mind'. When he had finished shouting at me, telling me that he was going to "ream me a new asshole" and confirming once and for all that I was a "totally f—king worthless piece of f—k", it was the turn of the factory manager to get the Gorilla's undivided attention.

I have no idea of the discussion that took place between the factory manager and our Gorilla. I imagine it was far from gentlemanly and suppose that the factory manager learnt some colourful new expressions to add to his vocabulary. But whatever was said, it turned out that deploying the Gorilla did not have the desired effect. Gareth was wrong – the factory manager actually stood up to the Gorilla's many threats including legal action for breach of contract – no contract had actually been signed. And, tails between our legs, we had to leave the site immediately, never to return. I heard that Gareth moved on from The Butchers soon after this event. I also realised I had no wish to spend my life lying to clients and firing innocent employees all to make the Gorilla and the man who trained the Gorilla able to buy even bigger Palm Beach mansions and luxury yachts.

---

(1) Masters of the Universe ITV 1999
(2) Top-consultant.com (for date: contact author)
(3) Top-consultant.com (for date: contact author)
(4) Financial Times 21 August 2000

CHAPTER 3

BABY BUTCHERS – COST-CUTTING CONTINUED

When I first started with The Butchers, consultancy was a minor sector probably worth around $6 billion per annum. Today, the worldwide management consultancy business is worth somewhere around $100 billion after growing by a massive 20% per year for the last fifteen to twenty years. Oversimplifying, one could say that at the time I began my consulting career, there were two main types of consultancy. At what we called 'the top end' there were the strategy houses like McKinsey, Boston Consulting, Booz Allen and Bain. These firms made a living mostly from writing reports for senior client management. It was then up to the client to decide whether they wished to implement their consultants' recommendations. If you had an on-going relationship with one of these firms, you could be sure of receiving a satisfyingly expensive stream of superb strategic analyses. As one leading businessman, Lord Hanson, commented, *"management consultancy has become one of the great growth industries of recent times. Hardly a single firm, government department or local council seems able to make a decision without the advice of these self-styled experts. The corporate world is now deluged with their expensively produced reports".*[1] Some journalists dubbed this *"the 'drop the report, send the bill, run' mentality"*[2]

But if these reports were really so wonderful, why didn't all these clients become so successful that they could finally dispense with their consultants' services? The answer was, of course that many of these great and worthy reports remained precisely that – just reports

– and never led to any action by client management. To quote Lord Hanson again, *"I have frequently gone into failing businesses and found the drawers of top managers littered with expensively commissioned reports".*[1]

Some of these firms had their own management publications reinforcing their image as management thought leaders. Others were active in encouraging their employees to churn out articles for worthy management publications like the Harvard Business Review and even books to support their public position as being on the leading edge of management practice.

Great and entertaining management theory wars were fought out between these top-end strategy houses, because the consultancy which held the intellectual high ground, was the consultancy which got the most publicity and the most clients.

Since the 1920s, it had been McKinsey, which had always been seen as 'The Thought Leader' in the industry. But by the 1970s their position had begun to weaken. A commentator wrote, *"McKinsey's growth engine seemed to stall. The economic turmoil of the oil crisis, the slowing of the divisionalization process that had fuelled the European expansion, the growing sophistication of client management, and the appearance of new focused competitors like Boston Consulting Group (BCG) all contributed to the problem. Almost overnight, McKinsey's enormous reservoir of internal self-confidence and even self-satisfaction began to turn to self-doubt and self-criticism".*[3] A confidential internal report in 1971 concluded *"that McKinsey had been too willing to accept routine assignments from marginal clients, that the quality of work done was uneven, and that while its consultants were excellent generalist problem-solvers, they often lacked the deep industry knowledge or the substantive specialized expertise that clients were demanding".*[3]

By the mid 1970s companies like BCG aggressively challenged McKinsey's position. With its two-by-two matrix, which introduced us all to the concepts of Stars, Question Marks, Cows and Dogs and their Experience Curve, BCG achieved major recognition, attracted some key McKinsey clients and threatened McKinsey's dominant position. In June 1997, McKinsey tried to fight back and pulled together a group of young partners for a three-day meeting to help build their intellectual defence against BCG's wondrous matrix. At first, this was apparently not too successful, *"we had three days of unmitigated chaos. Someone from New York would stand up and present a four-box matrix. A partner from London would present a nine-box matrix. A German would present a 47-box matrix. It was chaos,"* said one of the attendees.[3]

However, by the early 1980s, particularly with the publication of two books – *In Search of Excellence* and *The Mind of the Strategist* – McKinsey once again established a dominance in strategic consulting that has not been effectively challenged since. So by 2001, with annual revenues of $3.4 billion, McKinsey was considered to have over a 40% share of the strategic consulting market compared to just over $1 billion each in revenues of its two nearest competitors Booz Allen and BCG.

The other main group of consultancies at the time were the operational performance improvement firms like The Butchers, who tended to work out 'on the shop floor' with supervisors and hourly-paid workers, driving through changes in working practices and, more often than not, dramatic reductions in client personnel.

Like strategic consulting, operational performance improvement consulting probably also started as a clearly identifiable profession in the 1920s. A Frenchman called Charles Bedau went to America and, after several attempts to find a business opportunity, hit upon starting a management consultancy. Basing himself on Taylor's Scientific Management, he designed a system in which time and motion specialists with stopwatches could standardise every task in a factory or administration and give each task a 'B' value according to how long it took. Then each worker's productivity – how many B Units they completed for each hour they worked whatever their activity – could be accurately measured and compared to that of other workers. This gave management a hugely powerful tool to drive up productivity.

Bedau's new American company was hugely successful and he became immensely rich. At the end of the 1920s, working for the

American multi-national Kodak, Bedau brought his system and consulting company to Europe and quickly established a large and profitable business – particularly in Britain. Bedau used his wealth to fund an active social life where, by throwing lavish parties, he managed to enter the very top circles of Europe's richest and most powerful people. For example, he bought a large chateau in the Loire valley where he played host amongst other events to the wedding of the recently abdicated King Edward VIII of England to the American Wallis Simpson.

Bedau's downfall can be traced to his close relations with Nazi Germany. He was responsible for helping organise the highly controversial trip of the former British King Edward VIII to Nazi Germany just before the Second World War, where the ex-king and his charming wife were filmed cheerfully meeting a beaming Adolf Hitler. This was a huge propaganda coup for the Nazis. Later Bedau tried to arrange for Edward to visit America. But this trip was cancelled following protests about Bedau's close relations with the Nazis. Under pressure from negative publicity, Bedau was forced to give up his shareholding in his company, which then changed its name to X...... in order to avoid connections with its founder. During the war, Bedau worked with the pro-Nazi Vichy government in France. While in North Africa trying to build a Trans-Sahara railroad with the backing of the Nazis, he was arrested by the Allies and accused of treason. He committed suicide before his trial.

However, though Bedau himself was disgraced, the business he founded prospered. During the Second World War, with many men leaving their jobs to join the military and many women entering the labour force for the first time, management consultants using the Bedau system were supported by the government because of the contribution they made to improving productivity, particularly in factories making essential goods like armaments. Productivity improvement consultancy grew rapidly and many otherwise able-bodied men avoided the dangers of military service because their role as management consultants was seen as essential to the war effort. After the war, several consultancies adopted a version of the Bedau system for work measurement, though now each activity tended to be given a value in 'standard hours' rather than in 'B units'. Tens of other consultancies using a similar approach started up and grew rapidly throughout the 1950s and 1960s as industry in The West struggled to keep up with exploding consumer demand.

There were three main types of implementation consultancy – the head-cutters, the technicians and the technologists.

The head-cutters: Most notorious amongst these were, of course, The Butchers and their many off-shoots and imitators. They promised results – lots of them and fast. These results were usually people off the payroll (POPs). However, as I have hopefully shown (Chapter 2 *The unsubtle art of cost-cutting*) the need for people reductions was seldom linked to any overall concept of an organisation's future strategy and the numbers chosen for execution at dawn were often not the result of any particularly in-depth or honest analysis.

Another group of implementers were those we called the **technical consultants** – firms with in-depth experience of something like Total Quality, manufacturing, warehousing and logistics, HR processes and so on. Unlike charlatans like The Butchers, these firms could provide huge added value for their clients, but only within their limited specialised fields. The advantage of using them was that they probably were experts in their areas of competence. The danger was that, knowing little else, they could often fail to see what really needed fixing in a client's organisation and would gravitate towards optimising the parts of an operation, with which they were familiar, blissfully unaware of whether their work fitted in with or even prevented the organisation's overall strategy. It was not uncommon, for example, to see organisations with lousy customer service using logistics consultants to reduce their stock levels and thus making customer service levels even worse. Likewise, I've come across companies aided by accountancy-based consultants launching highly promoted campaigns to reduce working capital at a time when interest rates were at their lowest level for over fifty years and when in fact an almost insignificant increase in working capital would give millions in benefits from allowing expensive production facilities to be optimised through longer production runs and less changeovers.

The third group of implementers were the **technologists** – firms that combined consulting with the implementation of computer systems. At the time, something called Manufacturing Requirements Planning (MRP) was all the rage and it seemed that no firm wanted to be seen without it. Then came Enterprise Resource Planning (ERP) – another great hit with the management of large organisations with too much money and too few ideas of what to do with it. And just when the ERP craze was dying away, e-business came speeding on to the managerial radar as a must-have for the well-dressed organisation. Wave after wave of technology developments kept these consultancies growing at around twenty to thirty percent a year for the whole of the 1980s and 1990s and billions were wasted on massive computer systems of which many were about as useful as the proverbial pair of tits on a bull.

MOVING ON

After I had been in The Butchers for just over eleven months, I was contacted by a consultant who had just left The Butchers. He asked if I wanted to join him at another productivity improvement consultancy, which we'll call Baby Butchers.

Baby Butchers is perhaps interesting because it was typical of many small and medium sized management consultancies that were starting and growing rapidly at that time also offering 'business performance improvement'. Many of these were set up by people who had previously been with Butchers or some similar organisation. If you worked for what we called 'one of the majors' (major international management consultancies) you did not have to be particularly bright to realise that basically there were two possible ways to becoming extraordinarily rich as a consultant. You could work your way up the greasy and treacherous career ladder in the hope of becoming a partner or director. But there was a much quicker way – find (or more usually steal) a client and set up your own consultancy to deliver your first project. Then if you managed to sell another project to someone else during your first year of operation, you were well on your way to becoming quite satisfyingly wealthy. Many management consultancies were started this way. An ex-colleague in Italy recently took about twenty staff and several clients away from the consultancy for which we both had worked – he is now probably personally earning several million euros a year.

Apart from being representative of a large wad of productivity improvement management consultancies, Baby Butchers as I later discovered, was notable for three other things that I have experienced in several management consultancies:

- The way it avoided taxes.
- How it religiously tried to copy the consulting approach championed by The Butchers.
- The eccentric and domineering management approach of its wealthy owner.

TAX – TO PAY OR NOT TO PAY

Baby Butchers was much smaller than The Butchers. The story went that the founder and owner T.F. had tried to join The Butchers at a senior level, but had been rejected. So he decided to set up his own rival consultancy. Baby Butchers was just a hundred or so consultants, I think. Though if you do your sums, you'll find out that if you've got, say, a bit over one hundred consultants you're probably earning fees of close to fifty million dollars a year. So if you're only spending about ten to fifteen million a year on salaries and expenses, you've got a very very profitable business and can take home over thirty million dollars a year for yourself. Like most management consultancies, Baby Butchers started in the U.S. But it soon moved over to Europe when it realised the rich pickings to be had there. It was said that their first European salesman became one of the richest men in his home country of Southern Ireland.

Baby Butchers' European operations were registered in one of the British Channel Islands – a tax shelter with virtually no corporate tax – so most of the profits were kept by those in control rather than given away to some stupid tax authority. While most companies tend to at least make some effort to give the impression of themselves being good corporate citizens, you'll often find that management consultancies seldom suffer from such scruples – so much money usually flows in so easily that, once they've got their hands on it, their owners become quite loath to give it away to anybody but themselves. Hence a tendency among many smaller management consultancies to be constructed around clever tax avoidance schemes rather than operating in a more transparent and traditional way.

Though, it should be noted that apparently having creative relationships with tax authorities is not just the preserve of smaller consultancies. Accenture, probably the largest and most profitable consultancy in the world was reported to have only paid around 7% of its profits in tax from 1997 to 2000 compared to an average of 36.9% paid by the biggest companies in America. Moreover, despite having more than 2,500 stock-holding partners and more than 80,000 employees in 75 countries around the world, Accenture was, according to the same reporter, headquartered in Bermuda where the consulting gargantuan has all of three employees![4] The reporter described Bermuda as *"an offshore jurisdiction, which has been condemned by lawmakers as a place companies go to avoid paying tax"*. From this, I think one can be forgiven for being tempted to suspect that the Bermuda incorporation has more to do with tax minimisation than being due to Bermuda being a key consulting market for Accenture. In fact, this practice of apparent tax avoidance amongst management consultants has become so serious, that Congress in the U.S. is trying to bring in legislation preventing any consultancy involved in tax avoidance from getting government work. Accenture, for example, was reported to be facing the loss of more than $600 million of U.S. government business if this legislation is passed.[4]

But it was not only our employer Baby Butchers that avoided the unpleasant chore of giving away some of its goodies to the greedy and undeserving taxman. Very few Baby Butchers consultants paid tax either. It could even be said, but not proven, that Baby Butchers encouraged its employees not to bother with such trivialities like paying tax. This was particularly attractive for consultants living in high tax countries like Sweden, Germany and France. The whole scheme worked as follows:

Like most management consultancies, Baby Butchers had worked out that the more you get in fees and the less you pay in salaries and costs, the more profit you make for the owners. Baby Butchers paid quite low salaries. Though, as they were consciously set at a level considerably higher than those paid by The Butchers, Baby Butchers was always able to attract discontented Butchers staff whenever they needed more people. However, salaries were paid direct from the Channel Islands company to another Channel Islands company with which the employees had their contracts of employment and which then paid the employees. So, as the employees had their contract with a company based in a jurisdiction with no income tax, it was pretty much up to each employee to decide how much (or little) income they wished to declare to their own local tax authorities. Naturally, many employees also set up bank accounts in one of the Channel Island tax havens so their income could be paid to them outside their country of residence and/or work and thus without attracting the unwanted attention of their local tax inspectors. So Baby Butchers avoided the dreary and expensive drudge of administering a payroll process that would have had to conform to all the different requirements of all the countries where it had employees and the employees were free to choose how much of their income they wished to keep and how much their social consciences suggested that they should give back to society. Not surprisingly, most decided to keep everything and society could look after itself.

BUTCHERS REVISITED

The colleague who recruited me into Baby Butchers had assured me that this next consultancy did really good work, treated its people properly and were absolutely nothing like The Butchers at all. Of course, in reality it turned out to be very much like The Butchers, but in miniature. Most of the people had learnt consultancy at The Butchers, all the tools and methods were copied directly from The Butchers and the aims were the same as The Butchers – to give clients bottom-line cost savings, namely reduce their staff bills.

There were, however, a couple of differences:

1. Baby Butchers was less fear-driven than The Butchers

2. There were a group of us young consultants who tried to change the business model away from popping people and more towards genuinely improving our clients' operations

1. MORE GREED THAN FEAR

Consultants at Baby Butchers didn't seem to work in the same environment of terror as those at The Butchers. We didn't have a group of American directors unable to utter a single sentence without some blasphemy or swear word. Provided you didn't pay any taxes, the money was quite good and you did get reasonable promotions and pay rises. Moreover, there were other, slightly less conventional ways of increasing your earnings.

I remember a Baby Butchers management meeting held in Amsterdam. Although we didn't have any projects or consultants in Holland at that time, it somehow seemed to be a popular place for managers to hold their meetings – this was not just a characteristic of Baby Butchers – managements of other consultancies also seemed to prefer Amsterdam to other possibly more boring locations with a less interesting availability of nightlife. When checking in to the Sheraton

Hotel at Amsterdam airport once, I was surprised to notice that one of the largest British consultancies was holding a meeting there – I wonder why they had to bring their staff all the way over to Amsterdam just to talk to each other. Perhaps every hotel in Britain was full that week. In the thirty or forty consultancy company meetings I've been to, I have visited Amsterdam many times (thriving sex industry), Paris many times (great food and wine), Nice (sunshine), Geneva (close to weekend skiing), the Black Forest during the Munich Beer Festival, Cannes (sunshine and beaches), Verbier (excellent skiing), Barcelona (spring sunshine), Florida (more sunshine and beaches), plus many fine country hotels and chateaux (unlimited quantities of amazing food and wine) – but we never had meetings in Detroit, Birmingham, Lille, Hamburg, Manchester, Northern Sweden or any of the other nasty places where we tended to have our projects.

Although I was not part of the management group at that time, I was invited to the meeting because I had begun to propose the wild idea that you could get greater financial benefits for your clients, and therefore larger projects, by improving their businesses rather than just firing their people. At the start of the meeting T.F. ordered the largest bowl the hotel could find and filled it so full with money that the notes were overflowing on to the table around which his management group were seated. During the meeting, when anyone made what T.F. considered was a valuable contribution, the great leader rewarded them accordingly. If he judged the manager's comments as only a small addition to the proceedings, they would just get a few notes shoved casually and disdainfully their way. However, if like me they made a full presentation that our owner liked, he would pick up a great ball of cash with both hands and throw it contemptuously in the direction of the lucky recipient. Of course, the money flew all over the place leaving its target ignominiously scrabbling to gather it all up as the meeting continued around him. Although you felt embarrassed by your own greed, it was difficult to ignore the huge pile of money and stop wondering what you could do to get a useful part of it going your way.

The concept of handing out cash could have been quite motivating if done in a positive way. However, the intention here was to demonstrate T.F.'s domination, ownership and control over his management team and to humiliate them in front of their master and their peers. When looking at company cultures, we often picture organisations, which have been built up around one charismatic individual and his ideas, as being like mediaeval royal courts where you had an all-powerful monarch surrounded by fawning courtiers and courtesans. And all those courtiers and courtesans lived an uncertain existence, totally dependent on the favour of their master for their positions, their material comforts and their lives. Such was life at Baby Butchers. The prostitutes in the red light district were not the only whores in Amsterdam that weekend.

I spent three years at Baby Butchers and experienced many other amusing episodes where T.F. was able to demonstrate his general superiority and power over what passed for his management team.

Sometimes at company meetings a group of us were encouraged by the Supreme Being to go jogging with him in the morning. Inevitably, although he carried exercise weights and we did not, he ended up running faster than the rest of us and always completed the chosen course first. Then, of course, we all had to hear repeatedly about how he not only could run faster than the rest of us but could also do it in spite of the fact that he was both older than the rest of us and had the disadvantage of the exercise weights. I rather suspect that most of us could easily have outrun the man – but we all knew that it was better for our job security to struggle histrionically puffing and panting in his wake.

We once held a meeting at a luxury hotel in Spain, which, in addition to its five swimming pools, also had a small bullring. Sure enough, the first evening before dinner, we were ushered down to the bullring and a reasonably tame but still quite unpleasant-looking beast was produced – unfortunately very much alive and not yet ready to be made into steak. T.F. was first into the ring and we all shouted and cheered wildly as he chased the confused animal around the arena for a few minutes. The shouting and cheering was not quite so loud when we all realised that each of us would also have to 'fight' the bull and that none of our performances should be anywhere as proficient as that of the Mighty One who owned the company and all of us, its employees. It's quite difficult to purposely get defeated by a pretty pissed-off young bull without getting fairly mauled in the process.

2. TO POP OR NOT TO POP

Baby Butchers was a strange beast. When I joined, almost all the management had been at The Butchers or similar companies, had failed to reach lucrative senior management positions there and probably saw Baby Butchers as their last chance to make serious money before they were too old and tired to spend their lives in planes and hotels. They had little real understanding of organisations and only one simple product to sell – time-study workers, identify 20%-30% lost time and convince clients to reduce their workforce. However, there was also a bunch of us younger consultants, who were pretty disgusted by the whole Butchers approach. Most of the managers at Butchers were brutes not to be trifled with. But at Baby Butchers most of the managers were weak, ineffectual and would do anything for a quiet life. We later learnt, for example, that our European Operations Manager was arrested in the U.S. for being in possession of a large amount of paedophile material – which perhaps gives some idea of where his mind was as he travelled round projects like a well-paid tourist, never meeting clients and spending most of his time consulting his flight timetable rather than giving us the invaluable benefits of his many years' experience. However, fortunately this management vacuum allowed us juniors to experiment with new ideas in a way that would have been impossible at Butchers.

Both Butchers and Baby Butchers had a very simple management reporting system – all benefits and savings were reported to head office in terms of EPs (Equivalent People) or 'POPS' (People off the

Payroll) as they were affectionately known. So each week we had to report how many manweeks we had billed against plan and how many people we had 'popped' against plan. At Butchers the slightest deviation – not billing sufficient manweeks or not achieving sufficient POPs – was met with terrible retribution. At Baby Butchers, although we religiously reported our figures each week, nobody seemed to notice or care what the figures actually showed. This provided us young consultants with our opportunity to do things differently.

On one consulting project we were sent into a paper and printing works where about forty or fifty machines were manned by about forty or fifty workers per shift, where they had more work than they could cope with and where there was considerable machine down-time due to planning and scheduling problems. The standard Butchers approach would have been to try and propose that instead of one man running each machine, we could group the workers into teams and get a team of five or six workers running nine or ten machines – this, of course would enable us to fire twenty to thirty percent of the people. But we young consultants came up with the rather obvious realisation that, given the fact that the client had more work than they could handle, we could do something much more intelligent than firing a third of the people. We could instead improve maintenance and planning, increase machine up-time and enable the client to produce more output with the same number of machines and people.

Anyway we did the project, dramatically increased overall output and made loads of money for a very satisfied client – a client who was so satisfied, that they asked some of our consultants to stay on for another six months implementing further improvements in other areas of their operation. However, this novel approach gave us a problem with the Baby Butchers way of reporting project progress. The Baby Butchers management reporting system was based on informing the head office how many consultant manweeks we had billed and how many people were removed from the client's payroll each week – not how much money we had saved the client by producing more with a fixed level of staffing. So, although we did not actually fire anybody and made lots of money for the client, we could not report these financial gains – the consultancy reporting system did not allow it. And there was no way Baby Butchers was going to change its method of reporting results from EPs to such new-fangled concepts such as money earned for the client or extra profits. Without informing Baby Butchers' head office of what we were really doing for this client, the solution we found was to divide the weekly extra money our project made for the client by the average weekly cost of an employee – this gave the number of people, who would have had to have been fired to earn that amount of money for the client – a solution that satisfied everyone. Our client produced much more with a fixed cost base, while our management were able take comfort from the fact that we were reporting generous numbers of employees removed from the payroll, just like all their other projects. I later learned that this battle between the "slash and burn" approach of the old-timers and a more constructive consulting model proposed by the younger consultants was a battle which was fought at many of the productivity improvement consultancies around this time.

CAREFREE CONSULTING

Although I can now see that Baby Butchers was pretty unprofessional, at the time it seemed like heaven compared to The Butchers. I was working with a group of young people whose company I enjoyed and whose intelligence and commitment I respected, we had relatively little interference from management and we had some salesmen who got us some quite interesting work. With Baby Butchers we young consultants seemed to be able to wander round the world at someone else's expense and we got the chance to play around in other people's companies for a few months at a time without having to bear the longer-term consequences of our recommendations. None of us had much business experience and we were proud of the way we used to make things up as we went along. We used to joke that to succeed on a project, all you needed was to be 'one page ahead of the client'. Though, in general, I think we occasionally did some quite reasonable work.

We also got the chance to see some quite entertaining organisations:

There was a European supermarket and shop chain owned by an American retail giant, where we were sent in to reduce the staff levels. We did lots of efficiency studies following people around and generally getting in their way, before coming up with our recommendations about future staffing levels. These were then presented to management. After the visit of several bus-loads of unemployed and angry miners from the south of the country, sent in by the local unions to show solidarity with their colleagues in the shops, management decided that decimating staff numbers was not quite such a good idea after all. We left the organisation having removed a bundle of money but without having made the slightest change to their operations.

Then there was the huge dairy in Southern Ireland. The new chief executive called us in to review the operation, because he had the feeling that it was overmanned and inefficient. He was right – in a way. Huge numbers of people did sign up for work each day and over thirty percent of all hours worked were overtime at double the normal hourly rate – so the wage bill was massive compared to the modest output of the plant. The problem was that when you walked around, even at the supposedly busiest times of the day, the place was like the Marie Celeste – not a living soul to be seen anywhere. So it was rather difficult for us to do our usual efficiency studies on all the many staff when we couldn't find anybody to study.

What we gradually discovered was that the dairy was actually extraordinarily efficient – efficient at siphoning off vast undeserved subsidies from the European Union's farming budget. The dairy was owned by a farmer's cooperative, which had realised that you got more money by producing stuff nobody wanted (but was highly subsidised) than by making products that you had to go to the trouble of trying to sell to somebody or other. So, instead of breaking their backs to churn out the maximum amount of sellable produce from the place – as a normal business might do – they just contented themselves with making up to their European Union limits of products which they knew Brussels would buy from them, pay them to stockpile for a few years and then pay them again to destroy once they were past their sell-by date. Not a bad business really – getting paid to make something nobody wants, getting paid again to store it and then getting paid again to destroy it. In fact a pretty profitable business, especially when you could also sell off on the black market a considerable amount of the products that you had ostensibly stored and destroyed – checks by officials were few and far between and the local authorities were apparently very flexible in their attitudes to right and wrong once the appropriate amount of money had changed hands. Moreover, most people in the area had family members getting paid by the dairy, so nobody was going to blow the whistle. I say 'getting paid by the dairy' rather than 'working at the dairy' because many of those on the payroll had seldom if ever been to the dairy, actually had other jobs and would have be sorely embarrassed if asked to operate some of the equipment in whose use they were supposedly expert. The local unions were, of course, also fully involved in this profitable little game and it is not beyond the bounds of possibility that various criminal organisations and even terrorist ones were also getting their share of the booty.

There were other little idiosyncrasies we discovered. For example, somewhere out in the dairy were over two hundred purchasing books – this meant that at least two hundred employees were actively buying equipment and supplies. Of course, many of these purchases had more to do with the employees' homes and other jobs than they had to do with the dairy. I remember, during the third week of our study, meeting with a very peeved member of the management team. He had just used his purchasing book to buy a new fridge for his house – it had only been standing outside his office for a few hours, ready for him to take home that evening, when some eager workers noticed it and nicked it while he was out at a meeting.

In short, we had walked into a veritable den of thieves. Why the chief executive called us in at all is a mystery. Although fairly new to the company that officially owned the dairy, he should have had the gumption to realise that the place was a hornets' nest of quaint Irish rural corruption and local mafia rackets that should not be touched with even a clinically sterilised bargepole. We naive young consultants were, of course, totally out of our depth. The last thing this place needed was one of our efficiency improvement projects. Unfortunately, our project manager was a very highly principled individual, with a strict Catholic upbringing, who felt it was his duty to report our findings to the chief executive. This he did and we closed the project the very next day. We were quickly informed, the chief executive and the dairy management found our work both useful and interesting and that they would most certainly give the most serious consideration to the recommendations that we had presented. Goodbye!

THE ODD BUNCH

Like The Butchers, Baby Butchers could not exactly be accused of employing some of the world's finest business brains. A typical recruit to Baby Butchers and similar consultancies was someone who had moved away from their country of birth having married a foreigner. Such people would often find it difficult to fit in and get good jobs in their new countries of residence. So an organisation like Baby Butchers, which needed people who could speak the local language in the countries where they operated, provided an excellent opportunity for these people to earn a reasonable living. This frequently meant that people were hired just because they spoke a particular language and couldn't get another proper job. Don't get me wrong, many of my colleagues were really nice people, but just gathering a bunch of amiable displaced foreigners, who happened to speak a few languages and also to be unemployable, was perhaps not the best base on which to build a world-class consulting services organisation.

This, of course, meant that many of those hired by Baby Butchers and other similar consultancies were soon found to be quite unsuitable and unprepared for driving major business performance improvements for our long-suffering clients. Some, for example, had to be chucked out because being perpetually drunk affected their ability to turn up to work at all. I fondly remember the case of a certain Scottish gentleman, who shall remain nameless to save his embarrassment. He had problems getting to work on time. But this was tolerated until the day that the hotel, where the project team was staying, phoned us. The hotel management wanted to point out that our Scottish colleague had the unfortunate habit of drinking so much duty free whisky in his room each evening that he slept exceedingly soundly – so soundly in fact that he was unable to get up when he needed to have a pee during the night. He thus frequently mistook his bed for a conveniently placed lavatory and woke up each morning in a wet bed. Places like The Butchers and Baby Butchers could tolerate much human eccentricity, as long as money was being earned – but employing a drunken bed-wetter was apparently too much. So, after discussions with our head office, we despatched a consultant to the hotel, picked up the Scotsman, drove him to the airport and wished him well on his next career move. By the way, I think I forgot to mention – the Scotsman in question was our project director.

And there was George. George had dual nationality and therefore held two passports. As we later found out, this was quite useful for getting George out of the odd tight corner – usually concerning money or a lack of it. George was with us when we stayed at the Sheraton Hotel in Brussels for several months. On the top floor of the hotel with a fantastic view of the ugly Belgian capital there was an impressive swimming pool and cocktail bar. What we didn't know was that George liked to spend each evening up on the top floor entertaining lady guests and behaving like a millionaire – a very generous millionaire. George was apparently never one to refuse to buy anybody a drink or anything else that could be charged to his room. One day, when George had just disappeared never to be heard of again, we found out just how generous he had been – we were presented with his considerable bar bill.

There was an Irishman, R.J. whom we used to call 'road-runner' because, like the cartoon character, he rushed around at tremendous speed. Unfortunately, road-runner's rapid movements were not always accompanied by any great thought or direction and though huge distances were covered, little concrete progress was ever made. However, it should be said that he was a great guy and clients liked road-runner as he invariably gave the impression of enormous levels of activity – only his colleagues knew that most of this activity was essentially useless. Eventually, road-runner rushed out of the consultancy and emigrated to Australia, where one assumes that he is now speeding across that country's wide open spaces as rapidly and as pointlessly as he did when he worked with us.

Then there was Henry H........ Henry's problem was that he was like a virginal goldfish chucked into a pool full of sharks. He seemed to wander around in a kind of philosophical dream unconnected with the real world. Henry had a good education and wasn't congenitally stupid. But he also had a total and complete absence of anything that even slightly resembled common sense. When Henry was created, the Good Lord probably never intended that Henry should become a management consultant. But, unfortunately that is what he became – for a very brief period of his life. For several weeks, we managed to protect Henry from the harsh realities of this mortal existence by giving him a range of menial tasks that kept him well away from the client. He possibly could have continued this sheltered life had it not been for 'The Question'. Because Henry's consulting career came to an abrupt end the day he asked 'The Question'. For years afterwards, when many less colourful consultants were gone and forgotten, Henry remained a fond memory thanks to 'The Question'.

The occasion for Henry's demise was a sales presentation being given to a major industrial group in Sweden. This was a huge opportunity for Baby Butchers to sell a whole series of performance improvement projects in the many factories throughout the world owned by the group. So important was this business opportunity that our great owner T.F. flew over from the U.S. to personally lead this critical sales pitch. With him were a number of our executives and a few members of the team that we would use for the performance improvement programme once it was sold. The game plan was that T.F. would run the presentation, the various executives were to support him on particular parts and the project team were to 'shut the f—k up' and just look useful. This was a vital opportunity for Baby Butchers and T.F. wanted to make sure there were no slip-ups.

Anyway, the sales presentation was made to a sceptical client management group to convince them that paying Baby Butchers millions would result in a major improvement in their profitability and competitiveness. Particular emphasis was put on the fact that we would make 'real, measurable improvements in productivity.' At the end of our sales spiel, T.F. asked if there were any questions. "*Yes,*" Henry said. He had been bursting with enthusiasm to ask what he thought was quite a clever and useful question, *"how can we already say we know what improvements we can make and how we will measure them?"* There was a brief moment of silence. T.F. looked at Henry with incredulity – after all, the consultants weren't meant to ask such questions and especially never in front of potential clients. Probably for the first and last time in his wealthy life, T.F. was gobsmacked. The client's management team were undoubtedly just as taken aback as the faltering T.F. Probably never before had they been subjected to a sales pitch, where a member of the sales team seemed to be casting doubt on the value of the services his boss was trying to flog. Eventually a furious T.F. pulled himself together and gave a confused and unconvincing answer to 'The Question'. But that was most definitely the end of Henry's career in consulting. To this day, nobody really knows why Henry asked 'The Question'. It might have been malevolence. It might have been conscious professional suicide. But probably Henry was so naive and so otherworldly, that he failed to understand the bombshell he had just dropped on the man who owned the company for which he had, up till that moment, worked. Needless to say, we didn't get the project and we never saw Henry again.

There were many other similar characters and, as a project

manager at Baby Butchers and other smaller consultancies, it was often my job, when the time came, to inform them that they should probably find another outlet for their talents than productivity improvement management consulting. Firing people at Baby Butchers was a fairly straightforward affair. The unique employment contracts that Baby Butchers had developed through the shell company in the British Channel Islands made sure that employees had none of the rights that employees in normal organisations take for granted. For example, at Baby Butchers you were only paid for each day you actually worked on a project for a client. If you were unassigned – you did not get paid. If you were sick for a couple of days – you did not get paid for those days. If you had to take a day off for a family event like a birth or death – you did not get paid. Moreover, it was incredibly easy to get rid of people. All you had to do was drive them to the airport on Friday afternoon and say "goodbye, don't come back on Monday." That was it. No notice period, no employee rights. They were fired and they only got paid till the Friday they got the boot.

If they then wanted to claim unfair dismissal or anything stupid like that, they could always try suing the shell company in the Channel Islands that ostensibly employed them. Of course, nobody ever did – there wouldn't have been much point. Plus, given the fact that most people were strangers to the odd practice of paying taxes, nobody really wanted to draw too much attention to themselves.

However, he who lives by the sword dies by the sword. And my turn for the 'airport treatment' eventually came.

ALL GOOD THINGS COME TO AN END

I had just finished on the infamous Irish dairy project and was available for a new assignment. Our staffing manager rang me up and asked me to go to Denmark the following Monday to take over a project we had recently started at a fairly large factory producing a well-known brand of building insulation material. As usual, we had done a study and promised the client huge improvements in productivity. Unfortunately, the team sent in to deliver the projected improvements seemed to be struggling. The incumbent project director had been removed and I was asked to take over and sort out the mess.

Arriving at the site, my first move was to review the results of the studies, which had convinced the client to hire us. As could be expected, they owed more to the ambition and imagination of the previous project director than to anything that had actually been observed on the factory floor or in the administration offices. I reported my concerns to our head office and was instructed to continue with the project and just try and get some kind of results for the client. For a couple of months, we worked away trying to implement improved management processes and trying to train supervisors to run their areas more effectively – but with little to no concrete results. One of our biggest problems was that the previous project director had thoroughly pissed off the production director by daring to suggest that this was not the world's most efficient, most effective, most wonderful factory possible. So, the production director opposed our every move and instructed his staff to do likewise. After about ten fruitless weeks paying us to fight with his production director, the client realised that the whole thing was a huge waste of time and energy and closed the project. Though luckily for Baby Butchers he did not ask for his money back.

On the instructions of our European Operations Director, I wrote a report detailing what I thought had gone wrong. As could be expected, I was less than complimentary over the quality of analysis and the over-optimistic promises presented in the first part of the project. However, putting pen to paper was a ghastly mistake – because now there was a written record of us admitting we had all but lied in the first phase of the work in order to sell a project that we couldn't deliver. So if the client had tried to sue us and used 'disclosure' to get hold of my report, we would be well and truly up s—t creek without a paddle. Being an American owned company, Baby Butchers was always highly sensitive to the potential of being sued for failed projects. And we had a very mean firm of lawyers drafting our client contracts and warding off unhappy customers. I later heard that when T.F. saw my report, he was incandescent with rage – presumably not dissimilar to his reaction to Henry's famous question. As for his lawyers – well they apparently made it clear to him that whoever had written the report was a danger to the organisation and should be dealt with accordingly. The fact, that I had been instructed by my boss to write the report, was somehow overlooked as my boss – Ivor the Survivor (as we called him) – suddenly became invisible. Whereas, I was now a marked man.

I was fortunately, or unfortunately, oblivious to the furore I had created back in the U.S. and was eagerly badgering our staffing manager for my next assignment. There wasn't much work going in Europe at the time, so the staffing department, also unaware of the impending storm, took the decision to send me over to the U.S. for a few months to run a project there. That weekend, I had an emotional farewell from my girlfriend and headed proudly off to the airport on Saturday morning for my flight to the States. This was the first time Baby Butchers had ever permitted someone from Europe to manage a project in America and I was pretty pleased with myself and excited by the opportunity.

Arriving at London's Heathrow airport, I went to check-in and was surprised to find that my reservation had been cancelled. At first I thought this was some mistake and had a long but pointless argument with the airline staff. They were adamant. They had received instructions from my employer that I was not to board that flight. Slightly confused but assuming there had been some kind of administrative error and so not suspecting the worst, I found myself returning to London and having to wait in suspense till after the weekend to find out what had happened. A call to our Dublin office on Monday morning cleared up any confusion – no, there was no administrative error. I was not going to run a project in America. In fact, on the express instructions of T.F. himself I was well and truly out of a job and should never contact Baby Butchers ever again!

After my abrupt exit from Baby Butchers I'm embarrassed to

admit that I spent another couple of years grubbing for a living at the very bottom of the management consultancy evolutionary tree. A former colleague at Baby Butchers had recently got a job with a consultancy that we'll call The Plagiarists. Hearing of my predicament, he suggested I move over to join him there. So, having no useful qualifications to be anything other than permanently unemployed or a management consultant, I would have been foolish indeed to have turned down this offer.

The Plagiarists were founded by a quite ghastly little man who had stolen a client from Baby Butchers. He then used his first project to start amassing his millions. The man had one idea in his rather limited mind – to become rich. But as far as contributing to the development of management consultancy services and of human knowledge – forget it. All we did was copy Baby Butchers approach. At The Plagiarists we used Baby Butchers' documents, we used their training materials, we used their manuals, we used their management reporting and we even used their reference letters to help us sell projects, naturally after erasing any reference to Baby Butchers and photocopying them on to The Plagiarists' official company stationery.

So, thanks to the support unknowingly given by Baby Butchers we managed to sell a series of moderately-sized productivity improvement projects in a few countries round Europe. And because our owner also copied the legal and financial set-up used by Baby Butchers neither he nor his employees ever had the distasteful task of ever having to hand over any of our income to the tax authorities in any of the countries where we worked. So we consultants managed to keep the wolf from the door and even save up a bit of money in our offshore bank accounts, while our boss became a multi-millionaire.

But, although I had money coming in, even I could see that this was not a particularly useful way to spend one's time on this earth. There must, I assumed, be more sophisticated things we could do for our clients than the extremely basic but lucrative services that The Butchers and Baby Butchers and The Plagiarists were able to offer. So

I resolved to try and move up in the management consulting world and to get a job with one of the major players. But to join the first division, you needed an entry ticket and one way of obtaining that ticket was to get yourself an M.B.A. – Master of Business Administration (affectionately known by those who had one as Master of Bugger All). This is where the unpaid tax came in quite useful – a hundred thousand or so in the bank meant that I could easily fund my way through business school and hopefully onwards and upwards to new exciting and really value-added management consultancy – onwards and upwards to a better life I imagined existed where we could do great work for great organisations, onwards and upwards to Consulting Heaven.

(1) Contact author for reference
(2) Daily Mail 30 January 2002
(3) Source – confidential (contact author if interested)
(4) The Times Wednesday August 7 2002

CHAPTER 4

REACHING CONSULTING HEAVEN

The 1980s and early 1990s were bonanza years for management consulting. Some consulting companies grew at rates of anything between 20% to 50% per year. As Western organisations struggled to fight back against the seemingly invincible new competitors from Japan and other Asian countries, the biggest problem for consultancies was not finding clients; it was finding sufficient new recruits to staff all the projects they could sell. It was at this time that the big accountancy companies went seriously into selling consultancy and saw massive profit increases as a result. The next consultancy I joined we'll call 'The Family' because they called themselves a 'family' rather than just a consulting firm. *"We don't just like one another; we love one another, in a very creative environment,"* our owner once gushed to an obviously impressed journalist.[1] The Family was a leader amongst the new wave of consultancies and was expanding at around fifty percent a year – as one journalist wrote, *"growth, in fact, is one of The Family's biggest problems. The firm admits that its recruitment function has stumbled."*[1]

Whereas consultancies in the 1970s had been more or less split into the strategists like McKinsey and Boston Consulting Group and the operational improvement companies many of whom had split off from and copied The Butchers, the new breed of high growth consultancies managed to occupy a middle ground where they could offer a full range of services to their clients. Some expert commentators on consulting described how my new employer, The Family came crashing on to the consulting scene and rapidly grew to be one of the largest consultancies in the world:

"At its inception, The Family seemed to represent the best of both worlds of consulting, just the right mixture of academia and practicality..... It fairly exploded early on as businesses flocked to its sophisticated, complicated and pricey consulting offerings. The Family's growth was phenomenal and it added staff by the hundreds. By 1993 it was in the top ten of world consulting."

"The Family came along at the right time with a philosophy that proposed doing it all, from schmoozing with the CEO to lunching with the maintenance supervisors...And, of course, it could help with downsizing, reengineering, and the whole collection of other business school clichés and prescriptions that have come to define the industry of consulting"[2]

While the highly respected international journal, The Economist, wrote about the Family phenomenon, *"Few management consultancies have made quite so much of a splash, quite so quickly as The Family. Visit a business school and you will hear students discussing the newcomer in the same breath as McKinsey and the Boston Consulting Group"*.[3]

JOINING 'THE FAMILY'

While at business school, we had the opportunity of seeing various great companies doing what was called the 'Milk Round' – giving presentations at business schools and universities to try and encourage the best and brightest to apply to join their organisations. For me this was exciting – quite different to the recruitment techniques favoured by The Butchers and the other third rate consultancies, for which I had had the misfortune to have worked up till then. Here they weren't combing the bars and unemployment queues for misfits and deadbeats who could be overworked, underpaid and discarded at will thanks to quite dubious business ethics and shaky contracts of employment. The 'Milk Round' was professional, well-organised and for me appeared to be opening a door to a whole new world, where one could both be extremely well-paid and be proud of what one did rather than being continually ashamed.

Many management consultancies came to visit our business school, all extolling their fantastic training schemes, generous starting salaries and impressive client portfolios. One, in particular, The Family, caught my attention – it was, like most major consultancies, U.S. based. It had over a thousand consultants in The States, but was new to the British market and it urgently needed people to help it continue to grow its overseas business. But what most distinguished it from its competitors was the almost religious passion and enthusiasm of the employees making the presentation about their company. Instead of talking about money and promotion as the others did, they waxed lyrical about their 'Values' and 'Teamwork.' Jokingly, my fellow students and I started to refer to them as the Christian Scientists of Consulting. I was the only person in my year on the MBA course, who had ever worked in consulting and so I had some experience against which to compare The Family. They certainly sounded a whole heap better than what I had been used to. So, while the other students dismissed them as 'over-the-top' and 'brainwashed', I was fascinated – this was so different to the trickery, dirty-dealing and underhand practices that I had put up with for so many years at The Butchers and their various offshoots and imitators. Finally, after years of working in the dark underworld of consulting, it seemed I had the chance to emerge into the light and join an apparently world-class organisation. Perhaps Consulting Heaven was not just a figment of my imagination and really did exist after all. My fellow students sought jobs elsewhere – many with the more traditional management consultancies – but I sensed that there was something different about The Family and immediately applied to join.

A stunningly fast reply asking me to attend for interview showed that The Family were interested in my application – in fact, they were more than interested. A thing like myself was attractive to them for at least two reasons:

1. They needed people – coming to the British market with an original and exciting offering, they had sold work much faster than they could recruit people to staff their projects. They had work, they had billing slots and they didn't have the people to put in them.

2. Unlikely many applicants, I actually had some consulting experience, however questionable the ethics of the companies for which I had worked. So someone like myself could safely be put to work earning fees immediately with little to no training. In fact, once I joined The Family, I was so busy working on projects, that I did not get the chance to go on to the consultancy's on-boarding week for new consultants till after I had been with them for almost five months.

I went to one interview, then another and quickly got the job offer in May – four months before my one-year 'quickie' MBA course was finished. I explained to my prospective employer that I couldn't start work till September – I had another month's studying and exams left, then I had a two to three month summer project. But The Family couldn't wait that long – they had billing slots on projects to be filled. "No problem," they said, as soon as I finished my exams in June, I could join them. "But what about my project?' I asked – I couldn't get the MBA till I had finished my MBA project assignment.

Once again "no problem," said The Family – I could treat my first two months working with them as my MBA summer project. They even promised to give me time to complete the report necessary for me to be awarded the MBA (this turned out to be two days). To help me in my decision-making process, they also offered me a starting salary, which appears to have been the highest offered to anybody on my MBA course. Though this was not because I was God's gift to consulting. They needed warm bodies – fast. Plus they could sell me for up to five times what they would pay me, so offering me a few thousand more on my starting salary than they needed to, really made no difference to them – being able to bill me for the whole two months of my supposed MBA summer project made The Family a lot of money – in fact, almost twice what they would pay me during the whole of my first year with them.

Surprisingly, it turned out that I had made an unintentionally inspired choice. Rather than joining a big staid traditional consultancy with a well-worn and conservative service offering, I had stepped aboard a speedboat that was to accelerate past many of its larger, but less innovative, competitors. For quite a few years, The Family had a genuinely different and powerful approach both to selling to clients and also to actually getting measurable results for them – something many consultancies liked to talk about but which few will dare to promise to deliver. The Family experienced extraordinary growth. Within a few years, they went from about around thirty people in Britain to over five hundred in five to six European countries. Soon after, they were several thousand across the world.

But it was not just the speed of growth that was exciting. With The Family I moved up from the absolute lowest league of consultants scratching a livelihood doing third-rate work for some more than unsophisticated clients, right into the first division selling huge consulting projects to many of the world's greatest organisations. For many years, The Family successfully competed against and frequently beat the absolute giants of the consulting world – McKinsey, Boston Consulting, PWC, Accenture and many others. Before becoming a member of The Family, I experienced management consultancy's shadier underside. But with The Family, I found myself amongst the leaders playing around in many of the world's top-flight companies and public sector organisations. There really was a Consulting Heaven.

So, let me try and tell you what life was like at the top.

WHAT THE FAMILY BROUGHT TO THE PARTY

The Family were different from most existing consultancies, because they were probably the first to bundle elements of what the strategists, cost-cutters, technical consultants and technologists did into a single service offering. It took some years for The Family's competitors to successfully copy this. Quoting again from industry experts, who summarised why The Family were so different from the strategists, the head-cutters, the technologists and the technicians: *"Brilliant marketing is the hallmark of American business, and The Family was one of the best marketers of them all. It quickly grabbed the attention of the business press, as eager as CEOs to tap into the latest business school management fad. Amidst the backlash against the 'drop the report, send the bill, run' mentality, The Family joined the growing collection of consulting companies that crafted a message based on implementation. It recognised that the most difficult part of any business plan was putting the pieces into place and making it work."*[(2)] They then went on to describe the limitations of some other types of consulting, *"The McKinsey and BCG consultants could cozy up to the board of directors or CEO and dazzle with sheer brilliance, Accenture consultants could talk the language of technology and its many uses, the people from A.T. Kearney could analyse operations. The downsizers could cut and chop."*

Nowadays, everybody claims to be experts at implementing and getting results. So looking through the sales blurb issued by several of our competitors, it is difficult to tell them apart. But the messages they are all sending now, The Family were touting ten years or more before them:

"Our objective .... Is to partner with our clients to achieve sustainable improvements in their results" KPMG

"Our consultants are challenged to .....mobilise an organisation and effect change" Bain

"Assists clients in developing breakthrough strategies and

supports its clients in the seamless implementation of those strategies" Coopers and Lybrand

"Make our clients extraordinarily successful by creating real change for them" Deloitte and Touche

"Achieve significant improvements in revenue growth, operating effectiveness and management of capital" Ernst & Young[4]

There were probably five aspects of the way The Family worked, which set them apart from the competition for long enough for them to grow into one of the leading players in the world of management consulting:

1. A focus on people.

2. A unique culture.

3. A holistic view.

4. A passion for results.

5. Embracing technology.

1. A FOCUS ON PEOPLE

The Family took three of The Butchers' main methodologies – their techniques of productivity measurement, their process analysis and their use of tight management control systems to drive up performance. However, rather than adopting The Butchers' negative Scientific Management philosophy, The Family developed a kind of positive 'sixties Californian' view that people were resources to be developed rather than expendable objects to be discarded whenever it suited management. We framed our work as being about 'human resources development' rather than 'people reduction'. Today, this attitude is commonplace. But at the time, it was close to ground-breaking.

This led to us using a language with our clients, which they initially found bizarre but soon began to adopt themselves. We wanted to turn 'win/lose' situations into 'win/wins'. We never criticised people, we always 'gave feedback'. If we wanted to give feedback, we had to always give a 'benefit' (something we thought the person did well) before a 'concern' (something we felt they should change). We would never be allowed to argue with or contradict another person's idea; we would instead 'build on' what they said – even if it was inconsequential tripe. We didn't 'sell' to clients; we built relationships based on trust. We didn't tell people what to do; instead we had 'PSTB sessions' (Problem-Solving Team-Building) where we developed solutions jointly with the client's people. We didn't look for nasty things like obedience and respect for organisational hierarchy. Instead, we worked hard to get 'buy-in' and 'ownership'. We didn't train; we 'unleashed talent' and 'migrated knowledge'. We didn't run meetings; we 'facilitated decision-making'. Every meeting started with us collecting all the attendees' expectations of the meeting and every meeting ended with us opening our souls as we assessed whether we had managed to meet all the attendees' expectations. We didn't have organisational structures, we had 'boundary-less teams'. We didn't make money; we 'created value'. Although, fortunately for our owners, we did actually make exceedingly large amounts of money – for them.

2. A UNIQUE CULTURE

While other consultancies motivated their people with promises of pay rises, bonuses and promotion, The Family managed to get its employees to embrace a vision of the organisation and a set of work values, which spurred many of them on to a huge amount of self-sacrifice for the benefit of the company and those that ran it. Our managing director was quoted saying something that we had started to believe, *"We have built a great business. Now we'll go beyond that and change the world"*.[1]

We had a great vision, which seemed to be made up of all the types of words, which were fashionable at that time.

"To be the best in the world – the standard of excellence – at working together with leaders to build winning organisations. Help them transcend their aspirations to make a significant difference to their customers, people and shareholders. Make a positive difference to the people of The Family and, through them, the world. Leave a legacy."[1]

Looking back now, after all that has happened, after all the pillaging of our clients and exploitation of our own people that later followed, these words may ring a little empty. Moreover, if one really wanted to make a difference to the world, it's not obvious that the most logical route would be by becoming a management consultant. A missionary, teacher or garbage collector might be more appropriate career paths. But, be that as it may, at the time we employees really believed this stuff and we travelled liked madmen and worked like dogs to bring enlightenment and high performance to our, often recalcitrant, clients. On our projects, we achieved major changes in the performance of our clients' operations where all other consultants had failed. And what drove us through all the obstacles to change, thrown up by the client's people, was the conviction that we were there not just to bill our time and to make money for our bosses, but to actually 'make a difference' to people's lives.

As for our values, we were constantly reminded by our leaders, that 'living the values' was an essential part of our working lives. However wonderful your performance, if it was considered that you hadn't 'lived the values' you could miss promotion, be denied pay rises and even get booted out. If you ever wanted to stick the knife into someone's back, you would heap lavish praise on their performance and then just add as an off-hand remark, 'it's just a pity that they don't 'live the values'.

As our company diary reminded us every time we opened it, *"the character of our firm is defined by how each of us lives our core values."* There were seven 'core values': Excellence, Enthusiasm, Teamwork, Trust, Mastery, Fun and Results. When you received your performance reviews after every assignment and your progress evaluations every six months, one of the key criteria, against which you were judged, was how well you 'lived the values'. Moreover each project had soul-searching sessions based on what was called a 'Values Dipstick'. This was a questionnaire completed by each team member measuring how well the lifestyle and behaviours on the project matched each of the seven values. If the score was low, the project director was expected to take action to get it higher next time.

3. A HOLISTIC VIEW

At a time when most other consultants were either flogging report-writing, narrow expertise-based solutions or hopelessly cumbersome MRP systems, we managed to offer a much more holistic answer to our clients' issues. We were formed by bringing together a top-end strategy consultancy and an operational improvements consultancy. So we were able to combine a top down view of an organisation's overall direction with a bottom-up approach to motivating staff to achieve major improvements in performance. We were forever using fashionable tools like SWOTs, Industry Structure Analysis, Boston Boxes, Booz Balls, Balanced Scorecards and so on – things you would never have seen at The Butchers. And, unlike the downsizing so effectively pushed by The Butchers and their imitators, our improvement programmes were actually well integrated with all those wonderful things like gaining 'competitive advantage', 'value innovation' and our clients' 'strategic intent'.

4. A PASSION FOR RESULTS

Other consultants may have talked a good story about how they were dedicated to helping the client achieve measurable financial results. But when it came down to signing contracts with their clients, few would offer fixed price projects to deliver an agreed set of results. And even fewer would agree to be paid according to the results achieved, rather than just the manweeks used.

Getting a client's organisation to make major improvements in performance is difficult – if it had been easy, clients would do it themselves without the help of consultants. So offering to achieve a set of goals with an agreed number of consulting manweeks would mean that the consultancy had to take a risk. What if getting the results required more manweeks than originally thought? What if the client's people were resistant to change? What if market developments or competitor actions affected your client's performance? That could mean you were unable to achieve the desired results in the time estimated. And that could mean a consultancy having to give manweeks away free. This is something to which consultancies are by and large allergic. At a time when the consultancy market is growing by ten to twenty percent a year, you don't want people working unbilled for one client, to whom you have made rash promises, when they could be pulling in the cash with another. So most consultancies at that time would only work on 'time and materials' – this meant that they would get paid for all the consulting hours worked even if these vastly exceeded the original estimate given to the client. We, on the other hand, offered fixed price projects and we committed to achieving an agreed set of operational or financial results for that price, however many manweeks we actually used. When most other consultancies were peddling open-ended contracts in which the client had no real clarity on how much they would actually pay the consultants, our fixed price approach was quite attractive.

In addition to fixed price, we had another Unique Selling Proposition (U.S.P.). We were probably one of the only major consultancies willing to be rewarded according to the level of results achieved. Again, we differentiated ourselves from the crowd by agreeing to link part of our fees to the results we banked for the client. For many clients this was a refreshingly honest and open way of doing business – and not one that was common amongst our noble competitors.

And once we'd signed a results-based contract with our clients, in went the Christian Scientists of the consulting world, their eyes blazing with passion for our company vision, their every thought and action transmogrified by our seven values, their hearts pounding with the aspiration to 'make a difference'. Our owner described to a journalist how The Family worked *"almost always on fixed fees with fixed terms yet refusing to leave a client 'until he's ecstatic'"*.

This passion to cause lasting change was frequently recognised by our clients:

"The outstanding commitment and quality of The Family's consultants, working together with our organisation, has enabled us to deliver exceptional results"

"Too many consultants walk in, do a report, throw it on the desk, charge you an immense amount of money and walk out. The Family didn't do that. They wanted to stay with us and live through the problems, thereby helping us tremendously to reach a new level of business acumen"[5]

5. EMBRACING TECHNOLOGY

The final piece of the equation that helped The Family go from virtually nothing to thousands of consultants within just a few years was our ability to do stuff that was connected to IT systems. A few years after I joined The Family, we were bought by a monstrous computer systems group with tens of thousands of IT techies and other assorted propeller heads – people who thought it was normal to wear orange shirts, purple trousers and green ties all at the same time; people who thought that establishing a close personal relationship with the client meant going into client meetings, placing their laptop computers on the client's desk and typing in everything the client said; people who giggled uncontrollably at jokes most of us found old hat when we were ten or eleven years old; people who seemed to lack almost all the basic social skills that most of us take for granted.

Anyway, in spite of their personal shortcomings, many of them did know a thing or two about IT systems. Though understanding what they were saying could prove a challenge both to our clients and us. So, when $50m-$100m ERP systems implementation and consulting projects started to become all the rage with the major multi-national oil, chemicals, FMCG and pharmaceutical companies, being able to field innumerable crowds of system architects, integrators, programmers and so on, gave us a major advantage over the consulting houses that didn't have a technological leg to stand on.

CONSULTING HEAVEN

For probably seven to eight years, we at The Family had a ball. Of course, there were some problems – we worked so hard and travelled so much that most people got divorced, a few had heart attacks, there was the odd death or two and at least one suicide. But that didn't seem to matter – we blasted through client after client, selling monstrous projects and also delivering fantastic results. Unlike so many tired, stale, cumbersome and arrogant competitors, we actually did more or less what we promised. Time and again our clients would write us reference letters saying things like *"while other consultants talk, The Family gets results"* and *"I have worked with many consultants and I can say that The Family are the best in the world"* and *"It is inconceivable that we could have accomplished this transformation without The Family"*.

For example, we cut in half the production time for fighter aircraft and missile systems helping their manufacturer have some of the best-selling killing machines in the world; we assisted a no-hoper supermarket chain with an old-fashioned brand image shoot past its competitors to become the clear leader in its country; we pushed lazy, fat, rich pharmaceutical companies to become even more fantastically profitable than they already were; we turned round scores of banks and insurance companies; we were the leading consultancy in helping telecoms companies adapt to their new competitive environment and in the rapid launch of mobile telephone operations; – you name it, we did it – we completely turned round a whole heap of companies all heading for disaster if we had not been there. We brought enthusiasm, teamwork, innovative ideas, positive thinking to one heavy, over-structured, bureaucratic corporation after another and transformed them into newer, sleeker, slicker, slimmer almost unrecognisable versions of their former selves. We turned elephants into cheetahs. Our clients raved about how wonderful we were. And for our owners, we turned consulting manweeks into gold.

At last, after years with The Butchers and others in the sewers of the management consulting industry, I had finally reached Consulting Heaven.

(1) Consultants News (contact author for date)
(2) Contact author for reference
(3) The Economist (Contact author for date)
(4) Company websites 1998
(5) Client references

CHAPTER 5

DELIVERING VALUE AND MAKING A DIFFERENCE?

The big question to answer about management consultancy is whether clients actually get, and believe they get, value for the millions they pay for the mountains of management consultancy they buy. Consultancies and their clients tend to go quite quiet when asked whether it was all worth it and whether the reality that was delivered lived up to the initial promises that the consultants made. Quickly thinking back over all the consultancy I sold and saw, I would guess that about a quarter to a third was either amazing or pretty good, about a half was of questionable or no value and the rest was incompetent and often destructive to our clients.

One study conducted by the Cranfield School of Management[1] asked 640 consultants whether they thought they brought value to their clients and also asked 170 clients whether they believed they received value from their consultants. There were considerable differences in views between the well-paid consultants and the clients who paid them. A whole 71% of consultants said they brought value to their clients – unfortunately only 36% of clients happened to agree. So the clients' responses in this study quite closely reflects my experience of about two thirds of all consultancy probably being a waste of time and money.

The figures from the survey can be seen as pretty shocking:

- Consultants appeared to have admitted in a confidential survey that almost 30% of their work gave no value to their clients. You have to be pretty cynical to spend your life selling and delivering expensive consultancy that you know has no real benefit for those foolish enough to buy it

- Two thirds of clients are dissatisfied with the quality of work their consultants deliver – there are not many other businesses that could survive for long with so many unhappy customers

Yet, in spite of the general dissatisfaction with consultants' work, many managers are so dependent on them that they keep on buying their services. As one of the authors of the research said, *"some consultants are so embedded in the culture of the organisation that the client believes he has to go through them to get anything done"*.[1]

Sometimes, when working with clients, you wondered who was running the organisation. Several times, especially with the leading strategy consultancies, I have seen managing directors who spend hours locked away with their consultants, seldom listen to their own management teams and just use their management teams to rubber-stamp the decisions made by the managing director and their favourite consultants. As for the rest of the management team, well they were so afraid of upsetting the consultants and risking losing their jobs, that they allowed the management consultants to usurp their rightful positions. Moreover, what I have seen are apparently not just isolated cases – the author of the Cranfield Business School report goes on to say, *"I know a chief executive who won't do anything without asking the consultant. He acts on the consultant's advice, against his own best advice in the company."*[1] The author also noticed the same fear of criticising the consultants, that I have seen, *"people don't want to speak out on this issue. There is a taboo about it."*[1]

Some more recent, but less statistically-based research by a Harvard Business School professor and world expert on the management consulting industry concluded that consultants privately admitted that about 20% of their work was really excellent, about 60% was tolerable but of little value and around 20% was "junk".[2] The consulting expert then explains the main reason for the low standard of much consulting work – the focus on short-term profitability rather than on maintaining professional standards, *"in the professional services world, however, principles were sacrificed for cash. With one or two really rare exceptions, professional firms are not places that are driven by values and ideology any more. They are driven by almost a caricature of short-term financials."*[2]

I found this sentiment echoed by an e-mail I received from a consultant at Accenture, written three years after the public share offering (IPO) which made millions for each of their partners, *"we have gone from a firm which focuses on doing the right thing to a firm which focuses on what we can legally get away with. There is no question that the IPO has destroyed our culture along with thousands of careers. Partners, on the other hand, have made out like bandits laughing all the way to the bank."*[3]

So, assuming that at most a third of all management consultancy really adds value and makes a difference, it might be worth spending a short while looking at what distinguishes great consultancy from the majority of consultants' work which is either unhelpful or even destructive to its clients.

THE GOOD, THE BAD AND THE UGLY

THE STRATEGISTS

For decades McKinsey have worked with some of the world's most successful organisations. McKinsey has done projects for *"147 of the world's 200 largest corporations, including 80 of the top 120 financial-services firms, 9 of the 11 largest chemical companies, and 15 of the biggest health-care and pharmaceutical concerns"*.[4] It is said that their largest client in 2001 paid them $60 million for advice.

For example, they earned $9 million as a key adviser to CEO Carly Fiorina on Hewlett-Packard's acquisition of Compaq, they have done dozens of engagements for the highly successful Johnson & Johnson over thirty years, they have worked with General Motors helping improve competitiveness and have been a long-time counsellor to the huge German multi-national Siemens.[4]

However, for such an elite consultancy, McKinsey were also heavily involved in some embarrassing failures. McKinsey had advised Enron for nearly 18 years until it crashed and burned. Some industry experts were surprised that McKinsey managed to get out unscathed from the Enron debacle, *"I'm surprised they haven't been subpoenaed as a witness, at least,"* says Wayne E. Cooper, CEO of Kennedy Information, a research and publishing firm that keeps tabs on consultants. *"There was so much smoke coming out of the Andersen smoking gun that all the firefighters went after that one. McKinsey was lucky. They dodged a bullet."*[4] As McKinsey's long-term client evaporated under the leadership of an ex-McKinsey partner, Jeffrey K. Skilling, and tens of thousands of people were ruined, McKinsey's CEO could only comment, *"We stand by all the work we did. Beyond that, we can only empathize with the trouble they are going through. It's a sad thing to see."*[4]

McKinsey had been a key consultant to Swiss-Air which went bankrupt after a disastrous strategy of spending nearly $2 billion buying majority stakes in a whole series of smaller airlines including the chronically badly-managed and reputedly corruption-riddled Belgian airline Sabena. And there were Kmart and Global Crossing, which also filed for bankruptcy in 2001.[4]

Kmart makes an interesting case study. McKinsey worked for them from 1994 through to 2000, when they ended the relationship after disagreements over the new CEO's decision to pursue a disastrous price war against Wal-Mart. Getting out was probably a good decision for McKinsey as the price war left Wal-Mart as the world's largest retailer and Kmart in bankruptcy after over a hundred years in business. However, throughout the time that McKinsey advised Kmart, its client's competitive position steadily eroded. As one observer wrote about the time during which McKinsey advised Kmart, *"we know that Kmart continued to stay behind Wal-mart in deployment of technology, management of supply chains, strategic alliances with major suppliers and the product mix preferred by the customer"*.[5] Given that rather long list of apparent failures, it's difficult to imagine what value McKinsey could have brought to the struggling retailer. A study by McKinsey also highlighted the success of Wal-mart, the competitor to McKinsey's client Kmart, *"A study by McKinsey, the management consultants, found Wal-mart, whose revenues topped $200 billion last year, was responsible for a significant chunk of the overall improvement in productivity in the U.S. economy in the 1990s"*.[6]

As I've mostly competed against rather than worked for them, I've primarily seen their work with clients that weren't well served by the McKinsey colossus. They were therefore willing to let us come and help them, either while McKinsey were still there or just after they had left. So what I have seen would probably be classed as some of McKinsey's less brilliant projects.

What I observed, was that much of the work I saw McKinsey doing was not really strategy at all, but was either re-designing organisational structures or doing some benchmarking, both usually with the intention of reducing staff numbers and costs.

I personally found their organisation design stuff weak. It all seemed to be about drawing new organisation charts – moving the lines and the boxes on the organigram – rather than building the client skills and capabilities to ensure that the elegant designs, that they came up with, actually worked in the unpleasant reality of day-to-day operational life. Moreover, it was my impression that some of their organisation designs were overly influenced by what they knew the chief executive would like, rather than what was necessarily best for the organisation. And finally, I believe that it was questionable whether much of their organisation design work was really necessary: in my experience of a hundred or so organisations – really motivated, well-led, capable staff will make any organisation structure work however inappropriate that organisation structure may be. On the other hand, demotivated, poorly-led and inadequately skilled staff will fail, however brilliant the organisation structure within which they are placed by clever consultants. I therefore wonder whether some of the leading strategy houses might not have served their clients better by getting on with the much more difficult task of upgrading the effectiveness of their clients' existing organisations, rather than just taking their twenty pieces of silver to give clients smart shiny new organisation structures that the clients maybe didn't really need.

As for their benchmarking – it is said that, thanks to having worked with most of the world's leading organisations, McKinsey have built up an outstanding database of what constitutes good performance in almost any part of an organisation in almost any activity sector. I'm sure this is true. This allows them to establish very rapidly the kinds of performance levels at which their clients should be aiming and to advise their clients on how to reach the targeted levels. Again, I must stress that most of the McKinsey benchmarking projects that I have seen were probably not amongst the consultancy's finest. I've come across several McKinsey benchmarking projects that all looked a little shaky to me. I'll mention just two.

One was in a European national broadcasting service. McKinsey did their study and recommended how many people should be fired to reduce costs. McKinsey's results were disputed by those who had been involved in the study and who claimed that McKinsey had misused and misrepresented the data they had been given. Finally the McKinsey key client, the head of the national broadcasting service, had to apologise publicly for the number of errors in the McKinsey report and recommendations. If I remember correctly the client also had to rescind some or all of the dismissals that had been issued.

Another time I was working in a major electricity, water and gas provider. The company had just merged with some other utility companies and the chief executive asked McKinsey to do a number of tasks including a new organisation design and a comparison of the effectiveness of the hundreds of people in their various call centres, both compared to each other and compared to international benchmarks. The chief executive, a rather outspoken man who, his managers complained, spent more time with McKinsey consultants than he did with his management team, was particularly proud of the call centre for which he had been responsible prior to the merger. Conveniently, the McKinsey benchmarking also came to the conclusion that his was in fact the most effective call centre in the new expanded organisation. People at the other call centres complained bitterly at this result, pointing out that the so-called 'best practice' most efficient call centre only handled customer queries about electricity supply and billing, whereas some of the others had to deal with electricity, gas and water customers – altogether a much more complex situation requiring them to access three times as many databases and to interface with three times as many service groups as the supposedly 'best practice' electricity-only call centre. The moaners claimed that McKinsey were comparing apples with pears and insisting there was no difference. However, as far as we could see, their lamentations went unheard by a top executive, who was apparently more interested in listening to his consultants than his own people.

THE TECHNOLOGISTS

Certainly, there must be many many successful projects to keep the hundreds of thousands of technology consultants busy. But at several consultancies we tended to walk into situations where the technologists had failed and the clients now needed someone to quickly clean up the usually horrendously expensive mess that the technologists had left behind them.

One of the worst situations I ever saw, was when a part of the British government paid its technology consultants around one billion pounds for a major computer systems implementation. In addition to the billion pound cost, the organisation also had to pay their systems provider one hundred and thirty eight million pounds a year in service costs, which moved the organisation from having made a profit for the last twenty years or so into making a significant loss. The more we delved into the history of this enormous systems project, the more concerned we became about its massive costs and questionable results. I took a meeting with the programme manager to discuss the situation. Laughing, he admitted to me without any embarrassment that the whole expensive exercise had delivered "diddly squat".[7]

Nobody in the organisation seemed overly concerned at this disaster – it had just been taxpayers' money that they had squandered and fortunately nobody outside, like the press, had realised the true scale of the catastrophe. When I tried to warn them that a new similar project they were starting up with some other technology consultants showed all the signs of heading in the same direction as the horror story they had just completed, I was warned never to mention this again.

As we met with potential clients around the world, we came across many systems and consulting projects that had run expensively into the sand. There was a U.S. oil company that spent over $120 million on consultancy and IT support to implement a new system internationally and achieved no business benefits at all from the whole programme. A leading multi-national food company hired us for ten million dollars to get some financial results from their system implementation on which they had already spent tens of millions. Then there were numerous banks, insurance companies and supermarket chains, which had all thrown fortunes at technology consultancies without seeing anything for their money.

What you tended to find with major technology projects was that they start up with a huge fanfare and with the consultants promising all kinds of huge financial and operational benefits once the great system is up and running. However, months or even years later, as the whole thing grinds excruciatingly to a halt with money and people's time apparently disappearing into a huge black hole, clients soon don't care about the benefits any more. They drop their expectations to the minimum are just relieved when the basic parts of their system are finally working and there are no more headaches and disruption from the programme that once had such ambitious targets.

MAKING A REAL DIFFERENCE

I have mostly worked in what we called 'change management' consultancies. This meant that we both made recommendations to our clients about how to improve their operations and organisations and we took responsibility for ensuring that those recommendations were successfully implemented with the promised performance improvements being achieved. Not all our projects did deliver the expected results. But, when they failed, the client was usually so deeply involved in the failure that they found it difficult to pin the blame on us alone and I never heard of a client ever successfully suing us. Moreover, we always seemed to have some very very tough American lawyers, who made sure that any client complaints were quickly dealt with by us claiming any problems were never our fault but were due to client personnel not cooperating with our change projects. Sometimes, when clients closed down our projects due to their dissatisfaction with our progress, it was us who sued the client for breach of contract and anything else we could think of.

Nevertheless, for a period of some years, many of our projects were really good and led to clients giving us fantastic references. Although we did many things that differentiated us from much of the competition, I think that what most distinguished us was our openness and honesty when dealing with our clients. And a key aspect of this honesty was to make sure we gave our clients, not necessarily what they wanted, but what they really needed. Time and again, we would take the risk of challenging our clients' assumptions about what their organisations needed, rather than just taking their money to provide what they thought their organisations should have.

CHALLENGING THE CLIENT

When a client offers a consultancy a contract for, say, fifty million dollars to implement an MRP system, thirty million euros to get a CRM (Customer Relationship Management) system up and running or even just three million pounds or so for a trendy new matrix organisation design, it's awfully difficult for a consultancy to say 'no, thank you'. Most consultancies will obviously just take the money and, if the whole exercise gives no benefits at all, they can always fall back on the excuse that they were just doing what the client wanted. I've seen consultancies do this many times and have seen them run projects that they knew would give little to no value to our clients, but which at least kept large numbers of our consultants billing their time.

But for the few years, when we were really honest enough to want to give our clients value rather than just taking their money, the first thing we would do was to challenge them about their assumptions and their goals. We would ask them questions like:

- Why do they think they need to implement their fancy new system?

- What benefits do they expect from CRM?

- What are they really trying to achieve with a new organisation design?

- Why are they trying to buy business process reengineering?

- What is the point of redesigning their supply chain?

- And so on.

So, instead of just kicking off the programme the client management thought they needed, we would insist on doing a short (4-8 weeks) study to assess what the client's organisation really required. And, not surprisingly, we would find out either that client management had misdiagnosed the situation and had found the wrong cure or that they had completely unrealistic expectations about the benefits they would get from the projects they wanted to start.

For example, the management at a major IT services company with over thirty thousand employees asked us to produce a new organisation design. Our study confirmed that they did need to reorganise from small entrepreneurial fifty person units into larger industry-based divisions. But we also found that their real need was to develop the capability to sell and deliver larger more complex programmes than they had done in the past. So, while we did help restructure the business, the main thrust of our work was building strategic selling and large project management capability.

Similarly, a major FMCG (Fast Moving Consumer Goods) company asked us to redesign its new product development (NPD) process, as too few new products were coming through to market and most projects were over-running on time and cost. We found that the NPD process itself was OK and that it would have been a bit of a waste of time and money fiddling endlessly with the volumes of process flows and activity descriptions that a previous consultant had left them. However, what we did find was that the NPD staff were quite hopeless at planning their work, assigning the right resources, communicating valuable information, taking decisions – there was no dynamism, little leadership and almost complete organisational paralysis. So, instead of taking the cash for an unnecessary redesign of the NPD process, we convinced the client to let us run a programme strengthening the employees' skills in competencies like management, decision-making, work-planning, communication and so on. This project was successful and we put some life and energy back into the previously comatose organisation instead of taking the easy route and giving the client a superfluous, but potentially profitable (for us consultants), NPD process redesign.

Consultants should have a moral duty to use their experience to challenge the client's assumptions and make sure they get what they need rather than what they think they need. There should be a synergy between consultants and clients – clients' staff should have thousands of years cumulative experience of their particular activity sector, whereas consultants should have a collective knowledge of implementing new systems, redesigning supply chains, restructuring organisations and of best practice across a wide range of industries. However, too many consultants are afraid of upsetting their clients by telling them that their assumptions are wrong and so they obediently and gladly take their clients' millions, fully aware that they're probably not acting in the client's best interests by doing so.

(1) The Sunday Times 6 December 1998
(2) Fast Company 2002
(3) E-mail 16 October 2004
(4) Business Week Online 8 July 2002
(5) Business Week Online 29 July 2002
(6) FT.com 23 August 2002
(7) Client interview (contact author for further details)

CHAPTER 6

THE EASY ART OF SELLING MILLION POUND/DOLLAR/EURO PROJECTS

During the whole of the 1990s consulting continued to experience massive growth. In addition to all the normal stuff we'd do for clients – downsizing, restructuring, mergers and acquisitions, reorganisations, improving product development and so on – we were given a whole host of new things to sell, thanks to the outpourings of a string of management gurus, many of whom had probably never run a real organisation in their lives. These were the golden years of management fashions, fads and quick fixes. The tendency for organisations to leap at the latest instant solution from self-proclaimed gurus eager to make a name for themselves became widespread. In fact, this was such common practice amongst management, that one respected author, an ex-McKinsey consultant, wrote a book called *Fad Surfing in the Boardroom: Reclaiming the courage to manage in the age of instant answers* attacking this trend. Criticising managers for jumping from one fad to the other without looking for the fundamental causes of their problems, the author was brutally clear in her criticism of both management and their pet consultants when she defined Fad Surfing as *"the practice of riding the crest of the latest management wave and then paddling out again just in time to ride the next one; always absorbing for managers and lucrative for consultants; frequently disastrous for organisations".*[1]

The biggest fad was, of course, Business Process Reengineering (BPR), which created billions of dollars, euros and pounds of work for consultants. The author of *Fad Surfing* called BPR *"The Consultants' Full Employment Act"* and Michael Hammer, one of the authors of Reengineering the Corporation lamented that he wished he had taken a royalty on all the reengineering consulting projects sold as *"reengineering made billions for consultants".*[2]

Clients loved BPR, because they could easily understand what it was about and because it promised huge benefits. Consultants loved it because it provided a massive amount of revenue and because anybody you hired could do it. Previously, in consulting, you had to try and pretend you knew something about a client's business (healthcare, chemicals, defence, finance or whatever) to gain credibility and sell in a project. But with BPR, you could take someone straight out of college or off the street, teach them how to do some simple process flow analysis, call this 'reengineering' and sell these 'vanilla consultants' for seven to ten thousand pounds a week or more to any client in any line of business. 'After all,' we'd claim to clients, 'what was important with BPR was not knowing a client's business in detail, but rather the ability to conduct process analysis whatever the client's area of activity'. Although around seventy percent of BPR efforts were judged by clients and by industry experts as failures, they made many consultants quite fantastically rich.

If you couldn't sell in a large BPR project, there were other things you could offer – Balanced Scorecard, for example was a good money-spinner. There were also loads of enormous computer system implementations that needed to be cleaned up. Or you could sell Activity Based Management or Zero Based Budgeting or Six Sigma (if you had a few black belts) or some Total Quality Management or develop a customer-focused organisation or build a new vision or even create an empowered work-force. And finally, if none of that interested potential clients, you could shoot for the biggest prize of all – what we called 'Business Transformation', a massive change effort, which, as the internationally respected magazine, The Economist, wryly commented, *"would employ an army of consultants for a century"*.[3]

Several of my colleagues and I had once imagined that selling a million pound or dollar or euro project would be the ultimate sales achievement of our consulting careers. But in this gold rush, projects costing a million seemed to be hanging off trees. Soon we never quoted a price for a client that was less than a million. Then one of us sold a project for two million, then there was one for four million and then one for seven million. So that eventually, whenever we only sold a little project for just a million, we didn't even bother sending a 'go-ahead' message to the rest of the consultancy any more. Projects costing only a million were simply too small to attract attention. In fact, towards the end of this period of plenty, if you only sold for a mere million, you were seen as having in some way failed to meet our management's expectations.

There are obviously many different ways to sell projects to clients. Each client situation is usually unique, their need for consultancy will vary and they will each have a different buying process. Moreover, each management consultancy will have its preferred methods of selling. Some like getting a foot in the door, starting small and gradually building up their billing levels. Others go for a 'sh-t or bust approach' and push hard to get the big multi-million project from very first contact with the client. Some spend their lives replying to competitive Requests for Proposals (RFPs) and taking part in 'Beauty Parades' for one client after another. And others brilliantly exploit their networks of contacts to ensure that whenever there is an opportunity to sell consulting into an organisation, they are well and truly in there long before their competitors get the slightest inkling that something's going on.

To oversimplify reality considerably, let's say there are generally three main types of selling situations:

1. Clients who know they want consultancy support.

2. Clients who won't let you through the door.

3. Clients who are not convinced they need consultants and may even be hostile to them.

1. CLIENTS WHO KNOW THEY WANT CONSULTANCY SUPPORT

These organisations will tend to invite a few consultancies to discuss their situation and then to enter a competitive bid for the work. The bidding process may just involve submitting a written proposal or doing a presentation or both. Often there will be a first round, where a short-list is drawn up on the basis of written proposals and then a second round, in which a final few consultancies are invited to present their proposals to the client's management team.

Generally such clients will talk about a 'level playing field' where all the competitors are in with an equal chance of winning the assignment. However, all the consultancies will know that only a fool or a loser sends their team in to play on a level playing field. So all the competitors, while pretending to play the game fairly, will be desperately trying every ruse they know to stack the odds in their favour. One of the best ways to push things your way, is to get your people into the client's organisation before you present your proposal. A tactic we used was to say that it would be useful in preparing our bid if we could interview some key managers about their expectations for the proposed project. This gave us the chance to meet some of the decision-makers and influencers and to find out what their *'hot buttons'*, *'red issues'* and *'red flags'* were:

- *'Hot buttons'* are the things that turn them on and that they'll want to hear in your proposal.

- *'Red issues'* are the real problems they want solved. Sometimes these may not even be mentioned in the RFP and you may need to do a fair bit of digging to uncover these

- *'Red flags'* are the things you must absolutely not say as these will turn client managers against you

The interviews also let you try to prise out what the real decision-making process is. Will the whole management team as a group decide which consultants to choose? Are there a few dominant members, to whom you need to pitch your story? Or will it be the CEO alone who makes the choice?

Once you start to get a feel for how the decision will be made and you know how the main members of the management team tick, you can spin your presentation so it appeals to these individuals and avoids anything that might upset them.

To take a real life example, on one bid I met the European Supply Chain Director of a household name company. The man was arrogant, opinionated and convinced that he was God's gift to supply chains even though his particular supply chain was a mess and the company he worked for was going rapidly down the tubes having lost money for the last couple of years. Moreover, every time we mentioned some tremendous supply chain project we'd done for other leading companies and even produced glowing references, he just dismissed the other clients as idiots who didn't know what they were doing. This allowed us to adjust our bid so we didn't say anything that could have offended this clown. Similarly, through meeting some key people in a famous worldwide entertainments company, we found out that they were tired of consultancies that offered studies and reports. They were looking for someone who would achieve real measurable financial results. Although we were only a smallish consultancy at that time and were pitching against the best in the business, by basing our bid on being rewarded according to the results we achieved, we were able to win the contract against competition from several of the world's leading consulting mastodons.

If you've any contacts in the potential client organisation, you'll try to use these to find out about the problems and politics. Once I even found a fairly senior manager, who had just left a competitor against whom we were bidding for a potentially monster-sized consulting engagement. So I threw a bucket of money at him to hire him for a few days as an advisor to our bid team working against his former employer. This tactic paid off when he let a rather large and ugly cat out of the bag by telling us our main competitor's probable game plan for winning the business.

However, whatever small tricks you may use to get one over on the competition, generally these competitive situations are straightforward – the client knows they want consulting help and you try and convince them that you're the perfect partner.

2. CLIENTS WHO WON'T LET YOU THROUGH THE DOOR

Many other organisations simply refuse to talk to consultants. This can be either because they have strong management, who know what they are doing and therefore have no intention of letting consultants through the door. Or it could be because they already have one or more incumbent consultancies in place all eager to protect their privileged position and with no desire to let any more in. Or, of course, they may have had The Butchers in to do a 'slash and burn' sometime in the recent past and may now be fatally allergic to management consultancy in any form. With these clients you're probably best to walk away and wait till a change in their management or their competitive position causes them to feel more vulnerable and thus more open to letting a new team of consultants run riot in their organisation.

3. CLIENTS WHO ARE NOT CONVINCED THEY NEED CONSULTANTS AND MAY EVEN BE HOSTILE TO THEM

But the most interesting situations in terms of selling approach, client manipulation and dubious business ethics are those clients who are not convinced they need consultants and may even be openly hostile to them. The challenge here is to get them to open the door, however slightly, by allowing you just to talk to them. Because, once a door is opened, however tiny the crack, you'd be amazed at how many consultants can be squeezed through by even a modestly skilled salesman. Looking back now, it still seems incredible to me that my colleagues and I, most of whom had no real business or management experience, sold so much to so many clients, most of whom had not really intended to buy any significant amounts of consulting in the first place. The approach we used was so successful that in some years we converted over ninety percent of opportunities into million-plus projects. We even used to joke that on our team, *'you never got out of bed in the morning for less than a million'*. We found this hugely funny, though perhaps some of our clients may not have been able to appreciate our humour.

The purpose of this and the following chapter is to show how, during these years of plenty, any reasonable contact with a client could be turned into at least a million pound, euro or dollar sale providing you played your cards right. Like many of my colleagues, I never used to think of myself as a salesman. In fact, before becoming a management consultant, I had never really sold anything in my life. Yet, after just a few years learning the tricks of the trade from some true experts, I found that I needed just four to six weeks to take clients from being convinced that there was nothing consultants could do for them, to enthusiastically signing up for major consulting projects. I've seen pretty much the same approach used in several consultancies so I think it's sufficiently widespread in the consultancy industry to be worth spending some time on.

RIP-OFF! – THE MANAGEMENT CONSULTING MONEY MACHINE

FIRST AND SECOND PHASES – HOW TO GET A FOOT IN THE DOOR

When you've got a client who puts out a RFP because they know that they need their supply chain improved, their new product development speeded up, a new IT system implemented or whatever, you know they will be taking the whole thing pretty seriously and will have assigned a hefty budget for the project. So you can safely put in a multi-million bid as you can guess your competitors will be doing the same.

However, when a client is not convinced they need consulting help, if you start asking for a million or so to improve their organisation's performance you would clearly get thrown out the door. So what we used to do is find some way of getting into their organisation at low cost and low risk to them – we would creep in below the radar. Then, once we'd established our bridgehead, we would use our presence there to start expanding out to earn more and more fees, hopefully without our competition getting the chance to find out that there was a consultants' feeding frenzy taking place.

The way we used to get through the door in these cases was to say to potential clients something like:

- Why don't we send a small team to work with your people for four to eight weeks?

- Together we can review your supply chain, organisational effectiveness, service levels, structure, profitability or whatever.

- Together we can assess the opportunities for improvement and calculate what these would be worth to you.

- This will give us both the chance to see whether the benefits are worth going after.

- This will also give us both the chance to see how each other works and whether we can work together.

- Then you can decide whether you want to work with us to achieve the improvements or whether you want to just use your own people.

- And because we don't yet know what the opportunities might be, we consultants will take a business risk and conduct this first study at a greatly reduced price of only one hundred to two hundred thousand dollars or pounds or euros.

Provided you were reasonably credible, you found quite a lot of clients who would fall for this story and sign up to a short study of whatever area of their organisation they felt might be of interest.

I'm not sure why so many did let us in. They must have suspected that this was just a ploy to sell them a much larger follow-on project, which they probably thought they had no intention of buying. Perhaps many clients, who themselves only have experience of working in a limited number of organisations, are curious to see what outsiders think of their operations. Perhaps clients believe that it's safe to let consultants in as they, the clients, are not foolish enough to be taken in by the inevitable consultant claims that the client needs millions of consultancy help. Some clients may even believe that our First Phase team will give them a clean bill of health. So they could then go to their owners and say, "see, the consultants say we're doing a terrific job". But, whatever the reason, time and again, responsible business leaders and managers, who would slam the door in the face of double-glazing salesmen, Jehovah's witnesses and any other 'cold-caller', nevertheless agree to pay consultants hundreds of thousands to come into their organisations basically with one single aim in mind – to sell them a large consulting project. We used to call these first phases or studies 'paid sales' as the client would be paying us quite substantial sums of money to run round their organisation looking for something big and expensive to sell them.

Once the contract for the short study was signed, my colleagues and I in our First Phase team would take over. It was our job to ensure that around ninety percent of these studies led to major consulting assignments. Incredibly, for many years, they actually did.

Delivering major performance improvements once a project is sold to a client can be quite hard work. But the real 'Art' of management consulting is taking a situation, where a client probably had no intention of buying any significant work, and emerging a few short weeks later with a multi-million contract in your hands.

GETTING TO 'YES' – CREATING CLIENT DEPENDENCY

Obviously you're trying to use the time during the First Phase to sell the client a big project that will be profitable for you and hopefully provide something for the client as well. There are different ways of doing this. You could bring in a team of world class experts who truly understood a client's operations and had the experience and performance benchmarks to be able to tell the client exactly what their results should be and how the consultants could help them achieve those results. But truly excellent experienced consultants are rare creatures. In almost a hundred First Phases, I think I've only been in this happy situation four or five times, where my team were so knowledgeable about and experienced in the client's business that I could just let them loose and watch with pleasure as they tore through the client's organisation delivering world-class insights and creating a tremendous bow-wave of enthusiasm for working together with us.

More often, your team is so-so and may have limited experience of your client's area of work. Therefore you're not going to be able to blow the client away by the power of your insights and the breadth of your relevant experience. So instead you can try to sell by shaking the clients' confidence in their own people and the results they were achieving. We used to call this 'selling by creating client dependency', because the more worried the client got as you gradually but forcefully undermined what their own people were saying to them, the more they would switch their loyalties away from their own staff and start to bond with you. Then the more they bonded with you, the more they would become dependent on you to guide them. It is possible to sell a consulting project by doing lots of analysis and presenting lots of data, but if you can create client dependency, it's unlikely they'll ever ask you to leave.

The clearest way to see how we moved (manipulated) the client from scepticism to dependency and signing away millions is to follow the process we used during these First Phase studies. This process – what we called our 'Sales Process' – was so well-defined and frequently used that we had training materials, which explained in detail what we would say to the client each week and even each day during the First Phase study and how the client would react to our work week by week. So, while the client thought we were conducting a detailed analysis customised to their particular situation, we were actually just working our way through a highly regimented and well-documented sales routine.

Here, let's assume a First Phase of five weeks. Sometimes they were shorter and sometimes longer, but the process used was usually pretty much the same, whatever the length.

WEEK 0

Once the client had signed up to pay for a study, we would try and gather together the team that would be working on the assignment. We used to call this preparation 'Week 0' or 'Week minus 1' although during busy years, as people were often on other projects, we seldom had as much as a week and sometimes had as little as half a day to get ready. The shortest Week 0 that I had was less than two hours on a Monday morning in the car with my new team on the way to the client's head office to start the work.

Assuming, we did have a couple of days preparation, the team would meet either at our offices or at a decent hotel – the client would be paying our expenses, so there was no great pressure to keep costs down. During this preparation time we would:

- Gather what we knew about the client's organisation and activity sector.

- Have a first number crunch to see what that told us about our client's situation.

- Develop hypotheses about what the client's problems might be.

- Start to plan the interviews and studies.

- Start to set up meetings with key client people throughout the organisation.

- Suss out whatever other nightlife opportunities might be available in the places where the client was located.

- Check out which hotels offered bonus points for loyal customers that we could use for getting free hotel stays for our holidays.

- Go out for a couple of wonderful meals at great restaurants in order to help our teambuilding.

We would also start to think about our sales strategy – for example, how big a project did we want to sell? Would we restrict ourselves to the areas already agreed with the client or would we try to 'blow the scope' and expand our work way beyond what the client had originally intended? Was this a slow build-up or a wall-to-wall? How many people did we have 'on the beach', so how much did we have to sell here? How close were we to our sales targets, so how much did we have to get from this client to make our bonuses?

I would always use this time to assess how experienced and

effective my team were. If I had a strong team with a bit of relevant sector experience, then I could build a fairly ambitious and aggressive work-plan and also take the risk of having some fun by really 'blowing the scope' to try to sell a monstrous project. However, if the team was wet behind the ears or just made up of the consultancy's walking wounded, whom nobody else wanted, I would go for a much more conservative approach and only do a limited number of quite basic studies in order to get some results and sell a modestly-sized project, while avoiding exposing my team's weaknesses.

WEEK I

In the first week of the study, we would generally try and achieve three things:

A.   First Interviews

B.   Financial Overview

C.   Update 1.

A. First Interviews

In your initial sales discussions with a client, they may have told you what problems they think they needed solving. However, there is no guarantee that their diagnosis is right. In fact their diagnosis is usually only a small part of the problem – if the client really understood what was wrong, then they probably would have fixed it long ago without the use of expensive consultants. So you have to assume that whatever guidance you are given initially is at best only one element of the story and at worst completely erroneous. And sometimes, of course, the problems handicapping an organisation's performance are not what top management believes – the problems are top management itself and its failure to effectively carry out its responsibilities.

Another challenge you often have is that nobody on your team, including yourself, may have any experience of a particular client's area of operations, so at first you've got no idea about what to look for and where to look. I've had to analyse huge factories with teams who've never seen a factory before in their lives, review the ten year drug development process with consultants who couldn't even spell the word 'pharmaceutical', assess the effectiveness of a major teaching hospital with consultants whose last visit to a hospital was when they were born and turn round an oil rig construction company with a team whose only relevant construction experience were the Meccano sets or Lego bricks some of them had when they were children.

Sometimes, of course, you're lucky and you get a team, who really know what they are doing. But as your most experienced consultants will always be those who are most in demand on other projects, First Phase studies tend to be staffed by those people who happen to be available at the time. And availability is unfortunately not always the same as suitability or talent.

So, as you go in to a client, you urgently need to find out what is really going on – not what the client says is going on – and also you need to buy time for your team and yourself to get up to speed with what your client actually does. The tool we used to gain precious breathing space and work out the lie of the land was what we called the 'First Interviews'. By spending up to three or four days having ninety minute interviews with up to a hundred or more of the client's staff, you would find out an incredible amount about what is actually happening in the organisation, create the opportunity for your team to understand how a client's operations work and get a feel for where your friends and enemies were.

There is no magic in these first interviews – they are very simple. Though perhaps that is their magic. These interviews just contain a series of very general questions, for example:

- What is the strategy of the organisation?

- What do they need to achieve in the next 2-3 years?

- What would count as success?

- How would they measure that success?

- What does the organisation do very well?

- What could the organisation do better?

- What are the main opportunities for performance improvement?

- What percent improvement could be achieved and what would that be worth?

- If they had one message to give to the top director, what would that message be?

All very simple and unthreatening. In these interviews, we tended not to ask for detailed statistics on delivery performance, quality levels, post-operative death rates, stocks, operational efficiency, financial statistics or whatever. That came in Week 2 when we started the detailed studies. Here, during the first few days, we just had a general conversation about the operation – its strengths and weaknesses. But what was amazing in this conversation was how people quickly opened up and told you absolutely everything – it all came out, both the moments of organisational glory and all the dirty laundry. Skeletons are dragged out of cupboards. Unpleasant secrets are quickly unearthed. Political power-plays are soon laid bare. You find out who is fiddling their figures to make their department look good. You learn who is at war with whom and why. You discover which projects are heading for almost certain disaster. And you begin to pick up what is probably really worrying the people at the top.

Any reasonably-sized organisation is going to be a hotbed of intrigue, conspiracies, successes, ghastly failures and misdemeanours being swept quickly under the carpet. The interviews usually bring many of these to the surface – and once you know what's really going on, you can start to work out what levers you need to pull to create client dependency and to sell in a heap of management consultancy.

B. Financial Overview

The second thing you cover in this first week is to grab hold of a couple of years' management reports and any other numbers you can find and crunch them quickly.

The numbers will usually show you two main things:

1.   Meaningless and misleading data.

2.   Trends the client hasn't seen.

1. Meaningless and misleading data

Just by reviewing the management reports to see what numbers the client looks at each week or month, you can already get a feeling for how the organisation is being managed or mismanaged. Most top management reports have been built up over the years like layers of archaeological sediment and become heavy, stiff and inflexible. However, the environment for commercial businesses and government departments is constantly changing. Likewise, their strategies and goals also change with time. But you usually find that their management numbers don't evolve to support these changes in direction. So the organisation ends up trying to achieve one set of goals but actually measuring something quite different. They might, for example, be focusing on improving delivery performance or patient care or response times and often not actually be measuring any of these. And what you don't measure, you can't manage.

So, even before you've looked at which direction the numbers are headed – up, down or nowhere – you can get a first feel for the holes in the way the management team runs the place purely by finding out what numbers they look at each week or month.

2. Trends the client hasn't seen

Then, of course, you crunch all the numbers you can find to get a feel for the main trends. Are costs going up or down? And what about sales? And stock? And service levels? And numbers of deaths per hundred operations? And utilisation of key equipment? And percent of project milestones achieved on time and within budget?

These trends are useful to help the consultants quickly assess what is happening. But probably the client will already be aware of them. So showing you've got a nifty spreadsheet programme and drawing some graphs, however fancy and multi-coloured, isn't going to earn you any brownie points and certainly isn't going to worry management enough to push them to buy a mountain of consultants from you. You have to do something a bit more advanced with the numbers to really rattle the client's confidence in their people and themselves

However, life can get interesting when you start playing around with the numbers. A possible first game is to look for what we used to call 'the hockey stick'. This is when a client's sales or profits or quality or customer service has been flat or even declining for the last few years, but future projections for the next two to three years show a dramatic improvement to levels never before achieved. Then you delve back to projections made the previous year and, lo and behold, the same hockey stick graph can be drawn – static performance for the previous few years, but wondrously optimistic projections for the future. You go back one more year – surprise surprise, same picture. So each year, the client quickly forgets last year's optimistic and unrealised forecasts and makes a new projection that the next few years' results will miraculously be much better.

And having made these wonderful projections for their board or shareholders and having not achieved the forecasted improvement, the management team just finds all kind of excellent reasons for the unfortunate shortfall and once again blithely predicts great improvements in the future. Providing the reasons are at all plausible, boards and shareholders tend to have short memories and a client can get away with making optimistic forecasts and never achieving them for many years.

But if you find that this has been the client's game for the last few years, you're probably on to a goldmine. Once you show the client a couple of hockey-stick graphs and they realise you've sussed out what they're up to, they tend to become quite amenable to the idea of buying consulting from you to bring in the results they regularly promise and just as regularly don't achieve. Giving you a couple of million of their shareholders' cash is better than having you going around spilling the beans to all and sundry.

If there are no hockey sticks to be found, then you must try something else. Another good wheeze is to juxtapose and compare some figures in a way the client has never looked at them. Often you can achieve quite dramatic visual and emotional effects by taking one set of figures from the client's top management reports – usually these are the big picture figures like costs, revenues or profits. The trick is then to compare the trend of a big picture figure with a much more operational figure taken from the coalface deep down in the organisation and therefore normally invisible to top management.

You could, for example, draw a graph of the trend of profitability versus customer service. If you're lucky profitability might be stable or increasing, but customer service may be going nowhere or even decreasing as customers get more demanding. If this is the case, bingo! You've got a good story to tell. "Your people are content and lazy because profitability today looks acceptable. But you're giving lousy customer service – so, how's your profitability going to look next year and the year after?"

I was once doing a First Phase in a manufacturing plant in France, which was owned by one of the largest Swiss pharmaceutical companies. We drew a pile of graphs and noticed that although costs were regularly increasing each year, output was static. We asked the managers of the plant for their reactions to this. One of them just shrugged and said the great words, *"bof, ça ne fait rien, les suisses ont les poches profondes."* ("Oh, that doesn't matter, the Swiss have got deep pockets"). With relish, we played back the results of the first week's work to the Swiss German gentleman responsible for worldwide manufacturing and told him that we had the impression that the people at the plant weren't really trying hard because they felt cushioned from any pressure by the vast profits made by the company. The effect was truly wonderful. It was almost like turning a switch in the man's brain from, *'I don't like consultants and don't trust them'* over to *'those cheating conniving Frenchmen have been pulling the wool over my eyes for years. I'm going to send the consultants in to really shake them up. That'll teach them a lesson they'll never forget.'* Three weeks later, he bought a million plus euro project from us. Later we descended on several more of his factories and found the same story – extravagance, indifference and waste. After all, who cared about being efficient – pharmaceuticals are enormously profitable, so nobody bothered even trying to run a tight ship. We changed that. That was the first of a string of million plus projects we did in that company and all because some idiot confided in us, *"bof, ça ne fait rien, les suisses ont les poches profondes."* Never confide in a consultant, however honest and innocent they might appear.

C. Update 1

The climax of the first week is your first presentation to the client, what we used to call 'Update One.' When you go to see the client and their management team with the results of Update One, you've usually only been in their organisation for four or five days and are still finding your way around, whereas many of the client's managers may have been around the place for twenty years or more. They know the score and you definitely don't. Therefore you can make some hideous mistakes if you make any definite statements so early in the study.

In training our new analysts, we always used to tell them that in Update One, they should emulate the American TV detective Columbo and not Kojack. Kojack-type consultants are the experts; they know all the answers and just barge in and tell the client what needs to be done. The Columbo school of consulting is much more subtle and deferential. By posing indirect questions and by dropping hints rather than banging the table and pointing fingers, we let the client arrive at the horrible realisation that their world is collapsing around them and that they definitely need a boat-load of consultants.

In Update One, you tell the client that you're not going to give them any answers yet. You just want to feed back what their people are saying in the interviews and test with the management team the first impressions you're getting from chatting with employees and from the first trawl through the numbers. Although you tend to play down the results of Update One by saying you've not yet done any studies and so cannot reach any conclusions, there's usually enough material from the interviews and the numbers to send messages like:

- Very few people understand what the organisation's strategy is.

- Most people believe communication is very poor.

- Most middle managers find the management numbers all but useless.

- Departments don't work together and often have conflicting goals.

- Most people believe that the organisation could easily improve its performance by 20%-30%.

- Few people believe that customers or clients get good or excellent service.

- Few people believe that you can make any major improvements to the situation without outside help – from, for example, some nice friendly management consultants like us.

So, gently but firmly, you give this feedback and use this flood of negative energy from the organisation to test how top management see the situation. Sometimes, the people at the top just dismiss the results as their staff whingeing and moaning. In this case, you know you've got what we called a 'controlling/taking' client who will make the decision whether to buy consultancy or not regardless of what their people think. That calls for a 'top down' sales strategy – convince a couple of people at the top to buy a project and the rest will obediently fall into line.

I once was presenting to a new American division manager sent in to shake up his company's European operations. In the first meeting, I put on my most sympathetic and mournful expression, tilted my head to one side and started talking all about 'working with his people' and 'mobilising the workforce' and all that other 'we're all brothers' and 'tree-hugging save the whale and the environment' bleeding heart kind of guff. He interrupted me and said very firmly, "this company is not a democracy". I immediately stopped looking mournful, straightened up, forgot about hugging trees and worrying about the whale and started talking to him more about 'kicking ass' and 'knocking the place into shape' and 'driving through change' – all gung ho action words and sod the trees and the whales and the rain forest. And, of course, this was what he really wanted to hear from us.

However, if the management are rattled by the feedback and all worried and concerned about what their people think, then obviously you should adopt a quite different sales approach. In this case, your message is all about how **we** (top management plus your consultants) must work together to channel the energy of the organisation to achieve the 20%-30% improvement that their people say is realisable. With this approach, you're always using expressions like 'teamwork' and 'helping people' and 'breaking down barriers' and 'focusing on the customer'. Hugging trees and worrying about whales and that kind of stuff is absolutely what's needed to show that you're not just a bunch of greedy, environment-desecrating, pillaging mercenaries, but are really wanting to help their organisation because you're genuinely nice concerned people. And as you talk to management, you never use the word 'you', because you might end up saying 'you must do this' and 'you must do that.' Firstly, using 'you' can sound like you're accusing them of not running the place properly (which of course they are not). And secondly 'you' starts to suggest that they should start doing things independently of the consultants. And that's not the message you want to send. The subliminal message you want them to assimilate is how, hand-in-hand together with your consultants, they will move into the promised land of sustained performance improvement and happy fulfilled employees – hence you always talk about 'we' rather than 'you' long before they've even considered keeping you around after the first study.

WEEKS TWO AND THREE

The first week's interviews and number-crunching give you some indication where to look for everything that's broken in the organisation. Update One allows you to test your first impressions of the organisation and operations with the management team so that together you can agree on what areas should now be looked at in a bit more detail. In the second and third weeks, you launch your team into doing a series of studies of the juiciest opportunities for improvement. These might be the supply chain, sales force performance, project management, customer service, organisation structure, IT systems or whatever. Sometimes these studies can be really professional and involve loads of technical knowledge and numerical analysis. Blinding them with science is always better than baffling them with bullsh-t. So, if your team is strong and knows your client's business, you may try doing some fairly sophisticated sh-t to prove to your client that they desperately need your help. But if your team are a bit shaky and not really a collection of Einsteins, you may have to rely on just a quick sniff around a department to tell you whether the place is running like clockwork or on the way to becoming a disaster zone.

Luckily, we had two very basic but very powerful tools we used, when our consultants were a bit lacking in the old grey matter. The theory of these two tools, used by many consultancies, was that with them even a monkey could come back with what we called 'killer findings'. 'Killer findings' are discoveries of weaknesses or improvement opportunities that are so stunning that the client can't sleep at night and quickly agrees to let you send in an expensive team of consultants for an extremely long time to sort the place out. 'Killer findings' cut the loyalty bond between the client and their people and make the client dependent on the consultant.

The two of the world's most basic ways of digging out some killer findings are what we used to call DILOs and Brown Papers.

DILO stands for Day in the Life Of… All it meant was that you would send a consultant to just observe what went on in some department or other for a few hours in the reasonable certainty that if there were any weaknesses in the operation, these would become sometimes embarrassingly apparent in these few hours. Not very scientific maybe, but wonderful for theatrical presentations back to top management to get the emotions flowing.

I once did a study on a sales force in France. The first salesman I went to spend a day with visited two existing clients, sold nothing that wasn't already ordered and took me for a three hour boozy lunch at a restaurant where everybody seemed to know him awfully well. I did not need much more to tell me that there was no real sales force and no real sales force management process.

Another example; a huge steel company claimed to have a reasonable production and transport planning system. Now, steel tends to be heavy and, unlike gold or diamonds, not be worth too much per ton – so the most expensive way to transport steel is to hire a hundred lorries a day and put one twenty three ton roll of steel on each lorry. It's much cheaper to stick twenty or fifty or a hundred rolls of steel on a boat or a barge or train. Not having anyone on our team who knew anything about transport planning, we just popped into the office of the poor harassed little man who organised the transport and found out what a day in his life looked like. Each day he would order up to a hundred lorries all of them for deliveries the very next day. A copy of the one page fax sent to the transport supplier was enough to show top management that if they had transport planning, as their people claimed, then I was the Emperor of China – which I'm not. That was a killer finding.

Sometimes a Dilo could become a Wilo (Week in the life of) or even a Yilo (Year in the life of): at a theme park, we noticed that the five hundred or so administrative staff mostly took their holidays in the holiday periods – summer, Easter and Christmas. Normal, you may think. No! Because those were also the busiest times of year in the park. We drew a simple but wonderful one page graph showing that the curve tracing the number of visitors per week throughout the whole year (a Yilo) was exactly the inverse of the curve showing the number of hours worked by the 'busy' folk in administration. That was a killer finding. 'How,' we mused innocently as we discussed this curious phenomenon with top management, 'could the park run effectively at the busiest periods with only about twenty percent of the administrative staff at work? And why did it need so many administrative staff when there wasn't a holidaymaker to be seen?' Very soon, there were many less administrative staff.

The wonderful thing about a Dilo (or Wilo or Yilo) type approach was that you could use one short period of time or one quick aspect of the client's operations to pull out a killer finding which could forever shatter their confidence in their own staff. One fun example was in a steel maker in a country, where it always seemed to rain. The company decided to cover over part of its harbour because it couldn't load its products, rolls of steel, on to barges when it was raining. Unfortunately their expensive plans amounted to what we in consulting affectionately called 'building the church for Easter Sunday' – basically, they planned to build a loading shed which could fit in the largest barge that the company could imagine ever visiting them rather than the average barge. So, planning to make the building so huge was perhaps a bit over the top. But what was really silly, was that the length of the shed reduced manoeuvring space in the harbour and meant that they could only accommodate one barge at a time at the quayside rather than the two vessels, which they had been able to accommodate in the past. We wandered down to have a five-minute look at the harbour. We weren't engineers, but what we saw gave us another killer finding. We noticed that the front seventy percent of a barge is where you load stuff and the back thirty percent is made up of the wheelhouse and living quarters for the owner. Why, we asked ourselves, would you need to cover the back part? I mean, it didn't matter a toss if a bit of rain fell on the wheelhouse. It had a roof anyway! And the barge-driver (or whatever such a person is called) could always buy an umbrella if he or she really wanted to wander around the aft of their vessel in the rain. I remember presenting to a very embarrassed management team my schoolboy drawings showing that by making the shed about thirty percent shorter, they could both have their stupid loading shed to keep off the rain and also could maintain sufficient free space in the harbour to fit two barges in at a time after all. A killer finding – irrefutable proof to a management team that their people are either cretins or expensively taking the Mickey, irrefutable proof that the client needed someone like us clever consultants to wade in and put the place back on to the path of righteousness.

Obviously, you want to do as professional a job as possible when conducting your week two and three studies. And you do the best that your team is capable of in the limited time available. However, even if things don't go too well, with a bit of chutzpah and small dose of common sense you can usually dig up sufficient killer findings to comfortably cover the lack of substance in your team's work. Anyway, even if you really have done the world's greatest most excruciatingly detailed analyses, the things that stick in the client's mind and cause them to make the emotional decision to hire you are usually the theatrics of the killer findings rather the detailed data. We used to say that you could always beat a client into submission using 'death by numbers' – burying them under a mass of information. But the really effective way to sell was to 'take them into the Valley of Death' – cause top management to totally despair of the capabilities of their own people with a few colourful stories based on just a limited number of killer findings.

The other almost Neanderthal consulting tool, which provided a useful fallback if your team were not God's gift to consulting, was the Brown Paper. This consisted of taking a huge roll of brown packing paper and cutting off a piece about three to five metres long and one to two metres deep. You stuck this up along a wall in a large office, meeting room or even corridor. Then you would bring together a couple of the client's people and map out on the brown paper one of the key operational processes. This could be the new product development process, the project management process, the order-taking process, the production planning process, the operating theatre booking process or whatever. (The Butchers and their imitators were brown-papering processes half a century before *Reengineering the Corporation* made the word 'process' probably the most lucrative word in consulting history.) Once you'd mapped your chosen process, you'd walk employees past the brown paper, either individually or in groups. During the walk-through, you'd give them red and green Post-Its. On the green ones they'd write the strengths of the different parts of the process and stick them up at the relevant places. On the red ones, of course, they'd note the things that didn't go so well and needed to be improved and plaster these all over the brown paper. Naturally, for such is the nature of mankind, about ten percent of Post-Its would be a gentle shade of green and the other ninety percent would be lurid red. Then you'd invite the senior managers down to see the brown papers – ideally using one of their own supervisors to present the results. It always made a great impression on clients seeing their own people presenting this thing covered in red stickies that their own staff had written. After all, any client faced by some inexperienced consultant commenting on some important process can always go into denial and claim that the consultant has not fully understood the particular circumstances. However, when the people who work with the process day in day out have been encouraged to use the brown paper to show what a pile of crud the whole process is, there's nowhere the client can hide. Result – very worried clients want consultants to help sort out the mess. Moreover, your team almost didn't have to possess any knowledge at all about the client's operations to do the work. The client's people did everything. So you could reach this admirable conclusion using a consultant whose only skill needed to be the ability to stick a piece of brown paper on a wall in such a way that it didn't fall down during any important presentations. Brown papers could truly be said to transform monkeys into magicians.

UPDATE TWO

In Update One you probably didn't know enough about a client's organisation to make any definite statements that couldn't easily be shot down by client managers. So you had to do your Columbo act and just carefully test the water to see what a client would believe and what sort of sales approach would work best.

However, by the time you do Update Two (usually in the middle of week three) you've done a load of detailed studies, you've a pile of killer findings and you've got a pretty clear idea of precisely what kind of consulting project you should be selling. Now you don't need to play Columbo any more. Now a little bit of Kojack can be useful to start pushing the client towards the inevitable conclusion – signing up for a million plus project.

You tend to do Update One, individually with each client team member on their territory in their offices. The atmosphere is one of an intimate discussion. You are trying to get close to them and probing to understand what makes them tick – both as individuals and as a management team. You are testing to get a feel for their appetite for change. And you are searching to understand what levers can be used to make them buy from you. In Update One, you tend to say as little as possible and ensure it's mostly the client that does the talking because you learn by listening not by mouthing off.

Update Two is quite different. Here the impression you want to create is something like:

- We've done loads of terrifically detailed studies working closely with your best people.

- Together we've found lots of opportunities for making significant improvements.

- If we don't move quickly, bad things are going to happen and your results will go through the floor.

- Your people really want to work with us to sort the place out.

- The huge potential benefits we're beginning to identify will make our massive consultancy fees seem almost insignificant.

- This is a parade that you want to get in front of and lead rather than trying to stand in the way – so join us, don't fight us!

A good way to present Update Two is to bring the client out from the security of their offices and on to your territory (the offices they've temporarily allocated to your team) or on to neutral territory like a meeting room. The further the presentation room is from the safety of the top management's normal haunts and the closer it is to the day-to-day action the better.

When doing a pollution reduction study at a huge metal works, we brought the smart business-suited director away from the safety of his office in a city twenty miles from the plant and did Update Two in a supervisor's office just beside the blast furnace. A requirement for going in to the plant was that he, like all his employees, had to strip naked, walk from the so-called 'clean area' to the 'dirty area' and put on special clothing and then after the meeting he had to strip naked once more and walk through communal showers with his manual workers before donning his executive suit again. This helped get him in the mood that this place really was nasty and dirty and needed cleaning up. But what helped clinch the sale was the fortuitous poisonous gas leak that happened while I was giving the presentation. This forced us to break off our discussions as we all rushed out coughing and choking to find some breathable air. All this clearly made a great impression on the man. We may not have finished our presentation, but the big boss got two important messages firmly lodged in his/her brain – it was time to sort the place out and, unlike our client, we were down-to-earth practical people who weren't afraid to get our hands dirty and get stuck in however nasty the situation. We sold that project a couple of weeks later. However, usually Update Two is not quite so dramatic.

Sometimes, we in consulting talk about using Update Two to tell the client that *'this is the worst we've ever seen'* and to take the client down into what we called 'the Valley of Death'. The theory is that unless clients feel a great deal of pain from your assessment of their current situation, then they won't feel sufficient emotional pressure to take the leap of faith required to trust you with millions of their organisation's money. Our worry is that nobody jumps from the comfort of the familiar into the danger of the unknown until you have made the familiar so unpleasant that anything is better than retaining the status quo. In the First Phase team, we often used to discuss whether taking the client into the Valley of Death by whacking them with killer findings and an expressive 'this is the worst we've ever seen' was really a rather too primitive way of selling – it was what we called 'the deficit model of selling'. So we came up with a much more positive approach – 'the aspirational model of selling'. This meant that we would focus more on working with the client to create a dream about the future and spend less energy on the pleasurable pastime of torturing client's management with all the weaknesses in their existing operation. Sometimes the aspirational model did deliver the goods – a compliant client. But we frequently found that unless we caused the client management a goodly portion of discomfort and even pain in Update Two, we would have to do it later in Update Three or even Update Four to drive them over the edge into signing away their loot to us. It really seemed to be a case of 'no pain (for the client) no gain (for us)'.

MOBILISATION – FIRST TOWN MEETING OR BROWN PAPER FAIR

So far, you've interviewed and done studies with a load of the client's folks and you've been back to talk with individuals to check that the conclusions of your studies are not totally off the wall. However, most of the feedback that you've given has only been to a restricted number of top managers and you can run the risk that they don't like you or consultants or what they are hearing. They may even be regretting allowing you to search around in their dirty underwear and may now intend to stifle the initiative once you've finished the First Phase and push you out the door.

An excellent way to prevent this happening is to do what we called 'mobilisation'. When selling in the First Phase, we often tried to get the client agree to allow us to 'involve a critical mass of their people'. This was, we claimed, to 'create mobilisation' and 'build a broad consensus for change'. All good stuff and difficult to object to. Actually, the real purpose of mobilisation was to build such strong support amongst mid-management and the workers for what we were telling the client to do (buy a project), that there would be a riot if top management then decided to do nothing. Effective use of mobilisation allowed the consultant to corner the client in such a way that the only possible decision for them was to launch the consulting project we proposed and to do it **with** our help.

A great way to start generating this support amongst the grimy unwashed masses was to hold what we called a 'Town Meeting' or 'Brown Paper Fair'. The idea was that a couple of days after top management had seen the results of the first studies in Update Two, you would invite anywhere from fifty to five hundred employees to see the same presentation. Generally, you would walk people through all your presentation panels stuck up on brown papers in groups of ten to fifteen allowing them to see everything that management had seen and to add additional comments on Post-It notes. Usually this event had a deep emotional effect on the client's staff. Most people would be:

- Amazed to be allowed to see such detailed analysis and criticism of their operations.

- Delighted that the consultants were being so open and free with information.

- Pleased that finally someone had dared expose all the operational problems they faced in their daily work.

- Struck by the difference between us open and friendly consultants and how they had imagined consultants to be – arrogant and distant.

- Struck also by the openness and friendliness of the consultants compared to their own secretive and aloof management team.

- Impressed that we had found out so much in such a short time.

- Excited by the sense of energy and action.

- Enthusiastic about solving all the problems that had been identified.

At a brown paper fair you could make several hundred friends and create such pressure for action, that brave would have been the management team that dared say to their people, 'we've decided to think about what the consultants have said, but we won't be doing anything for the time being'.

Once top management started to get feedback from the first town meeting, if they were even averagely smart, they would begin to realise that survival meant getting on side with us and working with us (by buying a consulting project) because all this was going to turn from a parade into a stampede – a foolish man tries to stop a parade, only a madman gets in the way of a stampede. If the client was a bit smart, they might also realise that they were being manipulated and could even begin to get quite pissed-off. But by now, they would be finding that it was difficult to get out of the corner into which we were deliberately squeezing them.

Update Two lets the client start to feel that there are serious things that need to be fixed. The first brown paper fair lets them know that they have kicked off a new momentum and energy for change in their organisation and that it is becoming unstoppable.

WEEK FOUR

Hopefully your scene-setting for Update Two was so effective and your killer findings so powerful, that the client agrees that the priority now is not more analysis but moving forward. Given that some of your studies might, in spite of all your theatrics, have been a bit shaky and superficial, you're keen to fuel the rush onwards rather than spend too much time pondering the validity of many of the possibly inflated claims you may be making. Moving forward means designing the consulting change project that will galvanise their operations taking them on to a 'step change' in performance. It also means doing more number crunching to calculate the financial and operational targets for the change programme. So the focus for your team shifts away from analysing the 'As-Is' – namely, dragging unpleasant-looking skeletons from cupboards and shaking them to frighten client management into buying consulting support. Now you begin building the future state (the 'To-Be' in consulting jargon) and the implementation plan that's going to get them there. You move from destruction to construction, from beating the client up to lifting them up, from criticism to creating the future – and the future includes, of course, the million plus consulting project the client is going to buy from you.

Week Four is spent working with client managers and supervisors understanding precisely what effort will be required to implement the operational and organisational changes that you are recommending and quantifying the projected results of your efforts. Towards the end of this fourth week on site, you have Update Three with the client. Here you present the first draft of the Change Programme that you have been building with their people. Update Three allows top management to give their input and direction to this programme before the whole thing becomes set in stone. It also allows you to test the feasibility of the Business Case – the quantified benefits expected from the programme. Here you want to move fast, keeping the pressure on, accelerating the pace, getting decisions quickly – without giving the client too much time to contemplate the implications of what they are being driven to agreeing to. Without letting them think about how awful the next six to twelve months are going to be as a horde of inexperienced consultants descend on their organisation and their lives. Without giving them the breathing space to contemplate the effect on their cash-flow of a couple of hundred thousand plus very generous expenses flowing out each month into your bosses' pockets. Without a chance to realise the disruption that is about to be meted on their existence. Without the possibility of working out how they are going to explain the extravagance of a million plus going to consultants, when it could probably have been put to much better use elsewhere. Without time to think that it is their job as management to run the organisation properly and that if they were worth their salaries, they shouldn't be paying millions to consultants to do their job for them.

SECOND TOWN MEETING OR BROWN PAPER FAIR

It's not so difficult to convince a client that there are lots of things to improve in their operations. It's also not tremendously tough to convince them some consultancy help could provide some value towards getting things done a lot faster than would happen without the presence of outsiders to shake people out or their normal torpor. But, however impressive your work, the client may still be wavering or even totally dumbfounded by the amount of money you are proposing to charge them for your consultancy support. They might start considering trying to do the programme themselves with no consultancy support. Or perhaps they think they can get away with just a couple of consultants rather than the veritable army you are proposing. They might even, horror of horrors, suggest putting the implementation project you are designing out for a competitive tender to other consultancies to see if someone else can do it cheaper. And that would be a disaster for at least two reasons. There's always someone out there who will underbid you, so that they can get their greedy consultants in through the door and shove your excellent consultants out. Secondly, the more time the client has to mull over what you are proposing, the more likely it is that their enthusiasm will wane in the cool light of day and that they will try to slim the project down from the great bloated monster that you are proposing to something resembling an anorexic stick insect. An anorexic stick insect isn't going to feed your hungry bosses for too long. And it won't do your bonus too much good either. So, delay can be deadly. You need the client to sign on the dotted line and you need them to do it fast before what we called 'Buyer's Remorse' sets in.

Solution – you need one more dramatic event to nudge, push or bludgeon the client into submission. This is where the second town meeting or second brown paper fair comes in. After this, there should be no turning back for the client. After this, providing it goes well, they should have no option but to sign whatever you put in front of them.

The format of the event – a couple of hundred people being led through a series of presentations is the same as the first brown paper fair. However, while in the first big public event, you exposed everything that needed to be fixed with the organisation, here you present your project plan for implementing the improvements. The tone is all up-beat and go-go-go and let's stop worrying about the detail and let's leap into the future. You show the plans, the activities, the teams and the benefits case and you describe a brilliant new world that can only be achieved by working together with your particular consultancy (whichever one you happen to be employed by at that time). Once again, many people are so pleased to be involved at all, that their enthusiasm possibly displaces their natural caution and good judgement and a collective willing to get going pulls everybody along.

Top management are trapped. It's awfully difficult now for them to try and stop the tide. I've even seen groups of workers and even workers' councils say to senior managers that they want the project even before the bosses have decided whether they want to buy our services or not. Moreover, if you can get a really good level of pressure from below going, you can be pretty tough when the client tries to negotiate you down on price, time or number of consultants. Likewise, if most of the people are getting into bed with you, it's pretty hard for the client to start suggesting that they're intending looking for an alternative, cheaper consultancy company.

In short, whatever the client's concerns and however much they try to prevaricate, a well-run second town meeting or brown paper fair usually closes off any escape routes.

WEEK 5

Providing things have gone to plan in the previous four plus weeks, you use Week Five to finalise the implementation plan, to start choosing the work teams and to begin drafting the contract for the client to sign. You'll probably also have a series of price negotiations with the client as they try to reduce the fortune you're planning to remove from their coffers. Often you'll have chucked another ten to fifteen percent on the price of the project to give you some room to manoeuvre should the client need the emotional satisfaction of proving to themselves and their peers that although they have bought a massive consultancy project, they did however manage to 'really squeeze' the consultants on price. Given that you've pushed the client so far and so fast over the previous few weeks, it's good tactics to build in a bit of fat into the project price or staffing levels that you can give away. It's no skin off your nose and it makes the client feel good as they sign away their souls to your consultancy.

WEEK 6

In an ideal world, having sold a discounted door-opening five week First Phase, you start work on the much larger, really profitable second phase of your work on the Monday morning immediately after the First Phase ends. With an experienced First Phase manager this probably happens about half the time. The other times there can be a two to three week delay while you finalise contracts, argue about price, choose client team members and sort out some other bits and pieces. And in ten to twenty percent of clients, you get chucked out the door without any more work after the First Phase and then you have the onerous task of explaining to your management why they're not going to see lots of golden eggs this time round. And, of course, in The Butchers, if you ever got two no-gos, well you got fired.

CHAPTER 7

SOME TRICKS
OF THE TRADE

Whenever you're trying to sell a big consultancy project to a client who may not be convinced they even want to buy consultants, you're continuously in a very vulnerable position. It's always much easier for the client to say 'no' rather than 'yes'. After all, if the client says 'no', they can change their minds later or talk to some other consultants to see what they think or try to sort things out themselves or whatever. 'No' is simple, low risk and comfortable. Whereas 'yes' means committing buckets of time, resource and money. Moreover, 'yes' is high risk. Can the consultants be trusted? Will they deliver what they claim? Have they just used an 'A Team' to sell you the project and once the contract is signed, they'll send in a bunch of dross and move the 'A Team' on to the next unsuspecting client? If I were a client, I'd say 'no' to whatever exaggerated proposals my consultants came up with. However, fortunately for my modest bank balance and the gargantuan fortunes of my bosses, loads and loads of clients do say 'yes' without taking the time and the effort to really understand what it is they've just agreed to. When you buy a used car, you generally would be wise to check it out, poke around inside and kick the tires – why on earth don't clients do that when buying used consultancy? After all, used consultants are an awful lot more expensive than a used car.

Anyway, if for example, you're doing a first phase study with the intention of selling in a massive project afterwards, this vulnerability means that even the slightest thing going wrong can tip a client towards saying 'no' rather than 'yes'. And when you're running an inexperienced team in an unfamiliar environment probing out aspects of a client's organisation that they would rather remained hidden, there are at least a thousand things that can go wrong. For example:

- The works council or trade unions may not want consultants milking the organisation. They may feel that any excess cash lying around would be better off spent on the normally poorly paid workers rather than on high-living, highly paid consultants.

- When your study proves that the organisation is a basket case that will expire in the next few minutes unless it buys lots of consultancy from you, you run the risk of upsetting at least one member of, but more usually all of, the management team. Nobody likes being told that their baby is butt ugly. And when people are really pissed-off, they don't throw millions at you – they throw something else.

- Your team may not be highly experienced and some of your studies and conclusions may not exactly shine with the Arrow of Accuracy and the Sword of Truth.

- You only really have a couple of weeks at most to work out what's wrong and what needs fixing. After the first two to three weeks, you've got to get moving on to selling in the implementation project. So even three or four days lost by not pulling out some killer findings or just because some of the people you need to talk to are not immediately available can be fatal to your chances of coming up with a convincing sales story. Given that sometimes you may be working in three or four countries or even across two or three continents, you have to have pretty tight control on your team to make sure that every minute counts.

- You might make a few mistakes understanding the numbers

you're crunching and come up with some erroneous conclusions.

- One of your team might sleep with one of the client's people, get drunk in a restaurant the client often visits or have an argument with the staff in the hotel the client uses for his major meetings. I've done two of these – unfortunately only the latter two – and risked my bosses losing millions in fees as a result of my immature antics.

- One of the client's management team may send your team on a wild goose chase, because he or she has some pet theory that they use your team to test out and that anyone who has been there for more than a couple of weeks knows is total rubbish.

- You may misunderstand the political dynamics in the client management team and misread how the buying decision will be made.

- Perhaps you're just being manipulated by one member of the client's management to get at a rival and they've actually no intention of ever buying anything from you.

- And, of course, there are many more.

To compensate for their vulnerability as they're trying to sell, we teach our selling consultants certain tactics, which can help them manoeuvre clients to the glorious and necessary 'yes' in spite of the numerous obstacles in the way. While running Executive Selling courses for up-and-coming project managers at one major worldwide management consultancy, I listed over thirty selling techniques and tricks that we advised our people to use to persuade clients to buy large projects from us. Here I'd like to shed light on just a few of these tricks of the trade. I'll limit myself to five of the key ones here:

1. Presentations become working sessions

2. Using client Joint Teams to sell for you

3. The joys of Conspiratorial Selling

4. Turning your weaknesses into strengths

5. Managing the decision network

1. PRESENTATIONS BECOME WORKING SESSIONS

When you sell a First Phase or Study or Analysis, you agree with the client that you will give them a regular series of updates on your work. Often this can be every week. You make out that you are giving these updates for the client's sake, but in fact they are a critical part of your sales process. Nothing could be more dangerous than doing five weeks of work, then going to the client's management with the results and finding out that they don't agree with you. By touching the client and their management each week, you get the chance to continuously feel your way forward and course correct if necessary so that you produce a result that you know they will buy. Plus, by cosying up to them each week you get to understand their personalities, the politics and tensions, the things they want and don't want to hear, the levers to pull to make each of them say 'yes'. All in all, weekly updates are vital to your sales effort.

However, there's one other trick we often play with these regular updates. Clients are, in general, used to people like consultants giving presentations. But walking into a management team and giving a presentation is a risky way of convincing a group of people to do what you want:

• A couple of attendees may not be listening properly.

- There may be others who use the meeting to score points off each other.

- Others may see every meeting as a chance to voice off their opinions about anything that happens to come into their normally empty heads.

- Some may disagree with you on details, where either they or you don't have complete information at hand.

- And so on.

But above all, when managers go into a presentation given by consultants, they could either react by saying *'this is incredible, you consultants are so clever, we would never have come up with something so brilliant, we really want to give you a lot of our money'* or they could sit in judgement over you and try to find holes in your arguments. You don't have to be a genius to guess that most tend to follow the latter course. Ergo, first rule of making presentations to client management teams – don't! Don't ever present to a group any material unless each of the group have already individually seen, understood and reacted to that material. So, although you've committed to management to give them regular, even weekly, updates you manage to squeeze out of this foolish commitment as follows:

- You casually suggest that it would be useful to see each of the meeting attendees briefly one-on-one before each update 'just to get your guidance and make sure we're on the right lines'.

- At these one-on-one pre-presents, you take them through the whole update to find out whether you're in the right ball-park and whether they're personally in tune with you.

- You also test out how they think the other management team members will react to your material.

- Finally, to take their attention away from picking your presentation apart, you give them a task or a problem to solve before the formal update. This means that they use their energy making sure they don't look foolish at the upcoming meeting and, of course, distracts them from thinking too much about what you are proposing. This task could be just something simple like finding some key numbers or deciding in which areas your team should do studies or choosing which employees should work with your consultants or choosing the benefits targets at which the implementation programme should be aiming.

So, when you actually come to the so-called Update, you've already pre-presented, discussed and patched some of the holes in your material. This allows you to just give a brief resumé of your work and then use the rest of the time to work with the management team on making some kind of joint decision, such as those mentioned above – deciding in which areas your team should do studies or choosing which employees should work with your consultants or selecting which of their customers your team should interview or prioritising some streams of work in the implementation programme you want to sell them or setting performance targets for the implementation programme. Thus, quite subtly, you've changed the event that the client expected to be a presentation of new material (which you want to avoid at all costs) into a working session where, by taking some decisions jointly with you, the client's management team have 'skin in the game'. Later, as you reach the end of the first study phase, you can justifiably claim that your results and proposals are actually not *your* results but in fact the *joint* results of consultants and management team working together. That makes it quite difficult for them to then say that they disagree with the conclusions that you have reached as they have apparently been reached 'together'.

2. USING CLIENT JOINT TEAMS TO SELL
FOR YOU

There's always a risk that a client's management simply won't believe you, when your team tries to prove that a client must either buy a pile of consultancy from you or else their organisation will wither away or even promptly collapse. They may not agree with your approach, they may dispute your figures, they may find fault with your conclusions, they may even suspect the whole thing is an enormous smoke-screen designed to let you slip your people past them so your consultants can attach themselves to the very entrails of the client's organisation. And in many cases, they may be justified in suspecting some or even all of the above.

One infallible way of circumventing such objections is to use the client's own people against them. Nothing sells consulting better than a client's own staff telling the management that they should buy a monstrous consulting project. So, when selling the first study phase, we often suggest to a client that we can work more cheaply and more effectively if they assign some of their best people to work with us as part of a 'joint team'. 'This will make sure we get the right results fast,' we claim. 'And it will provide a great learning experience for your people,' we add showing our tremendous concern for the betterment of mankind.

Of course, what happens is a very simple and well-known process of 'role adoption'. Let me briefly explain. In the sixties and seventies, when all psychology books seemed to be written by American professors and based on studies done with American college students, there was a very famous experiment in which some students were to act as prisoners and others as prison guards. The experiment had to be stopped after just a few days as the normally happy-clappy, dope-smoking, flower-power, peace-loving students, who were playing the role of prison guards, started behaving with excessive brutality towards their former colleagues who were acting as 'prisoners'. Basically, as the students played out their roles as prison guards, they quickly developed both the mindset and some of the worst behaviours associated with their new roles.

A similar process (though thankfully without the brutality) works as you take trusted client staff and move them into a role as quasi-consultants. Within just a few days, as they work with you digging around and finding all kinds of stuff that needs fixing, the client joint team members start thinking and behaving more like external consultants than like loyal employees. Moreover, being part of the great investigation, they find themselves committed to the results. As they work with you, they inevitably find themselves examining their own organisation and their own departments in a new light. Often the client members of the joint team even become your most passionate advocates, spreading the word about how wonderful things will be when you've all fixed the nasty problems you've found together. Naturally when a client's most trusted employees present your project proposal to their management as the best thing since sliced bread, it's kind of tough for top management to reject what they're hearing in the way they would have done had it just been some greedy consultants pitching for business.

3. THE JOYS OF CONSPIRATORIAL SELLING

This was always one of my favourites. Normally, when you're trying to sell a project to a client, the client naturally sees you as a salesman. Therefore they are awfully suspicious about what you are up to and how eager you are to get your hands on their wallets. That's not a good position to be in. It's adversarial – you against them. You want their money – they don't want to give it to you. So we used to drum into our people that they need to be perceived by the client not as a salesman but as an 'executive peer' and as a 'trusted partner'. They should appear not to be selling to the client but to be working with the client to jointly solve a problem – for example, improving the client's organisation's performance, revamping their organisational structure, beefing up their customer service or whatever.

The mental picture we used to draw in our training was that our salespeople needed to move away from sitting on the other side of the desk from the client, trying to sell something to them. Instead they should be sitting beside the client jointly working together on some shared issue. It was all about becoming the client's equal – a trusted business advisor in whom they could confide – and not allowing yourself to be pigeon-holed as the client's inferior – a crafty salesman trying to dispose of some second hand consulting that nobody else was stupid enough to buy. This is a very important distinction when you're in a selling mode. If you try to apply this principle of sitting with someone as their equal rather than opposite them as an adversary or inferior, this completely changes the kind of relationship you try to build with them. It changes the way you deal with them and it has a significant effect on the words and phrases you use when with them.

We sometimes referred to this selling style as 'Conspiratorial Selling', because you and the client are working together to build the story that the top management team will eventually buy. So when presenting killer findings to an executive, rather than saying something like *'our studies show that over forty percent of deliveries reach customers late'* which is adversarial and unfriendly, you might say *'we're getting strong indications from the information your people have given us that we need to make major improvements in our delivery performance'*. The former statement might get the client defensive and cause them to start giving reasons or excuses for their miserable delivery performance. The latter way of presenting gets them thinking immediately of ways of making improvements, thinking of solutions.

Moreover, you also try to get one client manager to help you package your findings in such a way as to make them palatable to another client manager. Much better they use their energy on something useful like helping you sell to them, rather than wasting their time on something unpleasant like deciding whether they even want to buy anything from you in the first place. That's the joy of Conspiratorial Selling – you can manoeuvre the client's executives into selling to themselves before they've even thought through whether they want to buy anything from you.

4. TURNING YOUR WEAKNESSES INTO STRENGTHS

Because you're normally new to a client organisation compared to a client's management team, you'll always be in a weak position when carrying out your studies of their operations. One of the best tricks of an experienced consultant is to know how to turn your many weaknesses into strengths. Let me give two quick examples:

Too few or too many engineers:

- You've got to do a study of, for example, the work of two thousand or so engineers who design oil rigs and the client asks why none of your consulting team have any engineering experience. The real reason is that you have nobody available with the relevant background. But what you say to the client is something like, *"with two thousand engineers, you've got about twenty thousand years of engineering experience in your organisation, what you need from us is new ideas and approaches from outside engineering"*. Thus a ghastly and indefensible weakness – nobody on your team with the slightest idea of what engineers actually do – becomes a superb strength – the last thing you need on your team are engineers and you've allegedly gone to great effort to choose precisely an engineer-free team that can add a whole new dimension to the client's view of their operations.

- Or, you're about to do the same study for another few thousand engineers and this time the only consultants you can get hold of are actually engineers. Then, you tell the client that your team has been specially selected for their in-depth knowledge of the client's business, namely engineering. In fact, you claim with your hand on your heart, you wouldn't dream of putting anybody but an engineer on this critical assignment.

Your numbers are pretty shaky:

- Or, say you're in the middle of giving an important presentation with a whole bunch of numbers in it and someone from the client's management team starts to question the numbers. When attacked, inexperienced consultants will tend to try and defend themselves and their work. Then you get into a huge and largely useless discussion, about what the right numbers are, instead of keeping people's focus on the important issue – why they need to buy a project from you. But an old consulting lag might pause in their presentation and say something like, *"you're absolutely correct. These numbers might be right. Or they may be wrong. We don't know and nobody we talked to in your organisation knew either. Of course, they had opinions. But nobody really knew. And you can't run an organisation effectively if people don't trust your basic numbers."* You look histrionically round your audience to emphasise the extraordinary seriousness of the situation, *"so the real underlying issue here is",* you continue before the client realises that you haven't answered the question about the botched numbers, *"to work together to put in a management process that people believe in and can use".* In this way you can turn round a mistake one of your consultants has made in adding a few numbers and make this into a really critical problem for the client – getting decent numbers in their organisation is nigh impossible. Hopefully this little trick helps to give the client a crisis of confidence in their management information – all pretty smart really.

There's one other angle on where a weakness can become a strength. In most organisations, there's usually a fair bit of political rough and tumble going on. If you just do lots of analysis, however brilliant, and ignore the political tussles, you tend not to sell. However, if you are alert to all the politicking and games, you can exploit these to help you sell in your consulting project. Sometimes, however, you find yourself in a situation where an organisation is under so much pressure, that all the normal management processes have broken down and all that is left are warring tribes engaged in endless internecine battles – a kind of organisational Afghanistan. The problem with this is that all the analysis your team produces will just be used by the various factions to bombard each other and it's impossible for you to get together a group of managers who will agree on anything. Managers may even insult and abuse you as they try to find an outlet for their frustration. Selling, when normal law and order has broken down, is not easy and you often find that week after week you appear to be making no progress in moving the client forward.

However, you should never despair. There is a positive aspect to this situation. Nature abhors a vacuum. Organisations abhor a power vacuum. If management is not doing its job and there is a power vacuum, either the organisation disintegrates or people will begin to coalesce around any point of stability and control that emerges from the chaos. If that point of stability and control is you and your consulting team, then you can find that gradually people will start to gather behind you. When you have gathered sufficient support, buying a project from you as a unifying force can seem to be the only way for the organisation to break the vicious cycle of warfare and bloodletting. So, though you may never have the pleasure of actually presenting your results to anybody, you may still end up selling a very considerable recovery project.

5. DECISION NETWORK MANAGEMENT

One of the most frequently used selling tools I've seen, in most of the consultancies where I've worked, was 'Decision Network Management'. We would draw an organisation chart with the names of all the people who in any way could influence the decision on whether to buy in consultancy support. We would then assess what role each individual might have in the future decision around buying a project from us. Generally, we identified six different roles people could play:

Authoriser – the person who had the authority to authorise spending several million on consultants. Usually this person was one to two levels above the client who had originally hired us. What you tended to find was that someone like a division or country manager would have the spending authority to lay out one to two hundred thousand dollars, pounds or euros for the first study phase. But when you came back with the answer that the client needed to spend a million or more to pay for your consulting support for the second phase of work, this amount would be well over your immediate client's spending limit. So they would have to go to their boss or even their boss' boss. Because we selling consultants could anticipate this problem from the very first day with a client, we would actively work to get exposure to the client's boss, the authoriser, to start preparing them for what we used to call 'sticker shock' – the shock they would get when we told them how expensive the main project would be.

Buyer – this was the person who would make the decision – do we buy consulting services or not? Usually this was your main client. Though, as I've said above, they would normally have to go to their boss or even higher to get authorisation for the amounts they were going to spend with us.

Technical buyer – although the client might be the person, who decided to buy the project from you, there would also often be someone we called the 'technical buyer'. This tended to be the manager(s) responsible for the area(s) in which we proposed to work. The buyer would consult the technical buyer to make sure that, from his or her point of view as a technical expert in that area, what we were proposing was vaguely sensible. For example, if we were intending to supercharge a client's supply chain, the buyer would use the supply chain manager as a technical buyer or in new product development it would obviously be the product development manager.

Key influencers – throughout a client's organisation, there would be a number of people whom the top client trusted and whose opinions they valued. This could be because they had known each other for many years, because they had worked together on some key project or even because they played golf together. It was our project manager's job to locate the main key influencers and ensure that they were on our side if possible or that their influence was neutralised if we couldn't win them round.

Coach – the decision-making process in many organisations can be quite different from that which the organisation chart might suggest. Some organisations have centralised power in one or two individuals, others involve the whole level one management team, others are even more consensual and may look for agreement of twenty people or more for major decisions. We would always try to quickly find someone in the client's organisation, who could tell us how decisions were really made and coach us through managing the main decision network to get the right outcome – client buys huge consulting project.

Gate-keeper – was someone who had the power to exclude you from either information you needed or face-time that you wanted with key members of the decision network. This could be a secretary or even your client refusing to let you go and talk to their boss. You had to get close to gate-keepers and ensure they opened the gates for you.

Once we had worked out who in the organisation would play which roles in the decision to hire us or not, we would mark against their names their role and their temperature towards us

- Green – they wanted to buy from us

- Orange – they were uncommitted

- Red – they were opposed to buying from us.

Next the project manager would start to gather information on all the members of the decision network on what we called an 'Influencing Chart'. This would cover things like:

- Their background

- Their career aspirations

- Their WIIFM (What's In It For Me) if we hire these consultants

- Their green buttons, red issues and red flags

Then it was the project manager's task to turn as many of the decision network as possible into greens during the weeks of the study so that the decision about whether to buy a project became a done deal before we even asked the question.

To give an idea about how this whole decision network management process worked, I'll take an example from when my department manager was trying to sell a $10 million consulting project to a major division of one of the world's largest food producers. The project lead produced his influencing chart detailing the backgrounds, motivation and attitudes of the key players in the management team. The CEO was judged as being *"honest, positive to us, aspiring to retire leaving a healthy business behind"* but as *"not exerting proper management control over the organisation"*. One of the managing directors was viewed as a threat to our selling effort because he was *"Germanic, believing he knows all the answers and wanting to use McKinsey to help the company"*. The finance and IT director was seen as *"highly political"* and our project lead had the aim of *"shaking him out of his calmness, scare or excite him"*. The business development director was considered *"hostile to consultants in general"* and our aim was to *"take him out as the CEO's gatekeeper"*. Other executives were considered as either *"closed, conservative or empire-building"* and appropriate strategies were also constructed to either get them on board supporting us or else to side-line them.

Sometimes, though not with this client, if a manager was bitterly opposed to hiring us and could not be turned, we would just blow up all the faults we found in their area to totally discredit them and even get them relocated or, in the worst cases, fired.

---

1 Fad Surfing in the Boardroom: Eileen C. Shapiro Capstone 1996
2 Masters of the Universe ITV 1999
3 The Economist 6-12 May 1995

CHAPTER 8

WHO BUYS CONSULTANCY?

What kind of organisations buy consultancy? Is buying consultancy a sign of good management or an indication of inadequacy and failure? Isn't it management's job to manage? Isn't that what they're paid for? If so, why use management consultants? And why are so many clients apparently so ready to spend millions or even tens of millions on consultants to help them manage their organisations?

It is actually quite difficult to find out how much money many management teams do spend on consultancy. Consultants' fees can be hidden away in many different places on the balance sheet. There is no legal requirement for organisations to reveal in their annual accounts the amounts they give to their consultants and executives are not always totally honest about revealing how much they pay for outside help and what they get for it. In one of the cases discussed below, for example, a European TV and Radio broadcaster with an annual turnover of over two billion pounds, the British Broadcasting Corporation (BBC) claimed that by only spending £6 million on consultants, they achieved an impressive £255 million in savings on administration. But because the BBC is a publicly-owned organisation, they were eventually forced into opening their books to reveal the real facts about their disastrous use of consultants. Some time later, when the truth eventually came out, it turned out that they had actually been spending over twenty million pounds a year on, mostly American, management consultants and that their administrative costs had not decreased by £255 million, they had in fact gone up by £140 million. Most major corporations and government departments don't have the same level of public scrutiny and so their levels of spending on management consultants almost always remain closely guarded secrets.

Many clients, probably justifiably, feel it is a sign of managerial weakness to be seen to be throwing their shareholders' cash at consultants. I know that many of our clients made us sign confidentiality agreements that prevented us from letting anyone know that we were working for them. So, when projects did go particularly well, we found it quite amusing to see some executive, whom we knew, giving press interviews proudly claiming for themselves all the credit for the work that we know we did.

Some research done in America and Britain reveals how much major companies gave to their auditors for non-audit work – some of this will be for tax advice, but most will probably be for consulting. Huge as these figures are, they are undoubtedly only the tip of the iceberg, as they **only** concern consulting work done by the organisations' auditors – all work done by other management consultants will be buried somewhere else in the accounts. But at least these studies give some indication of the massive amounts of money that flow from major organisations to their 'professional advisers'. A U.S. study of 563 companies showed that they paid their auditors almost three times as much for consultancy as they did for audit. With some, the imbalance was more extreme, for example, Marriott International gave Andersen just over $1 million for its audit, but more than $30 million for information technology and other services.[1] And Andersen famously earned $27 million from consulting in its last year of existence from Enron, which had also used McKinsey for about twenty years. In the U.S., there are probably over 300,000 management consultants earning in excess of £50 billion a year in fees and in any year more than 250 of the 300 largest American organisations used management consultants.

In Britain, similar analyses gave similar results: Aviva a major insurance company – £43m in just one year, Unilever – £38.3m, the oil companies BP – £35.9m and Shell – £33m, GlaxoWelcome (Pharmaceuticals) – about £25m, Vodafone (telecommunications) – £22m. Twenty of Britain's top companies apparently spent well over

£400 million on buying consultancy advice from their auditors in just one year[2]. Overall, organisations in Britain spend over eight billion pounds a year buying the services of over 30,000 consultants.[3]

Throughout my time selling major consultancy projects to almost one hundred, mostly well-known organisations in over fifteen countries in the Americas, Europe and Asia, I constantly struggled with whether we were really providing any value to our clients:

- Were we really helping good management teams become even better?

- Were we just vainly trying to slow the decline of organisations which were on the slippery slope because their management teams were out of their depth?

- Were we just taking easy money selling pseudo-scientific mumbo-jumbo to clients who were simply not smart enough to see through our well-rehearsed stories?

There were, of course, some successes where I was really proud to be involved. Those tended to be organisations that hired consultants for a limited period of time to carry out a specific task and once that task was over the consultants left. Every management consultancy can boast of a few reference case studies demonstrating the fantastic results they have achieved. In these cases we tended to work with management teams who cared deeply about their organisations and worked passionately with us to turn their fortunes around in the face of seemingly impossible odds.

However, many of the organisations that I saw seemed almost addicted to management consultancy. Frequently there would be several major consultancies working for them at the same time and many of them spent millions on consultants year after year in what a leading international businessman, Lord Hanson, described as *"corporate cowardice"*.[4] In these cases, I got the impression that too many management teams were almost detached from their people and so, being unable or uninterested in communicating with their own staff, they spent much of their time closeted away making plans with their many management consultants. It seemed to me that on balance these organisations' fundamental problem was the inadequacy, greed or short-sightedness of their management teams. And we consultants were only too happy to take their money, in the full knowledge that we were just temporarily papering over the cracks and that, if we ever had the misfortune to leave, things would probably fall apart again. Many of these management teams seemed to me to be ensuring their own personal survival by continuing to pour money into the hands of their favourite consultants to do the job that they were ostensibly employed to do. Most often, they got away with it and were able to either retire with honour or in many cases get promoted without anyone finding out the real truth about their dismal performance.

But from time to time we would come across our clients' names in some of the most respected business press receiving a well-deserved lambasting for their continuous and conspicuous failure to do the jobs for which they were so handsomely paid. Having been deep within so many organisations, I know how difficult it can be for outsiders like the press to find out what really goes on inside major corporations and government departments. Nevertheless, when I see major consumers of consultancy mentioned in newspaper headlines like *"Corporate chameleon on the make"*[5] and *"Arrogant B......d counts the rewards of failure"*[6] and *"Pru and Corus in 'fat cat' row"*[7] and *"BT paying ex-chief £700,000 to do nothing"*[8] and *"Laxity and complacency exposed by AIB inquiry"*[9] and *"AIB chief's job safe despite £494m loss"*[10] and *"Line to disaster"*[24] and *"Hi-tech shambles of Britain's airspace"*.[11] I get at least a little satisfaction from knowing that occasionally the truth does partially come out. These headlines also give an indication of the poor condition of the management teams at some of our largest and most profitable (for us consultants) clients.

It may be interesting to compare two lists that were published in Britain. One is of the twenty companies that seem to buy the most management consultancy from their auditors.[2] The other is a study that splits major companies into four groups according to the pay and performance of the chief executives – the four groups are "The Great", "The Good", "The Bad" and "The Ugly".[12] "The Ugly" were those companies that had both significantly decreased shareholder value and yet chose to pay their chief executives often much more money than the successful companies.

None of the top users of consultancy fall into "The Great"; three of the twenty top users of consultancy are classed in "The Good" whereas four of the top twenty users of consultancy fall into "The Bad" and five into "The Ugly". While clearly not scientific nor statistically representative, this quick comparison does suggest that paying tens of millions to management consultancies over many years is more likely to be a sign of poorly performing, overpaid executives with a tendency to destroy shareholder value rather than of strong, value-creating management. Moreover, the poor performance of those companies using most consultancy, also could be seen as questioning the real value of all the consulting, which those "bad" and "ugly" companies bought. If the work the consultants had done was of any real value, why were their clients appearing in such a negative light in the press?

As I look back over all the more questionable management teams that I have come across, most of whom were regular consumers of millions of dollars and pounds and euros of management consulting, there seem to me to be four main types of situation where the top management and their consultants, rather than working for shareholders' or stakeholders' interests, could be considered to have almost hijacked their organisations and to treat them as their own personal property to be desecrated and plundered at will. I've called these four situations:

1. There's one law for the rich and another for the poor

2. We'll take the rewards but not the responsibility

3. Management as a fashion accessory

4.   It's only taxpayers' money

In this chapter, where I'm going to name a lot of well-known names of very powerful organisations and individuals, the risk of death by a thousand court cases is fairly high. So when talking about clients, who bought masses of consultancy from us and our competitors and yet so conspicuously appeared to achieve little to nothing, I will restrict myself to **only** quoting from information that is **already available** in the **'public domain'**. In many cases, my colleagues and I may be privy to much more information about certain organisations and individuals that, though totally and shockingly true, is probably quite unpublishable. I apologise in advance, that for obvious legal reasons, I will not make any comments about companies and individuals, that have not already passed the scrutiny of our learned friends in the legal profession and are thus already published elsewhere in the 'public domain'.

Nobody seems able to plunder a company and its shareholders quite like an American executive. Two key Enron executives, Andrew Fastow and Jeffrey Skilling, for example made over $60 million each from off-balance-sheet partnerships and shares sales before the company's collapse.[13] Dennis Kozlowski, the former boss of the U.S. conglomerate Tyco, and two colleagues *"stand accused of bilking $170 million from the company through a racketeering scheme involving stock fraud, false expenses and unauthorized bonuses"*.[14] Tyco also paid its chief financial officer a comfortable $47 million in just one year. Moreover, Mr. Kozlowski's generosity to himself with his shareholders' money is the stuff of which legends are made – $125 million of Tyco's money allegedly spent on his homes (including the famous $6,000 shower curtain, the $15,000 dog umbrella stand and the $2,900 coat hangers), $43 million allegedly given to charities as if coming from him personally and $1m allegedly spent on a 40th birthday party for his wife at which *"A life-size replica of Michelangelo's David carved in ice dispensed a seemingly endless stream of vodka from its private parts"*.[15]

However, the best publicly documented stories of when executives at our clients and their consultants (including us) took huge amounts of money from organisations, while apparently causing massive disruption and loss, seem to concern American consultancies getting into bed with top executives and apparently raping and pillaging British companies and government departments. Ever since the 1920s, American companies have dominated management consultancy and, whereas French and German executives have perhaps been more immune to their blandishments, in Britain it has always been fashionable for top executives to be seen to be implementing the latest American management ideas. This has made it very easy for U.S. consultancies to sell stuff, which may have been unnecessary or even destructive, to executives who lacked the ability to lead their organisations. Although I have seen some true horror stories in the U.S., with incompetent management and their consultants plundering organisations, these cases seldom seem to get the same degree of exposure as in Britain. Perhaps this is because the litigious nature of American society prevents journalists openly calling top executives things like *"incompetent, over-paid, complacent and arrogant"*. In Britain, the press are probably more critical of failing management and less afraid to reveal some of the great consulting catastrophes and the failures of the management teams who allowed them to happen.

1. THERE'S ONE LAW FOR THE RICH AND ANOTHER FOR THE POOR

I saw many management teams, which were ruthless in controlling their costs and their expenditures when it concerned their employees – reducing budgets and firing people were often painful annual rituals. Yet, when it concerned the survival, well-being and comfort of top management and their favourite consultants, there appeared to be no limit to the organisation's generosity. My colleagues and I lived very well from this situation, though often it was difficult to hide our disgust at certain executives' behaviour. Two examples:

"BT paying ex-chief £700,000 to do nothing"[8]

I think the largest single pure consultancy project that one major American consultancy ever had in Britain was a so-called 'transformation programme' that we sold to the privatised telecommunications company British Telecom (BT). The aim of the programme was to 'transform' it from an inefficient, bureaucratic nationalized monopoly into a commercially-oriented company able to compete in a deregulated industry, which was attracting some very aggressive new competitors. I believe our fees were well in excess of twenty million pounds and may even have reached as high as forty million pounds. At the time our average project size was only around one to two million pounds, so the BT assignment represented a massive chunk of work for us. The programme did have some very clear results and I believe from consultants who were on the project that it helped contribute to around 100,000 employees losing their jobs. But it is not clear that our work was a major success, as it was decided that the executive, who had apparently been the main driving force behind the project, should leave not long after its completion *"Mr. Hepher, 52, left BT by mutual agreement as part of a boardroom shake-up"*.[8]

Despite the veritable massacre, which took place amongst BT's ordinary employees, BT appeared to be as generous to its departing chief executive as it had been to us, its consultants. If the press reports are accurate, the executive in question does not appear to have suffered financially from his departure, as he would get paid his salary for a full year after his departure even though he was starting a new job almost immediately for Charterhouse, an investment bank, where he would earn well over a million dollars a year. *"BT agreed to pay Mr. Hepher £686,600 in salary until his service contract expires on August 5 1997. Other benefits worth up to £57,700 include the use of a BT company car and driver, personal telephone facilities, medical cover and financial counselling. The perks will end when Mr. Hepher joins Charterhouse on July 1 1996, but he will continue to draw his BT salary (for another year)".*[8]

The commentator clearly felt that this arrangement of paying someone for a year after he had left a job and likewise a year after he had already started his new job was not necessarily in BT's shareholders' best interests. *"BT shareholders and customers are likely to take a dim view of a package on this scale for someone who no longer works for the company."*[8]

Moreover, the new chief executive, who replaced Mr. Hepher, didn't appear overly impressed with the results achieved by his predecessor and by the massive consulting team we had in place there for a couple of years. *"When Bonfield arrived he also made clear that BT's culture had to change because, though it had been privatised 12 years before, it still ran more like a civil service department than a commercial company. He told me once that his plan to merge with the American carrier MCI Sprint appealed to him as much for the effect its employees would have as they tore like storm troopers through BT's Home Guard, than for any intrinsic business merit."*[6]

When things apparently didn't work out with the new chief executive, once again BT seemed to show remarkable generosity to its departing boss. *"BT chief executive Sir Peter Bonfield is to leave the company early, aided by an instant pay-off of almost £1.5 million. He will also be entitled to performance-related share and bonus schemes over the next three years, worth £1.3 million at today's price. A year's extra pension money, £350,000, will be paid into his retirement pot."*[6]

In spite of the generous financial package that this new chief executive received, two respected commentators did not feel that the chief executive had been overly successful. One wrote, *"The decision to leave follows a torrid couple of years, during which time BT's share price has plummeted from a high of 1358p to a low of 305p...... Last May, BT scrapped its dividend and delivered a £1 billion loss."*[6] And, under the headline *"Arrogant Bonfield counts the rewards of failure"* another columnist stated, *"By almost any measure you care to mention, Sir Peter Bonfield's term as chief executive has been a failure. When he took charge in 1996, BT was still the undisputed giant of the British telecoms industry, and had legitimate pretensions to be a world player in the telecoms business. By July of this year it was a company battling for survival, forced into the fire sale of many of its best assets simply to keep its bankers at bay""*[6]

The journalist then went on to compare the rewards received by the shareholders to the money given to the departing chief executive, *"Shareholders got a pretty poor deal too. In Bonfield's reign the total return on their investment was 94%..... In the same period Orange delivered a total return of 882% and Vodafone 311%. So few will mourn Bonfield, whose early departure, announced today, was revealed in these pages months ago. Typically, it was vehemently denied at the time by the company. Equally typically, and with an added layer of insensitivity and arrogance, he is now going with a wheelbarrow full of money."*[6]

So – here we have a company that fired something like a hundred thousand people to reduce its costs and yet seemed inordinately generous in handing out money to its chief executives and their management consultants, which in this case was fortunately the consultancy for which I worked at the time. We got very big bonuses those years. One law for the rich and another for the poor.

"Corus in 'fat cat' row"[7]

There seemed to be a slightly similar situation at the European steel company, Corus. It was at Corus that I sold the largest project of my career – the first phase was about six million euros and further work after this earned us several million more. I also sold three smaller projects to this client worth in all about four to five million euros. In addition to me, other salesmen from our consultancy also sold several million pounds of work to this client. So, although not as large an account as BT, Corus probably earned us in the region of ten million pounds for consulting of which about eight million would have been pure profit. Basically a very good and profitable client.

Not long after we had finished working for this client, Corus attracted the attention of the press for its apparent generosity to its executives at a time when it was tightly controlling the costs of its workforce. *"Corus, the former British Steel, revealed that Sir Brian Moffat, the chairman, saw his basic pay soar by 130 percent to £558,846 in 2001. During the same period the company made 6,000 of its workers redundant as the steel-maker languished under £1 billion of losses. The workers left at Corus in the UK were given a derisory 2 percent pay rise during the same period, half of which was mandatory, with the other 1 percent paid as a bonus."*[7]

Naturally not everyone was impressed by the company's 'one law for the rich and another for the poor' behaviour. *"Unions representing the steel workers at Corus, who earn £30,000 a year on average, were outraged by Sir Brian's pay rise. 'His pay increase is utterly indefensible,' a spokesman for the ISTC union said. 'It is absolutely disgusting that at a time when our members were being thrown on to the streets, the executives had their noses in the troughs."*

Typically for such organisations, the company rejected any attacks on its behaviour. *"Corus brushed off the union criticism, claiming that Sir Brian had taken on the work of two men when he became joint chairman and chief executive last year."*

2. WE'LL TAKE THE REWARDS BUT NOT THE RESPONSIBILITY

Another common characteristic of the management teams, for which we worked, was the ability to take the credit and the huge financial rewards when business was good, but a tendency to avoid any responsibility when there were problems. I saw this in many clients. However, those where newspaper revelations allow me to talk about this type of behaviour were clients such as Railtrack and AIB (Allied Irish Bank). Railtrack, the owner and operator of the railway network in Britain, became infamous for giving its top management generous performance bonuses at a time when an almost record number of people were killed and maimed in train crashes caused by poor maintenance of the railway network for which the company was meant to be responsible. In the same year, they also happened to pay out £225 million to consultants and freelance staff [3] – about ten million pounds of this, I think, went to us for a programme designed to improve Railtrack's project management.

"Laxity and complacency exposed by AIB inquiry"[9]

Perhaps the best-known example of a so-called 'rogue trader' bringing down a bank through disastrous investments and then management ducking and weaving to avoid its responsibilities was when Nick Leeson bankrupted Barings by losing $830 million. One of the bank's most senior executives admitted *"that the bank was too dazzled by the fraudulent profits and potentially huge bonuses generated by Nick Leeson to probe his trading activities"*. Yet, after Barings was taken over by the Dutch bank ING, the very managers, who should have been responsible for ensuring Barings' well-being, not only mostly hung on to their jobs but even threatened to sue ING if it didn't pay them their bonuses. Nick Leeson meanwhile, probably very accurately, described the Barings management as "bumbling fools" and "idiots".[8] Moreover, while Leeson was carted off to prison, such worthies as the Coopers & Lybrand auditors responsible for signing off the Barings accounts year after year managed to retain their licences to practise despite their firm having to pay £65 million to creditors.

One of our clients, Allied Irish Banks (AIB) seemed to have a similar problem to Barings. I had been involved in helping sell our first project to AIB, a project that we considered so successful that it was written about in a book by two of our most senior executives. AIB apparently experienced a mini-Barings – a trader, John Rusnak, at one of AIB's subsidiaries in the U.S., Allfirst, unfortunately ran up currency trading losses of $735 million undetected over a five year period. Yet in spite of a damning report, here too top management seemed to escape unscathed, their big salaries and bonuses intact.

Under pressure to explain the losses, AIB commissioned a report into the events. A business correspondent wrote, "*It makes painful reading. Ludwig's investigation makes clear that Rusnak was able to continue unhindered for five years, not through genius, but through an almost farcical laxity in controls and risk management at Allfirst and AIB.*"[17]

Some staff at the subsidiary lost their jobs, but all the key executives stayed in place. This example of senior management avoiding taking responsibility caused outrage amongst some business commentators, "*What is most worrying is the sheer complacency of chief executive Michael Buckley and his Dublin team when the first warnings were heard last May. Instead of thinking of Nick Leeson and other rogue traders and sending in auditors and senior executives to check matters out, they relied on local staff, whom have now been fired. This was inadequate. The board should have accepted Buckley's resignation and dismissed Allfirst chief executive Susan Keating, the line manager in charge in the final few months. This is a whitewash – or greenwash – which investors should challenge with some urgency.*"[18]

3. MANAGEMENT AS A FASHION ACCESSORY

A third situation which provided vast amounts of work for us and our competitors was when a chief executive or senior management team seemed to be hooked on the latest management fad – Business Process Reengineering (BPR), implementing some new computer system, setting up an Internal Market, jumping into some new growth industry, outsourcing, or whatever. In such cases, there was a tendency for senior management to believe that only they, and of course their consultants, were smart enough to 'see the light'- only they had a clear picture of the changes their organisation needed to make. Almost everyone else in their organisation was apparently too stupid or too resistant to change to embrace top management's new bright idea. By cosying up to such executives and encouraging them in their fantasies, we were able to sell in massive amounts of consulting. Our sales pitch, as we got quickly into bed with the chief executive with the big idea, was all about how they would need huge amounts of consulting support to convert the whole organisation to the 'new religion'.

I've seen top executives bring chaos and confusion to several organisations by calling in an army of consultants to impose the latest management fashion or fad on their employees. One huge and seemingly disastrous project was when a major American oil company spent over a hundred million dollars trying to implement a new and fashionable computer system that caused a massive amount of disruption. Moreover, as far as we could see, the system gave very few, if any, of the business benefits that had first been planned. At the time, the same system was being bought by all the other major chemical and oil companies. It seemed as if our client didn't want to be left behind in the lemming-like rush to buy the latest technological emperor's new clothes.

Likewise, the craze for BPR also led to organisations shelling out tens of millions to management consultancies – in this case to produce mountains of mostly useless process analyses. After all, the originators of the BPR craze admitted that around seventy percent of BPR projects failed to give results.

"Corporate chameleon on the make"[(5)]

Another enormously profitable period for consultancies was when many government departments tried to become more 'commercially-oriented' and tried to implement a kind of Internal Market, in which they bought and sold services to each other – a process which in general just caused an explosion in the number of administrators and bean-counters. Perhaps the best publicised example of this situation that I have seen where management fashion could possibly be considered to supplant experience and common sense was when John Birt paid the leading U.S. consultancy McKinsey and other consultancies tens of millions of pounds of the public's money to implement an Internal Market at the BBC.

The available information on how the director-general of the BBC tried to use McKinsey to transform the organisation into an 'internal market' gives a fascinating view of the clash that occurs when new management and their pet American consultants try to convert a whole organisation to a new management religion, in which apparently only they believe. Unfortunately, we had no part in this huge and lucrative programme. However, I did have a former colleague and very good friend, who worked in the BBC's strategy department at the time of the McKinsey project. I tried asking him what McKinsey did to earn the ten to twenty million pounds or so they were reportedly getting each year. He said that he didn't know, that he hardly ever saw them and that they spent most of their time locked away in a part of the headquarters building that had been set aside for them.

Two commentators have written such eloquent accounts of what appears to be a disaster for this client and a goldmine for the executives and the American consultants involved, that rather than trying to paraphrase their work, I'll let them tell this amazing story.

"Former BBC director-general John Birt delayed taking up a lucrative consultancy with a U.S. firm that earned millions in fees from the BBC during his time at the corporation in order to offset controversy Punch can reveal. Lord Birt stepped down from the top job at the BBC in January last year taking with him a total pay-off of £784,000. This "golden good-bye", attacked by a Commons select committee, comprised a final salary of £456,000, plus a termination payment of £328,000, related to his early retirement. He also receives an annual pension of £130,000."

"Barely six months after his departure, the newly ennobled Lord Birt was hired by the American-owned management consultants McKinsey and Company Inc as a special adviser on a huge, undisclosed salary. It was a controversial appointment because McKinsey had earned millions in fees while Lord Birt was head of the publicly funded organisation. Outside consultants were paid up to £22 million a year by the BBC, according to its chairman, Sir Christopher Bland, and the vast majority of the funds went to McKinsey."

"Lord Birt became director-general in 1992 with a mission to reform and improve the BBC. He believed the solution was management restructuring and McKinsey were commissioned at vast expense to recommend radical change. McKinsey and Company Inc. is a secretive management consultancy with a formidable reputation… McKinsey takes itself terribly seriously. Its website describes the company as "the United Nations of business consulting with one crucial difference: it works". Priced at £500,000 a year, a McKinsey adviser is hugely self-confident, intellectually precise, elitist, puritanical and obsessed with systems and structures. Like a cult, advisers encourage an aura of mystique and exploit the fears and power-jealousy of nervous, insecure executives running huge companies and organisations."

"A devoted disciple, Birt allocated McKinsey a permanent office at Broadcasting House…A major transformation occurred in 1996 with the implementation of an "internal market" at the BBC. A typically complex McKinsey project, it divided the corporation into dozens of new departments with extra "business units". Producers now had to negotiate with each unit to book a facility for a programme. This increased red tape and burdened producers. "I've got an identity crisis," said one at an internal conference. I started off as a production business unit. A couple of months ago I became a resource business unit and a couple of days ago an orchestral business unit. What does this mean?"

"None of the BBC's top management or staff were consulted by Birt …about this radical new system. It was almost as if McKinsey was running the BBC. "Birt always seemed to trust McKinsey's rather than his own management," said John Tusa, Former head of the BBC World Service. "Perhaps it was because they were completely obedient." Programme-makers deeply resented the McKinsey culture. They claimed that millions were wasted on "management counselling" and "role-playing" in business negotiations. One exercise in "working together" involved cutting out paper frogs and pretending to sell them to each other. Such training activities soaked up £15 million a year. Bizarre new *language known as "Birtspeak" was now used by BBC executives. Birt himself was likened to a McKinsey clone."*

"Hiring McKinsey was supposed to cut costs at the BBC, but bureaucracy and the number of administrators increased. Executives doubted they were getting value for money, but the fees paid to McKinsey were kept a closely guarded secret. Only Birt and personnel director Margaret Salmon knew the amounts as they were buried under "operational expenditure" in the BBC budget. In 1999, chairman Sir Christopher Bland acknowledged that the BBC spent up to £22 million a year of the £2.2 billion budget on advisers. When asked why the BBC had not previously released the figure, he replied: "We were probably a little coy about it."

But all good things eventually come to and end – even for McKinsey.

"The new director-general was not so shy about his view of McKinsey. He immediately axed 75% of the budget for outside consultants. "This is public money," said Dyke. "The public only give it to us legitimately on the grounds that we spend as much of it as we can on services for them."[5]

This picture of a seemingly run-away chief executive pursuing some fashionable idea with the obsequious help of his pet, well-paid consultants is reinforced by another independent outside commentator.

"But it's McKinsey's work at the BBC which is now being seen as the first major crack in the armour of perhaps the most illustrious organisation in consulting. The BBC's problems run deep, and to many observers the presence of McKinsey has made them deeper. The corporation has employed the Firm on a fairly regular basis ever since John Birt announced Producer Choice, his blueprint to reengineer the BBC two years ago. ... .BBC observers are arguing that Birt has lost touch with what's really going on. Programme-makers in particular are finding the difference between what the BBC says it is doing (as recommended by McKinsey) and what is actually happening to be huge."

"One example, just last year Margaret Salmon, the BBC's director

of personnel announced that the corporation had spent £6 million on consultants, but went on to say brightly that this expenditure had resulted in savings of £255 million, which was now going into programme-making. Programme-makers were immediately suspicious: all they knew was that their budgets were being pared considerably. Finally when the BBC announced in April that it had run out of money for new programmes and would have to freeze all commissioning, the sceptics were vindicated. The promised £255 million was nowhere to be seen. It had appeared somewhere in a McKinsey report, but was a classic consultant fudge: by reclassifying the same spending under different headings, large theoretical savings could be made."

Under a picture of the happily smiling John Birt, this report went on to conclude:

"The BBC now costs more to run while employing less people than ever before. The "savings" have turned out to be an extra staff cost of £140 million compared to four years ago."[19]

The expensive apparent failure of Birt and McKinsey to convert the BBC to their new great management idea was so massive that it attracted extremely passionate criticism from a vast range of observers. The following very personal comments about Sir John Birt and McKinsey give a powerful picture of the type of senior manager who appears to almost become dependent on their favourite management consultants rather than working directly with their employees to achieve their goals:

"It is not as if Birt's failings weren't apparent ….during his tenure as deputy director-general. Birt's shortcomings of excessive dogmatism and ponderous decision-making were clear well before his appointment. His interaction with colleagues was minimal. His presentations were laboured. His sense of humour and fun were nil. As initiative after initiative poured out from Birt and his myrmidons – from producer Choice to Bi-Medialism in the News – the message was clear: this was top-down, imposed change, externally driven by Birt's beloved management consultants." [20]

4. IT'S ONLY TAXPAYERS' MONEY

Perhaps the worst cases of management profligacy that I came across were in government departments and public sector organisations. The British public sector has always been a profitable area for consultants. But from the end of the 1990s up till today, there has been a veritable explosion in business within the British public sector as the government tried to espouse American management thinking in order to modernise the way it delivered its services.

Some of the most massive consulting and computer system implementations with the greatest multi-million budget over-runs were done by American companies like Accenture and EDS for a British government a little too eager to be seen to adopt modern American ideas of efficiency and automation. For example, a system for National Insurance payments built by Accenture in 2001 had a budget of £150 million, but actually cost closer to £250 million. Likewise, a system produced in 2002 by EDS for the Child Support agency, despite a massive budget of £200 million, ended up also costing about £250 million. In just three years, British government departments were estimated to have wasted well over one billion pounds on consulting and IT systems that were either hugely over budget or else scrapped after millions had been spent – a Benefits card payment system, for example, was scrapped after about seven hundred million pounds had been spent.[21] And current estimates suggest that the British NHS national programme for IT – NpfIT – will cost £30 billion, five times its original projected cost of around £6 billion.[22]

In my experience, the incredibly poor quality of the management that I saw in public services led to a vast amount of waste and lost opportunity. As one expert who was involved in more than a hundred consulting and IT projects explained, *In the public sector, you are not usually given any incentive for making decisions, you are more often rewarded for not making decisions. People who go into the public sector don't do so because they're great managers.*[23] And a journalist described how consultants and IT companies ran rings round British civil servants, *"through the 1980s and 1990s there were scandals and confrontations with contractors and suppliers profiting from soaring costs and overruns which were apparently out of control – such as the British Library, which grotesquely exceeded the original estimates of cost and deadline."*[24] Time and again, when working for government, I saw stupendous amounts of money being wasted as computer system developments went completely out of control and as consultants became comfortably ensconced in organisations that liked to talk about 'customer focus' and 'service delivery' but actually chose inaction and risk avoidance every time anything but the slightest change was proposed. In these situations, you tended to see our consultants 'go native' as they downgraded their ambitions to match the clients' aim of holding endless meetings but actually doing nothing. When I talked with our consultants, who had spent months or even years working with government departments, and asked whether they found it frustrating working within huge, immovable bureaucracies, they would just laugh and joke about how much they were getting paid, how little real work they had to do and how much free time they had. Often they would remark how much better their family life was now that they could leave home late in the mornings and get home early each evening. In many cases, consultants saw cruising comfortably within some government department or other as a well-earned rest after years of tough projects in real business.

The British postal service also seemed to have had some unhappy experiences with consultants and computer systems. This service was once called the Royal Mail. Then it expensively rebranded itself as the supposedly fashionable but meaningless 'Consignia'. A few years later, it decided that the whole name change had been a waste of money and so it went back to the good old-fashioned Royal Mail after having squandered millions on its worthless rebranding exercises. But this was small change compared to some of this management's other attempts to squander money. In a year, when they were trying to find ways of closing three to four thousand post offices and fire about thirty thousand staff, they gave at least thirty five million pounds to a whole host of management consultancies. In another effort, they appeared to have wasted close to two billion pounds on setting up and running a computer system, that they laughingly admitted had just added to their costs and not given any of the intended financial benefits.

Two other big public sector areas, where we consultants had a massive amount of work, were the railways and air traffic control. In a book trumpeting the success of our 'business transformation' product offering two top executives of one consultancy wrote about how we managed to transform a rail operator, Network Southeast (part of British Rail), into a *"customer-focused supplier of travel services"*.[22] The well-respected Economist magazine was less than impressed with this claim – *"This – take it from a regular user of the Network – is baloney"*.[25]

Railways – "Line to disaster"[26]

Just after we had completed a major consulting assignment aimed at improving project management at Railtrack, the operator of the British railway infrastructure, our client began to feature prominently in the press as costs for a major project went spiralling out of control. *"The fiasco over the West Coast upgrade, on which costs have ballooned from £2 billion to £13 billion in three years, led directly to the collapse of Railtrack last autumn"* explained one newspaper.[26] The paper went on to express total outrage at the apparent incompetence and ineptitude of Railtrack management, *"modernisation of the West Coast Main Line is fast becoming the most wasteful, incompetent and scandalously mismanaged project ever to be undertaken in post-war Britain. The cost has risen from an initial £2.1 billion to a staggering £13 billion, a six-fold increase in three years and an overrun whose size and speed dwarfs all others. The sum involved is now not only far above the cost of any other rail project in the world, including brand new high-speed lines; it is more than the total budget of most Third World countries, and a figure so ludicrous that it would have been vetoed by any government that had the ability to halt this fiasco."*

Announcing their plans for completing the work, Railtrack's

management, in typical public sector style, apparently oblivious of their own bungling, boasted proudly, *"when completed, this massive engineering programme will bring the West Coast line up to the standard required of a 21ˢᵗ-century high-speed rail link. All parties are determined to see the project through with the least possible inconvenience to passengers and freight"*.[26]

We got paid millions for our consulting services, yet on the key example where good project management would have mattered, we could hardly claim success for our efforts.

Air traffic control – "Flying into a disaster"[11]

For about four or five years, one of my employers sold project after project to Britain's air traffic control operator Nats (National Air Traffic Services). Most of our work was aimed at improving management processes, including project management. We used these projects as references for selling work to other clients as our client at Nats was so pleased with our work and how much it had improved the functioning of his organisation – *"the outstanding commitment and quality of the consultants, working together with our organisation, has enabled us to deliver exceptional results,"* a senior executive proudly proclaimed as he gave us a reference we could use when trying to sell our services to other potential clients.

Yes, Nats' results were exceptional – but not quite in the way the top management intended. Just like Railtrack, Nats attracted the attention of the press for their apparent bungling, incompetence and profligacy on a major project – building a new air traffic control centre. *"It has been a disaster more than ten years in the making, Britain's new air traffic control centre has turned the country's airspace into the bottleneck of Europe."*[11]

The press criticised project management and cost over-runs, *"The project was plagued with software problems and when it opened on January 27 it was more than five years behind schedule and £180 million over budget."* Moreover, even after opening, the control centre functioned terribly, *"the centre has performed disastrously, plagued by technical problems and staff shortages"* and *"since*

January, Britain has been responsible for more air traffic delays than 30 other countries put together."

The problems were numerous – the new hi-tech centre needed more staff than the old low-tech operation to do the same job, it could handle less planes and the typeface on computer screens was so small that controllers had difficulty identifying planes and their exact heights. Nats had been warned about the problem with typeface size five years before the centre opened, but took no action. In fact, the problems at the new centre were *"so severe that Eurocontrol has issued bulletins advising pilots to avoid Britain at the worst periods"*.

Pilots were apparently also not too impressed by Nats' performance, *"Swanwick has been a complete and utter fiasco all the way through"*.[11]

Nats management, of course, appeared oblivious to their own failure, *"A spokesman said, "Nats remains highly confident that Swanwick will be capable of delivering increases in capacity of at least 30% over the next few years"*. Nats bosses, the Government, also seemed unconcerned with the mismanagement, waste and pathetic performance, *"The Department for Transport, which holds 50% of the shares in Nats, said "The Government believes that Nats management are on the case and are doing their best to improve reliability and always with safety as the paramount consideration"*.

CONCLUSION: GREAT MANAGERS ARE NOT CONSULTANCY ADDICTS

In summary, yes of course we did do great work for some great management teams. But as I look at a study of about eighty major companies listed according to how much shareholder value they created or destroyed,[12] I can see three or four of our clients in the top forty or so companies, but I can see many more of our major clients in the bottom forty.

Recently, a newspaper did a comparison of the heads of two major retail chains, who were both retiring at about the same time. One of these chief executives managed to quadruple his company's share price in the last ten years of his long tenure and to take its market capitalisation to over three billion pounds. He was described as; "*a retailer and an entrepreneur...minded to build business organically...seize the opportunity in an instant......attention to detail, willingness to take risks, trading mentality*".[27]

The other CEO managed to almost halve his company's share price and reduce its market capitalisation down to just £139 million from a high a few years earlier of well over £600 million. The commentator underlined this gentleman's problems with decision-making and tendency to rely on management consultancies for advice, "*a manager with a penchant for management consultants...well-known for his ability to procrastinate ad infinitum.....likely to splash out on acquisitions.....inability to make decisions....tendency to surround himself with advisers*".

Concluding the comparison of the two businessmen, the reporter wrote, "*another difference between the two titans is the note on which they will leave their respective companies. ....(the former) has just unveiled a rise in comparable sales. .... (The latter) has been forced to dismantle the empire that he created...and may yet see the company disappear altogether*".

Commenting on the dismantling of this 'consultant-dependent' CEO's 'empire', the business editor of The Times suggested that McKinsey had played a significant part in the apparent failure of the latter of these executives, "*however, so complicated is the structure that those clever chaps at McKinsey helped to assemble that it will be well over a year before a clean and tidy..... business can be extracted from it*".[28]

In general, my experience suggests that good management manages and only very occasionally hires consultants for quite specific tasks – questionable management often hires consultants and too frequently appears to become almost dependent on them.

(1) Business Week Online – Accounting in Crisis 22 January 2002
(2) The Times 27 January 2002 (Figures from *Pension and Investment Research Consultants*)
(3) The Times 6 August 2002
(4) Daily Mail 30 January 2002
(5) Punch 16-19 June 2001
(6) Evening Standard City Comment 31 October 2001
(7) Times Online 5 April 2002
(8) The Times June 7 1996
(9) Evening Standard 15 March 2002
(10) Metro Business News 14 March 2002
(11) Sunday Times 25 August 2002
(12) Sunday Times 15 July 2001
(13) The Times Business 22 August 2002
(14) The Sunday Times 15 September 2002
(15) The Times 17 September 2002
(16) Financial Times 24 April 2002
(17) The Sunday Times 17 March 2002
(18) Daily Mail 15 March 2002
(19) Business Age June 1995
(20) The Mail on Sunday 4 November 2001
(21) The Times 14 August 2002
(22) The Daily telegraph 13 October 2004
(23) Contact author for reference if interested
(24) *Who runs this place?* Anthony Sampson, John Murray Publishers October 2004
(25) The Economist (contact author for date)
(26) The Times 29 August 2002
(27) The Times 12 September 2002
(28) The Times 16 May 2002

CHAPTER 9

WHY CLIENTS NEED HELP

There are obviously too many different client situations to generalise about why clients need to buy consultancy. Often clients do have good reason to buy consultants – for example, to develop new strategies, change their organisational structure, improve their systems or provide particular expertise that is lacking in their organisation. If this is the case, then consultants can often deliver value for money, provided they actually know what they are doing and have the right resources available to solve their clients' problems.

However, too often, clients choose to believe that their problems are due to strategy, structure, systems or a lack of expertise in their organisation. However, the real problem is actually a lack of management capability or a lack of cohesion in the management team leading to constant warfare between different departments. Before we went on to client sites, I used to always give a clear briefing to my selling team. My message to my consultants was that excellent winning management teams tend not to buy consultancy. Poor management, management that is at war with itself or management that is out of its depth do buy consultancy – lots of it! So, although our clients may think that they have bought us to provide strategy, structure, process improvement or whatever and although we would indeed provide these things, they were probably just symptoms of the underlying cause – inadequate management. This meant that although we would do all the useful studies and analyses and presentations and whatever management expected, if we were to be successful in selling a project, we had to quickly understand the problems within the management team and exploit these to get them to buy our services.

In many cases, it probably would have been better for the organisation to change the management team, rather than leaving them in place and allowing them to squander millions on consultants. For example, when discussing how he managed to extract an extra £100 million a year in profits from the Forte hotel group, which he had recently bought, the chief executive of the acquirer, Granada, explained that they just replaced a management team that had been heavily reliant on consultants with one that could manage without consultancy help.[1] But the management teams who use most consultancy were often those who should be replaced and they were hardly likely to be amenable if we suggested they should fire themselves. So there is a small moral dilemma here – weak or inadequate management is usually excellent for consultants but also usually catastrophic for organisations. As the example below hopefully shows, you can redesign structures, streamline supply chains, implement fancy new computer systems and reengineer processes till you're blue in the face, but if you don't sort out the weaknesses in the top management team, all your efforts will lead to very little.

Here I reproduce a part of a case study of a project that one major consultancy used on its training programmes as it was so typical of the situations we faced with our clients. This also gives quite entertaining descriptions of some of the main members of the client's management team, who probably all still hold senior management positions somewhere in the world today. As you will see, assuming our descriptions of the key management members are accurate and I have been repeatedly assured that they are, the executives were out of their depth and spent much of their time on interpersonal rivalry rather than on developing the business with over a billion dollars of sales, for which they supposedly had responsibility.

Below, is how our consulting team described the company and some of the interesting characters that made up the top executive team. I think the descriptions speak for themselves, so I won't make any comments.

COMPANY PROFILE

The corporation is a medium-sized multi-national in the retail market turning over $20 billion at a net profit of 9%. The local client for whom we worked had a turnover of $1.2 billion and a net profit of less than 3%. There were 22,000 staff. Over the years the product/price position has become confused, market share has dropped from 25% to 16% and costs of transport and warehousing have risen resulting in decreasing margins. About 70% of sales are achieved on Friday and Saturday. Staffing of the shops, particularly on Fridays and Saturdays, when they do most of their business has historically been a high mix of part-timers and students. The turnover of staff is typically 70% making training a continuous and costly activity. There is a typical functional conflict between the two key departments:

–   Buying and Merchandising believe they always buy the right stock which the Retail Operations Group fail to sell
–   The Retail Operations group think they know what the customer wants and could have told Buying and Merchandising that the stock they have bought will not sell

THE MANAGEMENT TEAM

MANAGING DIRECTOR – GEORGE

George is a typical expatriate, who has languished in an emerging nation for the past 20 years. He rose in the executive hierarchy on the back of competent performance in the Buying function of the local retail market leader which had grown to that position on the back of the largely white immigrant population. He has held the current post of MD for the past two years during which time the general retail market has been buoyant. He has made very few changes during this time, hardly anyone has been fired although there is clear evidence of incompetence everywhere you look.

The lack of pressure from the market-place has allowed him to use his preferred boardroom style of gathering consensus for the majority of agenda items. His office location is next to the boardroom, but on a separate floor from all but one of the other eight directors. The door remains closed for the majority of the day as he even takes his sandwich lunch in relative privacy. His political and personal radar remain switched off as he seems unaware of the frustrations of several of his board colleagues who are more action-oriented individuals.

George has taken to reading the latest management thinking and has started to create a vision of what might be possible for this sleeping giant of a company that he now heads up. One thing stands between him and that vision – competence – his own and that of the over-promoted individuals in the top 100 management positions. Promotions come easily in the good times!

Meeting behaviour

George's meetings rarely had agendas that had been circulated beforehand. George would frequently spend the first 15 minutes working out with the attendees what he and they wanted to talk about. Most of the discussion was unstructured.

During the meetings, George was not seen to make any decision of substance and became extremely agitated if the mode of the meeting looked as if it was heading towards heated discussion or disagreement. He frequently stated that he expected that sort of behaviour to take place outside the boardroom

BUYING AND MERCHANDISING DIRECTOR AND DEPUTY MD – HENRIK

The previous CEO, whom he knew from another company, had brought Henrik into the company. In his view, he had turned round the first Group company he had worked in and was given the position of Deputy MD as a reward. He interviewed George, now the MD, and two of the other directors for their respective positions and recommended that none were offered the jobs they now hold!

He has brought with him a number of Buying Directors who have formed a comprehensive organisation controlling the profitability of the product lines. He was charged by the Board to implement plans for increasing margins by 2%. None of these plans have taken shape or been implemented. Any questions in that area are met with discussions over the pace and complexity of such changes.

His main interaction outside his own function is with Helen, the Personnel Director, whom he would call a friend although he does not take this as far as social interaction, continuing to maintain his aloofness from the Board. He repeatedly insists on reference being made to his position as Deputy MD, although his difficult relationship with George, the MD, means that he does not share any of the role nor participate in any shaping and visioning of the company future.

He spends much of his time travelling around the world 'searching for new supply bases in emergent economies'.

He claims to be completely disinterested in company politics, but others view such statements with scepticism. His relationship with George is distant, born from his views on their relative competencies and their diametrically opposed management styles. He views the other Board members as having no vision and making no real changes in their areas.

Meeting behaviour

He turns up punctually to all meetings. His inputs are very carefully considered, highly factual and delivered as matters for little discussion. His inputs amount to less than 5% of the total. It appears that very few, if any, of the agenda items are put up by him or are related to his function or area of expertise.

RETAIL DIRECTOR – JAMES

James is a professionally qualified accountant who was Finance Director of the company for 2 years before becoming Retail Director at the same time as George came on board as the new MD. He has a good network of staff in the finance department who carry out 'odd jobs' for him without going through the new Finance Director, Mike, who is quietly furious about this behaviour.

James has started to introduce new concepts in the shops, which look attractive and are selling more product. Unfortunately he has also gone down market in the price structures and the company needs to sell 40% more items to make the same gross profit number. James seems to have omitted to complete the thorough analysis of the consequences of this change. This analysis clearly indicates the cost base growing out of control and the net profit number decreasing rapidly. The budgets for the cost base are largely held by other board members and James does not consider them to be his responsibility.

James sees himself as the new visionary within the retail market and constantly overwhelms people with his loud monologues on his latest concept. Publicly and vocally, he is a huge advocate for the change programmes the business needs, but privately he continues to fuel the fires that rage between Retail and Buying. He has a personal agenda to get control of the whole value chain.

In contrast to the prudent behaviour of most accountants, neither when he was Finance Director nor now does he see the need for budgets below Board level. He has openly discussed massage techniques for the Retail results to improve the picture to the Group Board.

On a personal level, he is very affable with other Board members and his staff who enjoy his management style, which is refreshingly open in contrast to Henrik. However, the staff regard him as a buffoon.

Meeting behaviour

James contributes significantly during meetings taking more than half of the air-time available. However, his inputs are largely confrontational, dismissive and largely miss the point. His style is to talk loud or louder than the others and to dominate the discussion by talking so rapidly that others cannot get a word in.

James comes to the meetings prepared with data to show how his functional area, Retail, is doing very well or would be if others – Buying – did their job properly.

PERSONNEL MANAGER – HELEN

Helen is a career HR person who has moved up the hierarchy mainly by changing company. Her impact at every level of the company is low, although she is a very likeable personality. Her mannerism often gives the impression of strength in management style, but this soon recedes when a firm response is given.

She has been in position for 6 years and as such has seen the going of at least 2 Managing Directors during that time.

She has brought little innovation or change to the HR function within the company but serves as the management tool for hiring and firing, doing much of the latter herself. The issues of high staff turnover are endemic in the Retail business. There seems to be little awareness of this in Helen's function and no plans to attack the issue.

Helen is great business friends with George, the MD, and spends more time with him than any other Board member. She spends very little time with James, Retail Director, and seems troubled in his presence.

Meeting behaviour

Helen has almost no voice at the meetings, contributing nothing other than mild support for George. Silence appears to be golden in her life.

CONCLUSION

I was working in another country at the time of this particular project. But I had many good colleagues who were involved. If I remember correctly, we did a lot of work out in the organisation trying to improve performance and we earned a lot of money for our efforts. But we never effectively tackled the problems at Board level. Eventually, I think, the Managing Director was fired and the shops were sold off to another company with a more effective management team, which reversed their declining fortunes.

I have recently received from sources within a major consultancy, their descriptions of the executive team at one of the world's largest motor car manufacturers. They make quite fun reading – but perhaps we should save those for another time.....

CHAPTER 10

FAR OUT IN THE
FAR EAST

As consulting markets in the West became over-saturated, fad-surfing became unfashionable and competition began to push down prices for consulting manweeks, many of the major consultancies began to cast their eyes eastwards towards Asia as the potential most profitable new business opportunity. Between 1994 and 1997, for example, McKinsey opened offices in Shanghai, Beijing, Bangkok, Kuala Lumpur and Singapore. Some consultancies made a success of their expansion eastwards by mastering the unique commercial approach necessary in many developing countries, but not all. Quite a few others abandoned Asia during the Asian financial crisis. A big challenge for the consultancies entering Asia was learning to live with a business culture that was somewhat different to what they might have been used to in the U.S. or Europe.

One of the many regrets I have, as I look back at the numerous high, medium and low points of my career in management consulting, is that I spent most of my time in Europe and the USA and only ever did one short piece of work in Asia. For, although the Asian project I was on was brief for reasons that I will explain, it was a real blast! As we say in consulting, working in Asia 'accelerated my learning curve'. And this acceleration was in three areas:

- **1. Professional** – this was my first real experience of working with the hordes of wonderful folk in our massive IT systems division and my first exposure to the chaos that they considered to be professional client service and a well set up project. I was later to have the pleasure of co-operating with them on an opportunity that was even more challenging than my brief foray to help them out in Asia (Chapter 12 *The great systems swindle*)

- **2. Commercial** – I was privileged to experience business practices that make the Irish dairy (with its fraud and theft) and an Italian meat processing plant (with its management being whisked off to prison while we were doing our study) both look like innocent kindergarten games

- **3. Social** – the consulting team seemed to indulge in a variety of after-work activities, which made anything one had ever done in places like Amsterdam seem rather tame in comparison

1. PROFESSIONAL – AN INTERESTING APPROACH TO SELLING A PROJECT

How we actually sold the Asian project is a little unclear as is often the situation with projects that end up as basket cases – in consulting, as I suppose in most other walks of life, when things go horribly wrong, the people responsible start muddying the waters so that any blame going around doesn't land at their door. Also unclear is whether we ever got any money for all the work we did. I suspect that finally, we made a monstrous loss, as we neither got any fees paid nor our considerable expenses refunded. However, our project team had a great time. I do know that the salesman was fired immediately after the project collapsed and went to work for a competitor, where he was given Germany as his territory. I imagine he is now having rather less fun there than he had when he was 'working' Asia.

Roughly what might have happened was as follows. This consultancy had about four or five thousand management consultants and tens of thousands of people in our IT systems division worldwide. Pretty much throughout the company, IT systems people did not talk to management consultants and vice versa. We management consultants tended to look down on the systems people as a lower order of human being, perhaps able to 'sell boxes and wires' but totally incapable of understanding complex business issues – those were our domain. They, from their side, quite rightly judged us as arrogant, uncooperative and inflexible. We used to joke that the relationship between IT systems and consulting was not so much 'hands-off' as 'f-ck off'. So, to the great distress of our owners, who had the dream of providing seamlessly integrated IT systems and management consulting for our clients, we on the ground lived in a state of permanent hostility and mutual contempt and only spoke to each other under the greatest of duress and usually just to trade insults.

One result of this was that, in spite of our public claims to offer a full service range all the way from strategic consulting through to change implementation to IT systems development to IT systems outsourcing, it was difficult to get systems people and consultants in the same room without a fight starting over who 'owned' the client and whose approach and methodology would be used. Another result was that the systems folk decided that, if we consultants weren't going to co-operate with them, then they would just copy most of our tools and techniques and build their own management consultancy to compete with us. This they did quite effectively – again much to the chagrin of our owners who had intended us to work together and not against each other. It did get embarrassing sometimes when our salespeople would go knocking on the door of a potential client only to find that the IT systems consultants had been there the week before proclaiming that they could do exactly what we so-called 'strategic consultants' could do, only much cheaper.

However, sometimes (rarely) we did work together. Unfortunately this tended to be in cases where the systems people had got into so much trouble, that they had no other option than to ask for our help to dig them out of the enormously deep holes they had deservedly got themselves into. This, of course, just served to reinforce our prejudice that they were well and truly incompetent. Naturally it also strengthened their belief that we were arrogant and unapproachable. In summary, lots of infighting, plagiarising of ideas, territorial rivalry, price competition and mutual distrust and, naturally, little active focus on providing the best service to our clients.

Our client here was the national airline of a large Asian country. This particular airline was having a few problems at that time. One of these problems was that the U.S. Federal Aviation Authority (F.A.A.) had made threatening noises about removing this airline's permit to fly to the States following a number of incidents including the impounding of a jumbo jet due to concerns over its airworthiness and the accuracy (or otherwise) of fault and maintenance records that were kept by the flight crew. In the airline business, it's generally not a particularly good idea to get banned by the F.A.A. – if an airline loses the right to fly to America, there are not many other countries that would want its planes causing havoc in their airspace. Moreover, once word got out that the F.A.A. considered the airline's planes a crock of sh-t, apart from the pilots and the crew, there's probably not that many people who would want to fly with them even if they could maintain a few of their routes. So, this airline had what we called a 'Red Issue', a real problem that management had to solve – if it didn't smarten up its act in maintenance and do it fast, its survival could be under threat.

One other small difficulty the airline had was that, like all major enterprises in this particularly charming country, it was used as a personal piggy bank by the ruling family and their thousands of hangers-on – a piggy bank from which they believed they were entitled to withdraw cash in large quantities, without ever having made any deposits. So money, that could have usefully been employed doing such mundane things as, for example, maintaining the aircraft in a condition that would enable them to stay airborne when intended, was instead diverted to buying unbelievable quantities of foreign luxury goods and to filling up numbered Swiss bank accounts, which would come in useful when the kleptocratic ruling family and its circle of sycophants were finally and deservedly thrown out of power.

Hearing about this particular airline's airworthiness and cash problems, the salesman and two of our aircraft maintenance experts from our IT division's consultancy put an ingenious offer forward to the airline's cash-strapped management. Our people knew from experience that most airlines tended to carry far too much stock of costly spare parts. We would, they proposed, work with maintenance to reduce the stock levels of spare parts to what was essential using modern stock management techniques. Unnecessary spare parts like excess wings and engines and gyroscopes and so on could then be sold to other airlines, which would pay full price for them. Part of the money the spare parts sales generated could then be paid to us to run a consulting project aimed at substantially improving the airline's maintenance methods and standards. All in all, an offer the airline shouldn't be able to refuse. So, the airline agreed to let us start to explore how much excess stock could be sold off and to design the maintenance improvement project that we wanted to sell to them.

Our two experts kicked off the first phase of our work and after a few weeks of struggling with a lack of information, atrocious record-keeping and a general unwillingness to do anything in a timeframe that could be measured in anything less than years, they did manage to produce a listing of all the stock that was theoretically held by the maintenance department. Gleefully they viewed page after page of extremely expensive parts, which were way in excess of the airline's operating needs and would fetch millions when sold on the world's aircraft parts market. Now they were ready to start the process of flogging off the excess stock, generating the money and selling in the main part of their maintenance improvement project.

Being rather mature and experienced people, the salesman and two maintenance experts out in Asia did not feel any need to get involved in all the warfare between the IT people and us strategic consultants. Thus, while contemplating how to design and sell the maintenance improvement project, they genuinely saw that, while they had huge knowledge of aircraft maintenance, their little team could benefit from the help of someone with a broader background in designing and selling organisational performance improvement programmes. So they contacted our Transport and Travel consulting director. Fortunately for me, none of his underlings were enamoured by the idea of a couple of months working with our lifelong sworn rivals in a faraway country in Asia. They looked around for someone else and ended up offering me the assignment. A couple of days later, I was sitting comfortably in the business class section of an intercontinental flight – incidentally, not with the airline in question. Although I was instructed to fly tourist class with our client, given what I had heard in the incredibly brief briefing I received before packing my bags and heading off to the airport, I decided to choose a more reliable carrier.

2. A COMMERCIAL CULTURE TO MAKE YOUR TOES CURL

I remember seeing a list in a business newspaper of world's most corrupt countries in which to do business. If my memory serves me correctly, Nigeria came gloriously first with Pakistan a proud close second – though it may have been the other way round. Anyway, the particular Asian country, to which I was sent, was most definitely comfortably up there in the glorious Top Five in terms of institutionalised corruption and general moral rottenness. During the first weekend, I took a little time off from the various social activities, which seemed unavoidable, and had a look through the selection of literature available in the hotel bookshop. I bought a book called 'The Business Culture in ………. (the name of the country)'. One of the key messages in the book was that to win any major contract, you would have to grease the palms of an extremely large number of people. But, the book warned, it was fatal for a foreigner to offer the necessary bribes – this would be seen as a personal insult to your potential clients and would definitely lose you any chance of doing business. After all, you would have cast a slur on your client's honour and integrity by suggesting that they were in any way corrupt. However, fortunately the appropriate method for bribing your way to winning contracts was helpfully explained by the book:

- Find a local partner

- Add about twenty percent to the price of your bid

- Pay this twenty percent to your local partner as commission

- Your local partner would then take contact with all the people involved in awarding the contract and distribute the twenty percent in appropriate quantities, to the appropriate people in the appropriate way

- Providing your local partner's palm-greasing was better than that of your competitors, you would win the contract

- Nobody's honour would have been besmirched and so everyone wins apart from the rival companies whose palm-greasing is less generous or less gracious than yours.

However, what the great book didn't mention was that there was an extremely effective short-cut and more reliable alternative to the above process – namely, pay massive bribes continuously through a local partner to influential members of the ruling family kleptocracy. This was, as we were to discover to our cost, the sure-fire route to success.

Our salesman was not naive and our company had already had a number of contacts with one of the largest local trading houses – a massive enterprise owning factories, shops, property and a few banks. This trading house had also set up its own management consultancy and was keen to find a foreign partner who could bring in some know-how to help it grow its consulting business. In our discussions with the directors of the Asian consultancy, we had already reached preliminary agreement on how they would help us sell the project to the airline. Then the plan was that we would work together to staff the project with experienced people from our side and some of their people, whom we would train during the project to develop local skills and competence. By the time I arrived on the scene, our local partners had already begun making contact with the airline's managers to assess who would make the buying decision and how much loot would have to be distributed to ease the whole sales process. So, in one way at least, the project sales team had effectively assessed the local commercial culture and adapted their sales approach to it. But there were other aspects of doing business in this delightful country that were unfortunately overlooked or at least underestimated and these errors of judgement led to our rapid undoing.

Joyously I left a grim European winter to arrive in the humid thirty degrees sunshine of Asia. On my first day on the project, the project lead took me through page after page of a lengthy computer listing of all the maintenance parts stock held by the airline. The incomprehensible numbers and aircraft part codes meant nothing to me. But he explained that the place was a goldmine of excess stock. "Here," he said, pointing to something or other, "there's at least three years' supply. And here. And here……." And so it went on. Apparently, in his expert opinion, there were millions here that could be sold with no trouble – it would be easy, he reckoned, to sell on the maintenance improvement project once we had started generating so much cash.

Avoiding the massive and unpleasant-looking spiders hanging in the trees between the maintenance department's offices and the stock areas, we set off to check a few of the juicier items on the stock listing. If I remember correctly, we were looking for wings for Boeing 737s and 747s and gyroscopes – apparently gyroscopes are incredibly expensive. Now, you'd think, especially if you were fairly inexpert like me and had only seen an aircraft wing when you looked out of your plane's window, that they are fairly large and it would be quite difficult to lose five or ten of them, even in quite a big stock building. But we searched and we searched and didn't find ten wings, nor even five – we found one! And that was considerably less than the number on the wondrous stock listing. "Well, maybe they're somewhere else," the project manager concluded as he turned his attention to the next juicy item on the list – gyroscopes for Boeing 747s. Eventually, we actually did find one of these. But though it was listed as new – it most definitely was not and had seen better days with at least one other airline before arriving to gather dust here. We tried a few other parts – with the same depressing results. Either the parts were simply not there in the quantities listed or else items described as new had actually been used before and had been refurbished with widely varying degrees of professionalism.

How to explain this strange set of circumstances? Possibly, the stock listing that our experts had produced was simply wildly inaccurate. Possibly many of the parts on the listing had actually been used up long before, but due to poor record-keeping, were still showing as available. So perhaps all the missing wings and invisible fuselages and second hand gyroscopes and so on were all part of a series of administrative errors. There were, however, other less innocent explanations for the parts stock discrepancies. These explanations owed more to the colourful local commercial culture than just being due to poor book-keeping. One idea that was floated was that airline executives were selling off many parts and pocketing the income for themselves. Moreover, from several sources we heard rumours that a local supplier of spares was in cahoots with maintenance management and was knowingly supplying second-hand refurbished parts but getting paid for them as if they were new and that the conspirators were splitting the proceeds of their profitable little enterprise.

Now before Boeing and Airbus set their lawyers on me and have my book banned, I would humbly draw their attention to a warning issued by the Italian civil aviation authority ENAC to over three hundred airlines and aircraft maintenance operators in January 2002.[1] The warning concerned at least one company suspected of stripping down old aircraft, taking out used parts, falsifying documentation to make the parts appear in better condition than they really were and then selling them on for use in civil airliners. ENAC advised airline maintenance departments to check that all second-hand parts already installed on aircraft actually could be safely used. Now, I'm sure the whole thing was a misunderstanding and that all those involved will be shown to be innocent – those with the best connections into the Italian government, the Mafia and the police will no doubt be proven to be the most innocent of all. And I believe totally the Italian traffic minister, when he claimed that at no time has passenger safety ever been put at risk from this allegedly illegal trade in used aircraft components and accompanying false documentation. But if such an unfortunate allegation can surface in an only moderately corrupt country like Italy, the mind boggles at what might really be going in a moral sewer like the Asian country where we were working.

Anyway, the bottom line was that the supposed goldmine, which was due to fund our maintenance improvement project, was unpleasantly empty – what was not clear was whether the gold had simply been honestly used, but its use had not been accurately recorded, or whether there were more sinister explanations for the huge shortfall. We had no way of finding out whether there had ever been any gold in the first place or whether some enterprising individuals had got there ahead of us and had dug out most of the gold before we could get our hands on it. We did find a little bit of inventory here and there, but it was arguable whether it was really excess to the airline's requirements and in no way was it sufficient to fund the project that we had hoped to sell.

That left us with a rather embarrassing, but more challenging, situation – we had the project that the client needed, but the client didn't have the cash that we needed them to pay for the project. We now had two choices – either we could pack up and go home or we could stay there and try to find some other way of helping the client generate the money necessary to pay for our project. I had just arrived, the weather was fabulous, we were having lots of fun and we had planned to go to a well-known holiday island the next weekend. So we were not in the mood to give up so easily and resolved to fight on – after a wonderful weekend, of course.

For the next week we took a conference room at our hotel and started to work on alternative ways of getting this client to buy our project. As we couldn't flog off aircraft parts to get some cash, we decided to focus on maintenance productivity instead. We got hold of records on how long the maintenance department took to complete their 'A Checks', 'B Checks' and 'C Checks' – these are compulsory regular maintenance operations undertaken after specified numbers of flying hours or distance travelled. The A Checks are the shortest and most frequent, while the C Checks are fairly lengthy overhauls. I, naturally, couldn't tell the difference between an A Check and a hole in the roof. However, our maintenance experts were on familiar ground and calculated that with better planning of work and on-time parts supply, we could reduce the calendar time taken for these compulsory maintenance operations by up to thirty percent and thus increase the availability of each aircraft. This in its turn would, of course, allow the airline to increase the flying hours and thus the income generated by each aircraft. All in all, an elegant solution. We were elated. We now had our 'Business Case' – the commercial rationale that we could use to show the client they could save money by investing in a large project with us and an excellent reason to stay out there in Asia rather than returning to drab, cold, old Europe.

Excited by our breakthrough, we prepared the presentation that we would give the next week to the head of maintenance and his management team. We conferred with our local partners and showed them our conclusions. In the meantime, they had been sounding out our potential client and believed that the right amount of money distributed at the right time would smooth the way to the desired contract. At that time, they too seemed optimistic about our chances.

However, looking back now, I'm not sure we could ever have been successful in selling this project. There was too much murkiness about what was going on in maintenance, especially around how much money was being spent, with whom and for what. I'm not sure anybody in maintenance management actually wanted any changes – they were comfortable with the way things were. There were also equally murky things apparently going on outside maintenance. One of our major competitors was reputedly in cahoots with a leading member of the ruling family. According to information later received by our partners, when our competitors heard that we were trying to use selling a project to the national airline as a bridgehead for entering into a market they believed they had sewn up for themselves, they had their contacts send a message to our client via the head of the airline that we were not to be hired under any circumstances. Our potential client was apparently also informed that if there was a project to be done, our competitor with links into the local abominably venal ruling family were more than happy to do it instead of us.

Who knows what the truth really was. Perhaps we could have sold the project; perhaps we never had a chance. However, given the way we behaved during our presentation to the maintenance management team, we managed to kick ourselves so effectively in the b-lls that even if we had had a chance of success going into the meeting, we were dead in the water as we came out.

In the famous book, the book of how to do business in that exotic country, it states very very clearly that you must never, repeat never, in any way make your client lose face in front of his colleagues. While we in the West often like a good healthy argument, in many Asian countries this is abhorred. Arguing with your client in the East, or being seen to criticise them in front of others is unforgivable. And this was a trap we went crashing into. Unfortunately for us, our project director was a fairly large fellow even by Western standards – compared to our Asian clients, he was huge. He also had a great booming voice, many years of experience and the strength of his almost religious convictions. Enthusiastically, his great voice amplified by his passion for his subject, he started the presentation by telling the maintenance management team what a mess the whole maintenance operation was. His intention was to convey the enormous potential for improvement if we could work together. However, given the man's physical presence and uncompromising stance, what actually came across in this culture, where confrontation and personal criticism are absolutely unacceptable, was a withering barrage of accusations that had both the client and us other consultants cringing. By the time our project director handed over to me to explain the project design, the client had completely closed down. There were no questions, no comments, no words exchanged. At the end of our presentation, the client team walked out without a word. We had insulted them. We had shamed them. They had nothing whatsoever to say to us.

The next day, our salesman sat for over three hours outside the maintenance director's office waiting for the chance to repair the damage done the previous day. Inside the office, alone and clearly visible through the glass walls sat the maintenance director. The maintenance director simply ignored our salesman that day and the next and the next. We also tried to get access using our local partners. They too were denied an audience. Meanwhile our London office who was paying our salaries and ever increasing expenses was starting to ask when we would get a contract and when they could expect to see some money flowing in to them rather than out from them. After about a week of being stonewalled, our partners advised us to walk away and let them try to make some headway once we were out of the client's sight. I don't think we ever heard from them again.

3. SOCIAL – A NIGHTLIFE TO MAKE YOUR HAIR STAND ON END

In order to be near work, we stayed at a hotel close to our client's offices out by the international airport rather than in town. And there's generally not much happening in the evenings at hotels on industrial estates by international airports – in this country or any country. Moreover, the hotel was not yet fully built. It was having what is called a 'soft opening' – that means that its various facilities were only gradually being brought into use as building work was completed and local staff hired and trained. So, there weren't many people staying there either. The first night at the hotel was thus a fairly quiet affair – dinner in a ninety percent empty restaurant followed by drinks in a ninety percent empty bar. But there was, fortunately for us, one other person in the bar that first night – Bob an American salesman of something or other. Bob said he knew the capital well and invited us to join him the next evening on a visit into town. Bob had one address in his address book for that city. It was a nightclub called the Tanamur. Bob said we wouldn't need any other addresses. Bob, despite being an American and a salesman, was right.

So, on the evening of day two of my time in that country, five of us crowded into a rickety taxi and headed into town to check out Bob's recommendation. The Tanamur turned out to be a fairly lively nightclub packed full of locals and foreigners. A few minutes investigation revealed that there were probably three types of girl at the place. Locals who had genuinely gone out with friends to have a good time and didn't want anything to do with foreigners. Then there were ordinary working girls and students who were interested in supplementing their meagre incomes with a little evening work – usually servicing the sexual desires of the many foreign businessmen. And finally there were full-time prostitutes.

As management consultants travelling around the world at our clients' expense to help organisations in need, we are often faced by great moral dilemmas, for example:

- If we need to prove 30% ineffectiveness in a client's operation in order to sell a project but our inexperienced and untrained junior consultants can't find it, should we just falsify the results of our studies to make sure we win the work? Or should we tell the client they don't need our help?

- If we believe that a client management team is making a wrong decision, but agreeing with them will give us work while disagreeing with them might get us shown the door – what should we do?

- If a client asks us to help implement an incredibly expensive, but probably useless computer system, do we turn down tens of millions in fees by telling them they don't need the system? Or do we just take the money on the basis that all we are doing is helping a client implement their decision? That the decision was wrong and would distract, perhaps fatally, client staff from the more important task of serving their customers would not be our problem.

- If there is an apparently endless supply of small, dark, young, fabulously attractive Asian girls available at very reasonable prices and willing to provide a quite wide range of services, do we do our bit and help support the local economy or do we rush back to our hotel rooms to watch CNN News night after night?

Fortunately, we management consultants have great experience in finding the right answers to such tremendous moral dilemmas that might confound lesser beings. In the first taxi back to our hotel that evening were four people – myself, our salesman and two young ladies, who seemed to find us two men both extremely interesting and attractive and, incidentally, with whom we had already agreed the services to be provided and the price to be paid. As we reached the hotel and headed off to our separate rooms, our salesman tried to do a deal with me whereby, when we had both completed our business with the ladies in question, we would call each other and swap partners for a second round of what we consultants call 'service delivery'. I declined. I felt this might be taking the idea of teamwork slightly beyond the levels encouraged by our management. So, when I had finished with the various things that one does on such an occasion, I despatched my partner to the taxi that was waiting to take the two girls back into town. The next day, I learnt that our arrangements broke down slightly. The girl whom the salesman had chosen was incredibly drunk and apparently liked to talk – a lot. When I had already finished my business and gone to sleep, he had hardly got going. Fed up at having to wait so long, my partner and the taxi driver decided to leave without the second girl. Although the salesman did eventually get the services, which had been agreed, he also got several hours of one-sided conversation, much of it in the local language of which he understood not one iota. The next morning, he looked extremely tired and not all sexually satisfied.

However, we tough international management consultants are not deterred by setbacks, however great. The next evening saw us taxiing back towards the Tanamur. As did the one after that and the one after that and the one after that. In fact, we ended up having such a whale of a time there in the capital, that we dropped our plans for jetting off to the holiday island for the weekend and instead moved in to a hotel in the centre of the city – coincidentally quite near to the Tanamur nightclub.

One thing I did find interesting was how much one finds out about a person's character by the type of female companion they choose to purchase each evening – but probably I've said enough about consultants and whores for the time being.....though telling the difference between the two can sometimes be quite difficult, except that whores tend to be better looking and more honest in how they go about earning a living.

---

(1) BT Business Section 4 February 2002

CHAPTER 11

THE ROT SETS IN

THE MARKET TIGHTENS

By the mid 1990s, there were at least three major changes within the business world, which posed a threat to the further growth of management consultancy.

Firstly, a new generation of managers moved up to positions of power within many Western corporations. Unlike many of their predecessors, these managers had been to business school and didn't feel the need to hire in consultants to the same degree as their predecessors. One leading businessman summed up this tightening of the market when asked about his use of consultants, *"I am not closed to an external perspective that consultants might bring. But I think M&S suffered from that in the past. There was an expectation that there were consultants working on everything. We have very consciously swung it to the other end of the pendulum"*.[1]

Secondly, as Western companies improved their performance and the Japanese and other Asian economies moved into recession, the apparent threat from the Far Eastern Tiger Economies competitors seemed to diminish.

And thirdly, many of the products we had been selling, like Business Process Reengineering, Balanced Scorecard and Business Transformation had begun to lose more than a little of their lustre.

However, there were now hundreds of thousands of management consultants who needed a place to bill their time or else they were out of a job and their bosses would miss their bonus targets. Basically, we moved into a position where there were probably too many consultants now chasing too little business. Unlike the growing market we had enjoyed for the last twenty years or more, the new conditions meant that the pressure on us to sell warm bodies became enormous, irrespective of whether our clients actually had a need for consultancy help or not. Naturally this led to a decline in standards of work and a decline in the value provided by consultancies to their clients – if you manage, for example, to sell a client a million dollar project they don't need, however successful the project, you're not going to provide much value by delivering it. For some consultancies just surviving started to become an issue.

WHY IT USUALLY ENDS IN TEARS

Having seen so many management consultancies, both from the outside and the inside at all stages of their development, you start to see a pattern emerging of how consultancies are formed, grow and then often decline. There are times when you can expect a consultancy to give you true dedication and great work and others when you should be prepared to be taken to the cleaners time and time again, if you're not extremely careful. There are probably three main driving forces behind the formation of most management consultancies:

1. Get rich quick
2. Jump on the band-wagon
3. New service offering

1. GET RICH QUICK

There are consultancies that are born when their founder just steals a client or two from his previous employer. Usually they also steal a few consultants and electronic copies of all their previous employer's training materials to assist their start-up. They then regurgitate their previous employer's approach without the slightest change or innovation. Sometimes, as we saw with The Plagiarists (Chapter 3 *Baby Butchers – cost-cutting continued*) they even steal client reference letters and photocopy them on to their own company paper. The founder(s) then becomes disgustingly and undeservedly rich, without having created anything new or having had a single idea of their own – apart from how to rapidly inflate their own bank balance. If one of these consultancies comes knocking at your door, then beware. They were conceived from stealing someone else's ideas. They have become rich from endlessly reapplying a well-worn approach created by someone else. Unless you are absolutely sure that you want to buy second or third hand ideas mechanically reapplied with only the slightest customisation to your unique organisational situation – then don't go near these consultancies. They will serve you badly because they only know how to do one or two things and those things are not even new or original, they are borrowed or stolen from someone else. Like The Butchers, they may do them well. But it is unlikely to be exactly what you really need. And in these consultancies, with their tried and tested business model for making money, innovation and creative thinking about a client's business issues are generally not encouraged.

Only very weak managers employ consultants who just regurgitate and mechanically implement ideas that were becoming old and stale even as the consultancies were first being formed. Fortunately for such consultancies, there are many very weak managers in the world.

2. JUMP ON THE BANDWAGON

Every few years, there comes a new management fad which sells so well that a huge market is created for people who claim to be able to supply something that looks like, tastes like or slightly smells like the original version. Nature abhors a vacuum. And there's nothing like an enormous unsatisfied market in something our clients don't understand to fuel the formation of a myriad of new management consultancies and boost extraordinarily rapid growth for any incumbents fast enough on their feet to jump in front of the new parade.

The last big seller was 'e-business' when loads of self-serving experts told us that all organisations would suddenly do most of their business over the Internet. Those, which didn't adapt, the gurus threatened, would die. Billions were spent on organisations becoming 'e-enabled'. There was a feeding frenzy for management consultants. Loads of new ones appeared with trendy names which reflected how amazingly different they were to the boring and greedy major players. And the major players desperately scrambled to develop their own e-offering. Salaries for anyone who could spell the word 'Internet' soared and people became multi-millionaires overnight. Then the bubble burst, Internet company stocks collapsed and bankruptcies were widespread amongst the fashionable new consultancies with the trendy names. Meanwhile most of the majors, who had failed dismally to exploit the e-wave, breathed a collective sigh of relief as their new competition was decimated and frightened clients came running back to safer pairs of hands.

Before that, there was the Business Process Reengineering (BPR) craze. However, whereas e-business led to the rise and fall of many new consultancies, BPR led to the explosive growth of many previously fringe players in the consultancy market. For years the major accountancies had been prevented from growing due to a finite number of organisations to audit. Many had envied the huge fees and seemingly unlimited growth of management consultancies. So to get their part of the consultancy cake, most of the larger accountancies had set up management consulting divisions. But these lacked a compelling product to sell and so tended to be small compared to their auditing business. This usually left the consulting partners as very much barely tolerated newcomers and clearly second-class citizens, always under the thumb of the well-established audit partners. BPR changed all that. BPR gave these consultancies something that was easy to understand, easy to copy, easy to implement with armies of inexperienced staff and easy to sell to clients with an apparently insatiable appetite for this latest set of the emperor's new clothes. The growth of most consultancies doing some kind of BPR was impressive. The growth of the accountancy-based consultancies was phenomenal – some had tens of thousands of consultants. When it was sold to IBM, PWC had around thirty thousand management consultants. By the end of the BPR craze, many of these consultancies had become significantly more profitable than their huge auditing parents and typically, many accountancies would be earning five to ten times as much from selling consultancy as they earned from their audits.

3. NEW SERVICE OFFERING

Then there is a group of consultancies that are set up because the founders genuinely believe they have a new service to offer clients, which is not currently available on the market. They don't usually need to steal clients and ideas because they have the capability to develop some ideas of their own. Likewise, they aren't just following the Gadarene Swine on the latest band-wagon. They are pioneers trying to go in a different direction from the crowd, because they passionately believe that they have something new to offer. And it's probably the word 'passion' which distinguishes these consultancies. Because they believe in something higher than just gorging their bank balances and more original that quickly copying what everyone else is up to, these consultancies have a true conviction that they are adding value to their clients as well, of course, to themselves.

Such consultancies may have a difficult first year or so as they try to convince clients to have the courage to try something new. But once they have got their first clients, things tend to move quickly. Such consultancies are great for clients because they are like missionaries dedicated to spreading The Word. They tend to be truly committed to showing that their approach adds value and they will work all hours to achieve results for their clients. Moreover, their staff have a passion for their work as they are driven by a belief in their product rather than just the need to sell more manweeks and bring in an unceasing flow of fees. For many years (Chapter 4 *Reaching Consulting Heaven*) The Family was one of this group.

Also, as these missionary consultants are usually reasonably small at first, they can keep sufficiently busy by skimming the market just picking off the low hanging fruit – clients who really need what they are selling. It's only once they get larger and their offer becomes less novel, that the pressure to sell whatever you can takes over from the passion for excellent delivery to clients.

Though, one danger with these missionary consultancies is that demand for their services can outstrip their capacity to supply useful bodies. Then they either have to turn work away or else they are rushed into recruiting people, whom they would normally not consider, and they are pressured into putting new and modestly trained consultants into positions for which they are clearly not ready – what we in consulting euphemistically call 'stretch' roles. So beware, if you're talking to a bright newish consultancy with a great original service to offer. What they can do may be great for your organisation, but check out that the people, whom they are proposing to put on your particular project, have been with them for more than a couple of days and make sure that they have successfully delivered the consultancy's offering at least once.

LOTS OF CONSULTANTS WITH NOWHERE TO GO?

But what happens to the jump-on-the-bandwagon consultancies, when the fad they have been riding starts to become old hat and demand begins to fall? They have built up a massive money-making machine. They have a structure where the bosses are earning a fortune on the backs of thousands or even tens of thousands of hard-working pawns, who are often only capable of delivering one basic thing, for example BPR. What do they do once clients are no longer interested in paying through the nose for armies of business process reengineers? First they start dropping their prices just to try and win contracts to keep their people in work – it's a very expensive pastime to have say one hundred consultants earning over a thousand pounds a week each unassigned or as we say 'on the beach'. As an industry observer wrote in an article titled *Consultants face their darkest hour*, "*Many big clients have put big projects on hold. This has had a dramatic effect on the hourly rates consultants can charge clients. They have been on a gravy train until now charging up to £2,500 for a day's work. But insiders said that things have got so bad some have been prepared to work for nothing*"[2]

The bottom-line for fad-followers is that once your profitable fad starts to lose its appeal, you're left with hundreds and maybe thousands of hungry mouths to feed. And if you wish to retain the level of income, to which the fortunate few at the top of the pyramid have become accustomed, you have to keep on selling those people's time, whether there is market demand for their services or not. Now you may be lucky and another lucrative management fad may create massive new demand for some other kind of consulting. Then you can just try to quickly rebrand your people by, for example, putting loads of your business process reengineers through a two week training course in e-business and then selling them off as e-business experts to clients who couldn't tell the difference between e-business and a hole in the road. As the HR Director of one consultancy said at a management meeting I attended at the time when the BPR craze was dying and we had loads of BPR consultants whose time we couldn't even give away, never mind sell, "*we need to respray people so they fit into requirements*".[3]

But if the next fad doesn't turn up at the right time, you've got an awful lot of hard selling to do just to keep your employees busy and the money flowing your way in a market that has a declining desire for what you can offer. And you always have the threat hanging over your head that, as soon as your people aren't billing millions, they're costing millions.

Running a management consultancy can seem a bit like running on a treadmill which keeps accelerating and doesn't have a stop button – once you've got going at a reasonable speed, you have to run faster and faster just to stay on. With consultancy, once you've reached a certain size, you have to keep selling warm bodies to anyone to do anything just to keep your head above water. At that point you don't care what a client's real problems are nor how to give them the best service. All you are interested in is getting though the door, selling something however small to establish your presence in a client's organisation and then using that bridgehead to keep on funnelling more and more warm bodies into that client. Consultants like to talk about building long-term relationships with their clients. Of course, they want these relationships – after all, it's in the consultants interest to have a safe and secure place to push expensive consultants who have nowhere else to go.

But what about clients? Is it in their interest to have the same firm of consultants hanging around for several years as part of this wondrous long-term relationship? Probably not – for several good reasons:

- If the consultants really were any good, they'd help clients solve their key organisational issues and then would no longer be required.

- The longer a consultancy stays with a client the more its people 'go native' adopting the client's way of thinking and working. And the more the consultant resembles the client, the less able they are to bring new fresh challenging ideas.

- The longer a consultancy hangs around, the more clients' managers become dependent on consultants and the more they abdicate difficult decisions to the consultants – consultants who often have a fairly limited repertoire of solutions to offer.

The same sorts of problems arise for the missionary consultancies like The Family. They get a great idea, it sells well, they build up to hundreds even thousands of consultants and vast sums of money are accumulated by the big chiefs. But gradually the big idea that underpinned their growth loses some of its freshness and excitement. Then somebody else comes up with something even newer and fresher leaving you looking decidedly like yesterday's news. But like the bandwagon-jumpers, you now have many mouths to feed, so you have to keep on selling, however obsolete your ideas and skills may be. And this pressure to keep on selling more and more of the only thing you know does not make for good unbiased client-focused consulting. It turns you from passionate missionaries spreading The Word into desperate product salesmen eager to shift as many units per day on to their clients for as high a cost per unit as a client will stand. You end up just like a refrigerator salesman trying to sell yet another fridge to everybody in a town where every home already has at least one.

Consultants may have great skills and ideas, which can be useful to you. But they are also under incredible pressure to sell warm bodies. So, please make sure you buy the consultancy you need and don't just end up, like so many clients, by becoming a lucrative parking space for your pet consultancy's excess inventory of people who need billing slots!

FROM SWEET TO SOUR

I remember being with one major worldwide management consultancy as it moved from the phase of having a great product that clients wanted to buy to the phase of just being another me-too supplier of bodies, an indistinguishable face in a crowd of consultants clamouring at would-be clients' doors in the eager rush to sell their people.

Over the previous few years, we had done some fantastic turnaround projects for some quite major organisations and we had built up an enviable group of talented and experienced consultants held together by a shared pride in the quality of our offering and in the excellence of the results we achieved for our clients. But competitors became better at copying us, they claimed to be able to do what we did, they were cheaper than we were and business became harder to get. This put pressure on our management – pressure that they, because of personal greed and political cowardice, were ill-equipped to handle. By their panicked reaction to the tougher business situation and the breathtaking cynicism they showed in how they treated both **our consultants** and **our clients**, they almost wrecked the company:

1. By treating **our consultants** as a disposable commodity like toothbrushes or washing powder, they destroyed the spirit of loyalty, teamwork and dedication which had made us great and which had enabled us to deliver fantastic results for our clients

2. By trying to sell anything at any cost to **any client** they could find to keep people busy, they got us bogged down in a series of badly prepared and poorly executed projects, which pretty much trashed the impressive reputation we had all worked so hard to build up

Let me now try to show how the whole thing can go so badly wrong, at our people's and clients' expense, when the pressure to sell consultants' time dislodges any concerns about quality standards, real client needs, fairness or professionalism.

I. UP OR OUT! – TREATING PEOPLE AS COMMODITIES

As a tightening market for our services began to put pressure on our billing rates, our management did a very simple calculation. They worked out that if they could reduce the consultancy's salary bill and maintain or just slightly reduce our weekly billing rates, then they could protect profit margins and their bonuses. But, of course, our management couldn't just reduce consultants' pay, when they themselves were clearly amassing millions. The troops wouldn't have stood for that. Because of at least five years of stunning growth and market success, we had built up a group of consultants with a fair breadth of knowledge and experience. This, of course, meant that they were capable of delivering better results for clients than some of our competitors, who just had hordes of 'green peas' (inexperienced staff on their first consulting assignment). However, in the eyes of our management, experienced consultants meant expensive consultants and expensive consultants meant less profitable projects. What they had to do, they realised, was to find some clever excuse for replacing expensive consultants with cheaper ones. So, with mind-boggling cynicism, they cooked up a story, whereby they claimed that in order to accelerate the development of our people in a company with the slogan 'People Matter', they felt it best for all employees if they introduced an 'Up or Out Policy'.

The Up or Out Policy was very simple. Our vice presidents decided that consultants would be allowed a certain length of time in each grade of the company hierarchy. If, during that time, they were not promoted to the next grade up, they would automatically have to leave the company – with no compensation, no redundancy payments, nothing. If you were an associate consultant, for example, you had two years to be promoted to consultant. No promotion in that time, of course, meant you were fired without compensation. Consultants had three years to make it to senior consultant. Senior consultants had two years to get up to managing consultant. Managing consultants got three years to fight their way to becoming Project Managers. And Project Managers had five years to clamber their way up to becoming Vice Presidents. Needless to say, there were no limits at all for time in grade for our most expensive people, namely our Vice Presidents – after all, it was them that thought up the policy in the first place.

Our vice presidents claimed the purpose of the Up or Out Policy was *people development* and *growing skills* and *leveraging the talent within the company'* and *'being an organisation where People Matter'* and *'fulfilling our mission to become leaders within the consulting profession'*.[4]

But you don't develop people by booting them out the door when you yourself refuse to promote them. You can hardly claim that *'People Matter'* if you chuck them out of work and replace them after they have given you and your clients years of dedicated service. You don't become *'leaders within the consulting profession'* by replacing many of your most seasoned consultants with cheaper juniors still wet behind the ears and who probably couldn't tell the difference between a supply chain and a pile of bricks. And you don't create an environment of trust and teamwork, when you deliberately set your people against each other as they start to fight for the limited promotion opportunities that will save them from getting fired.

Thus the decision to treat talented consultants as easily replaceable commodities had a disastrous effect on morale – it turned people from co-operating into competing and it destroyed the sense of teamwork and togetherness that had once made us great.

But it had an even more awful effect on our ability to deliver quality work to our clients. Different consultancies obviously have different market positions. Some are known for hiring supposedly the most brilliant MBA students and providing their clients with leading edge analytical skills. Others have armies of technology-literate staff to drive through multi-million pound systems-based change programmes. And yet others have hordes of worker bees, who have been trained to religiously follow a few limited but effective methods and procedures set down in stone by their bosses.

Our niche was that we brought both knowledge of clients' businesses and the ability to cause major performance improvement together in a way that was unique and specially tailored to each client's particular situation. So we needed consultants with real-life work experience and we tended to hire people with anything from two to twenty years in line management positions before they went into consulting. For someone like myself in Sales, who had little to no practical knowledge of any of the areas in which I was sent to sell projects – areas like steel-making, pharmaceutical supply chains, new product development, manufacturing missile systems, launching satellites, building offshore oil rigs or whatever – the easiest way to convince a client to buy a project from us, was to have someone with years of experience in the client's particular sector. Then I could claim to the client that I could bring in expertise from causing performance improvement in organisations in almost all activity sectors imaginable, while Joe (or whoever), who would be a key figure on the project, had worked most of his or her life in the client's own industry. This was a great combination and it worked time and time again in landing us whopper-sized projects.

So the kind of person, who was most effective in helping me sell major projects, was someone who had perhaps spent up to twenty years in some industry or service sector, whose children had grown up and left home and who had decided to spend the last ten to fifteen years of their career as a consultant to get a bit more variety in their work and build up their pension fund. The Up or Out Policy, of course, went completely against our model of delivering successful projects through experienced people. Because now what mattered to our bosses was only how much our consultants cost in salaries, rather than how much they contributed to our clients. And what experienced person would now leave a safe line management job to join us knowing that they would be automatically fired after a couple of years if they weren't promoted quickly enough? There is a saying that 'every army needs people who can dig a hole and shoot straight' – you can't have everyone demanding to be generals, except of course in the Italian army. Likewise, consultancies like ours needed good solid experienced people who could gain credibility with and work effectively with client supervisors, middle managers and front-line staff. We needed people who had a certain professional weight and who didn't mind doing this year in year out and getting paid a solid sixty to eighty thousand pounds per annum. Deploying a flock of bright, ambitious and impatient green peas was not always the most effective way of getting results. It certainly wasn't the approach that had made us successful. So, this policy was truly and utterly a disaster for us who actually had to sell and deliver projects.

At first, the Up or Out Policy was received with consternation. Then, as we realised our vice presidents were serious, there was shock and disbelief. The effects of the implementation of Up or Out were almost immediate. Previously, most of our consultants had been very flexible in accepting whatever assignments they were offered – even if these didn't match their career aspirations. However, now Up or Out was in place, consultants who were near the end of their time in grade naturally started to get concerned about whether their next assignment would give them the development opportunities they needed to get promoted. If the opportunities weren't there, they would refuse the assignment. This, of course, led to a shift of energy from serving clients to engaging in lots of pointless internal arguments over whether we could force consultants to take roles on projects, which did not give them the development opportunities they needed to get promoted, and would thus lead to them getting fired through no fault of their own.

The implementation of this policy also led to a visible split between project managers like myself, who actually had to face clients daily and deliver high quality results, and vice presidents, who started to hide behind the rules and conditions of Up or Out, however ludicrous the ensuing decisions. How could I honestly say to clients that we had experienced teams ready to deliver world class results, when I knew that internally we were at war, that our experience base was being decimated and that Up or Out was preventing us recruiting the kind of people who would be most useful to our clients?

In organisational development, a useful concept is that of the 'psychological contract' – this is the unwritten set of expectations that exist between employer and employee. Normally, for you to get the best from your employees, for example, the employees would expect to be treated fairly, to get management support with difficult problems and believe that they and top management had shared values and goals. We had always had a fantastic psychological contract between our people and the company due to our shared set of values and common belief in the need for professional integrity. This was the basis for our ability to form multi-national teams anywhere in the world and from the very first minutes to be working effectively together to solve previously intractable client problems. The Up or Out Policy destroyed that psychological contract and started the slow and painful decline that led to the eventual disappearance of this consultancy as a successful several thousand person independent operation.

Now, Up or Out in itself is not necessarily bad. McKinsey, probably the world's leading consultancy, practice it very effectively. When new recruits first join McKinsey, they already know that only one in five of them will ever make it up to partner. All the others will, at some point or other, be forced to leave. However, McKinsey doesn't just dump them out on the street like our hopeless management did. Instead, McKinsey helps them get good jobs. This allows McKinsey to build a huge network of former employees, the McKinsey alumni, who have a positive attitude towards and loyalty to their former employer. McKinsey continually cultivates its alumni network and as many of them rise to top positions in major organisations, they can create a market for McKinsey services. They can also severely limit the growth potential of McKinsey competitors like us. While trying to sell projects we frequently got blocked by board members who were ex-McKinsey.

Actually, the Up or Out Policy started to fall apart within the first full year of operation. In the initial policy documentation it was stated that *'there will be no exceptions'*. However, when the first Up or Out promotion round came, it was found that, as the number of promotion slots at each level was limited, some very good people had reached the end of their time in grade and therefore must be fired, even though we needed them. So clients saw some of the most experienced consultants, on whom they had come to rely, announcing that they would be leaving our company and that someone new would replace them on their projects. And project directors were informed that some of their most talented people were being shown the door. Of course, this situation was ludicrous.

Finally, some project directors found the courage to protest. There was confusion amongst our senior executives. Again lots of internal politicking and lots of distraction from our primary business goal – serving the client. Eventually, after some key people had gone, top management backed down, slightly. A memo was issued *'the Executive Group has decided to abolish the mechanistic application of time in grade with immediate effect'.*[5]

However, our executives were not prepared to admit that the whole thing had been a ghastly, costly and time-consuming mistake. So the memo from our managing director ended with the transparently untrue and pathetically hypocritical words: *'I would like to see the change to Up or Out not as the ending of a policy, but as a beginning, as a resurgence of our passion for people development in ourselves and in each other'.*[5]

2. CALLING IN THE CAVALRY –
POOR CLIENT SERVICE

Just as the Up or Out Policy cast a blight on the relations between our top management and our people, so the desperate rush to sell, sell, sell polluted our relations with our clients. Our vice presidents and salesmen were under pressure to produce more clients and more projects to keep the company and their bonuses growing, as the market for our services stagnated. So they would promise almost anything to almost anybody and then leave it to us middle level project managers to sort out the mess, while they disappeared off to important internal meetings in Florida and Cannes or took their skiing holidays.

Perhaps the best way to illustrate this, is to describe how I wasted about two years of my life digging one consultancy out of one nasty hole after another.

I had spent the previous few years reasonably successfully helping to sell largish performance improvement projects and having the satisfaction of seeing the teams that took over the projects actually delivering a significant part of what we, the sales team, had originally promised our clients. These were good times. We produced results. Our clients were often delighted and bought more work from us. Also they would host visits from potential new clients and proudly show them all the improvements we had achieved together. Our clients became our most effective salesmen as they told one visiting organisation after another, *"we couldn't have done this without ...."*. There was a spirit of passion and excitement in the company. It was almost a pleasure to come to work. This was the way management consulting should work in an ideal world. But, as we all know, the world is not ideal. Anyway, we became big, the top people got greedy and the competition got smarter. Fishing for clients became an altogether more difficult task, clearly requiring more skill and cunning than most of our vice presidents possessed. So in their desperate attempts to claim sales successes for themselves, they would throw all kinds of poorly prepared rubbish at us project managers, in the hope that we would turn at least some of it into gold dust. Let me give you two case studies in how not to sell consulting projects

A. David Craig – the oil rig expert

B. The corridor test

A. DAVID CRAIG – THE OIL RIG EXPERT

I was at home one Monday having just finished an assignment. I got back from a morning run in the local park to find an ansaphone message from my boss at the consultancy. I rang him back, was instructed to get to the airport as fast as possible and make my way to Oslo to attend a project start-up meeting with a new client at five o'clock that evening. I did ask my boss, how come they had only just found out the project was starting – I got a garbled and unconvincing story. I asked who the client was – my boss didn't know. I asked what the client did – my boss didn't know. I asked what the project was about – my boss didn't know. I stopped asking.

I grabbed a shower, called a taxi, got to the airport and literally ran on to a flight that was a few minutes from leaving. As I had no luggage, I managed to run off the flight on arrival in Oslo, push myself past lots of polite socially-conscious Norwegians to the front of the taxi queue and get to our Norwegian head office at about ten minutes to five. Almost immediately I was shown up to a meeting room and the head of our Norwegian consulting practice (let's call him Olaf) came in gabbling away in what I suppose was Norwegian with two men, who turned out to be the potential client's managing director and HR director. I still didn't know who the client was nor what they did. When Olaf switched to English and introduced me to the client mentioning the name of the client's company, I was none the wiser as, unfortunately, I had never before been to Norway and wouldn't have known the difference between a pillar of Norway's commercial life and a failing fish and chip shop.

We all shook hands, sat down and Olaf placed the contract letter for the project on the table and started to talk about the great work I was about to embark on with this client. Seeing the contract letter for the first time, I quickly started trying to read it upside down to get some inkling of what was up and especially find out exactly what Olaf had promised this client.

Eventually Olaf finished his introductory platitudes and launched into the meat of our discussion with the client – how a team led by me was going to spend five to six weeks investigating the opportunities for this client to improve the way it built oil rigs. Oil rigs! I thought. I don't know anything about bloody oil rigs. Visions of standing miserably in the middle of the North Sea with a bunch of sexually frustrated Norwegian oil drillers – this didn't sound like it was going to be as much fun as hanging out smoking and joking in Amsterdam or as swanning around the Far East. My heart sank at the likely disastrous effect this project would have on my social life. My mind buzzed as I desperately tried to think of something extremely intelligent to say about what I personally could contribute to the more effective building of oil rigs.

The two clients looked at Olaf with consternation. "We thought you were going to do two days of interviews and then tell us what we need to do," they said. Apparently I wasn't the only person in the room, who was seeing the project contract letter for the first time in their lives. Olaf looked somewhat perplexed, "didn't you get the copy of the contract we faxed to you?" he asked. The clients shook their heads.

The HR director (we'll call him Wulf as that's, I think, a Norwegian-sounding name) picked the letter up and started, like me, to read it for the first time. Though he was lucky, he could read it the right way up and he could read the whole letter – I had only managed to cover the first page and that was reading upside down. I had no idea of what was on the second page. His eyes widened as he began to grasp what Olaf the Oaf had been trying to slip past him. "We don't want many weeks of studies," Wulf said, "we just want the interviews."

Olaf the Oaf's previously cheerful grin rapidly vanished as Wulf began to sink his great project, the project that would have helped Olaf meet his challenging sales target to get his bonus. But Wulf was very emphatic, "then after the interviews," he continued, "we can decide if we want you to do anything else for us."

Olaf the Oaf stuttered and stumbled for a few moments. Definitely not much warlike Viking blood in him. This was not quite what either he or I had expected. Then suddenly his face lit up again as he had a tremendous Norwegian brainwave. Turning to me, he said, "David, you're really the expert in this area. Why don't you explain our approach?" He then leant back to allow me to take centre stage. He had dug himself into an embarrassingly big hole in his desperation to sell something to this client – it was now up to me to get us out of the mess. It's what we in consulting who had played rugby called a 'hospital pass' – you chuck the ball to a member of your own team just as a herd of the meanest, ugliest players on your opponents' team are about to leap on top of you, so it is your team-mate, rather than you, who ends up in hospital. Idiot that I was, I dutifully caught Olaf the Oaf's hospital pass and began to duck and weave my way past all the client's well-founded objections to Olaf's plan of swamping their company with expensive and inexperienced management consultants. It wasn't easy, but gradually I managed to close the gap between a client, who thought they had agreed to a couple of days of interviews which would, Olaf the Oaf had promised, apparently give them the answer to the Meaning of Life and Olaf the Oaf, who had rather hoped that the client had somehow agreed to a three hundred thousand dollar first phase of work, which would then lead to a multi-million dollar consulting project and of course an increase in Olaf's salary and bonus.

Actually, things turned out quite well. I explained why we needed to do more than just a few days of interviews and all the tremendous value our studies and improvement programme design work would bring the client. The client eventually agreed and we got permission to start our project – the five to six weeks First Phase. At the end of this First Phase, with the help of a Norwegian project manager who managed to gain great credibility with this client as he fortuitously turned out to have spent most of his life in the oil rig supply business, we managed to sell on a quite major business performance improvement project, then another, then another. But this time we were lucky. Olaf the Oaf's greedy and cynical bungling of the sale could have cost us dearly.

Not what one would generally call a well set-up project. But a lot better and more easily salvageable than my next experience.

B. THE CORRIDOR TEST

At the time of this next little horror, I was running a First Phase study at an oil refinery somewhere in Europe. Things were going to plan at the refinery and in spite of this leading world-wide oil company's history of seldom buying significant amounts of management consultancy, we looked to be on track to selling a bit over a million euros of work. While at the refinery, I used a few spare moments to keep in touch with colleagues on other projects. One consultant, who had once worked for me previously, was involved in a sales pitch to improve the effectiveness of new product development at a company which made a product range, that all of us use at least twice in our lives – nappies for the young, incontinence pads for the old. They also made other sanitary products aimed at absorbing unpleasant bodily fluids. I got the impression from the consultant that there was something wrong with the project set-up and that things were not going too well. I asked my vice president if I could pop over to the other project for a couple of days to see if I could lend a hand. But, as each vice president was only looking after themselves and didn't give a damn about anyone else, my boss saw her interests best served by keeping me at the refinery. Given that she was sleeping with our managing director at that time, what she decided nobody dared oppose. She wanted me there to ensure that her project sold – the new product development project sale was someone else's problem.

A week later, I talked to the consultant again – if anything, things were now even worse on his project. Again I asked my vice president if I could help – again she flatly refused my request. However, the next week, we signed a consulting contract with the oil company. A results delivery project manager took over from me. If the vice president had kept me around for even just a few days to help the new project manager with the start-up, that would have eaten into her project's profitability. As far as this vice president was concerned, now her particular project was sold, I could go to hell in a hand basket for all she cared. So I was taken off the team. The fact that I had just worked my b-lls off for over a month to sell the project was no longer important. At that time, in our company, gratitude was in short supply. Moreover, if you were sexually involved with the consultancy's CEO, as she was, you didn't need to worry about making friends.

Finding my next assignment was the responsibility of our overall operational manager. And he had a big problem that needed solving. The new product development project had finally gone belly-up – after four weeks there were no results and at a major presentation of hot air by the consultants to the management team, the client managing director had stood up and announced that he was very disappointed with progress and would be asking for his money back. Our company went into a bit of a panic and the call went out to send in the cavalry. I was despatched immediately to the project that I had been trying to get on to for several weeks and told to sort things out and sell a second phase of work to this discontented client.

On arriving at the project site, I first reviewed all the stuff that the team had done over the last month. The review didn't take long. The situation was clear. The project director had apparently never seen a new product development process in his life and was way out of his depth. His team manager had even less experience. And the team – well they had just been wandering around in a haze of ill-informed ignorance. Lots of interviews had been conducted. A few business processes had been 'mapped'. But all with no real sense of direction and absolutely without result. An hour after arriving there, I had a meeting with the client, the managing director. He was actually quite pleasant and helpful, when he had every right to beat me up good and proper. But the he was a true gentleman and actually trusted us. Moreover he genuinely wanted a major improvement in his new product development and still hoped that we could help find the secret of making his people get their projects completed in something that had at least some relationship with the originally projected time-frames and budgets.

So, rather than chasing us round the block and threatening to sue us as we so richly deserved, the managing director offered us the chance to get our act together and do something useful for him in the remaining two weeks. It didn't take long for me to realise that the way out of our problems here was a classic case of 'turning our weaknesses into a strength' (Chapter 7 *Some tricks of the trade*). The worst thing I could have done would have been to try to defend the work done, or rather not done, by the current team. Standing up for them was not the way to win this particular war. However, by turning our weakness into a strength and blaming the client's culture for our lack of progress, I could actually use our unforgivable failure to achieve anything against the client as a pressure point to get him to buy a project from us. The whole game went like this:

On my second day on the project, I went back to see the Managing Director to tell him what we were going to do about the mess. When I saw him, I started by apologising for the team's work. *"I'm really sorry"*, I said, *"but my people have fallen into exactly the same trap as your staff. They've got lost in the detail of the product development process and have lost sight of the fact that what is important is not whether a particular decision gateway is in week twelve or thirteen or fourteen or whatever and not which committee takes which decision. What is important here is not the technical side, but the human side. You have a reasonable product development process. It's as good or as bad as anybody else's and you could play around with it till the cows come home, but that's not going to give you the results you want. What is wrong here is not in the process itself, but in the behaviours of the people who work within the process. There's too much time spent on analysis and too little on action. Decision-making is slow and badly planned. Communication is inadequate. Key people are not doing the right work creating skills bottlenecks. There's little sharing of knowledge or people between projects. Delays and problems are not dealt with quickly and so on....."*

The managing director started to nod in agreement, *"that's right,"* he said, *"when I come to work every day, I get the feeling that people are talking and talking, but nothing's really happening."*

Internally, I could breathe a monstrous sigh of relief. Luckily, I had hit the right button. Encouraged, I went on, *"it would be completely wrong for me to try and sell you a project to improve your product development process. The process itself is good enough. What is needed here is a programme to train and develop your managers and supervisors in planning their work, in effective meeting management, in personal effectiveness, in decision management and in project management. The programme needed here is all about making your people more effective, not fiddling with the details of the process as your people and our team have been doing for the last four weeks."*

He liked it, I guess, because two weeks later we signed a contract and immediately started work on a half million-dollar project to strengthen management and coach and develop the people in new product development. This wasn't the biggest project in the world – but this was an awful lot better as an outcome than some of the alternatives like having to give the money back and getting our reputation in that country besmirched by such a failure.

And what about the vice president who was responsible for the sorry state of this project? Where was the person, who would get the big bonus if the project sold? What was he doing when the whole thing went down the tubes? What was his contribution to the rescue operation? One would imagine that he would be there on the client site working all hours with the client and the project team to turn the situation round. One would hope that he would be using his huge experience to really add vast amounts of value. The minimum one would expect would be that he was on the phone at least a few times a day giving me advice, help and support. One would have assumed…….. But this was a management consultancy under pressure because our product was no longer selling like hot bread. This was a consultancy where a lot of extremely well-paid people faced the prospect of having their millionaire living standards considerably reduced if our sales didn't improve. This was a consultancy where some wealthy arses had to be covered quickly, when anything started going wrong.

As soon as I got to the project and sussed out that it smelt unpleasant, I got on the phone to this particular cheerful, rich and diminutive individual. He would really like to help me, he said, but was unfortunately really really busy. Moreover, the week after I arrived on the project, he was taking his son skiing and obviously would be out of touch. And, equally obviously, there was no way he could change that arrangement! I pointed out that by the time he got back from his skiing holiday, the project would be over and that, given what little his team had achieved so far, the project might even be over a lot earlier than that. My brave, supportive vice president was by now bored of this conversation. He curtly suggested I contact one of the more junior vice presidents to see if they could help and then he had to end the call, as he had to go to a very important meeting. That was the last I heard from him, until of course, the project had been saved, at which point he returned from skiing to claim the credit and the bonus

And finally, what about the 'corridor test' – now, I must say that the next story is only hearsay. Happily, I never actually knowingly saw anyone perform the 'corridor test'. And even more happily, I was never asked to perform one myself. But as we worked with the new product developers, these courageous people who had dedicated their lives to finding better ways to absorb our various unwanted bodily excretions and other excess fluids, we were told that they tested their new products both in the laboratory and on volunteers. Apparently, while testing the comfort and absorbency of new incontinence devices, they would ask staff to wear them. Then, as the staff went about their daily routines, rather than using the toilet for those things for which one normally uses the toilet, the testers should just let go there and then. So as they walked around the corridors of the building, with their various fluids and other things outside rather than inside their persons, they could comment on the efficacy and comfort of the products – hence the name 'corridor test'. If this apocryphal tale is actually true – then once more it shows there are worse jobs in this world than being a management consultant.

---

(1) The Times 23 August 2002
(2) Contact author
(3) OPEC (Officer, Principal and Executive Consultant) Meeting 29 November 2001
(4) Confidential internal memo
(5) Confidential internal memo

CHAPTER 12

THE GREAT SYSTEMS SWINDLE

THE DANGERS OF TECHNOLOGY

Just as a tightening consulting market led consultancies to sell more and more dubious projects in order to find somewhere to park our excess of warm bodies, so increased competition in the IT systems and technology consulting market also led to a rash of poorly planned, inadequately staffed and badly executed IT system implementations.

Most ordinary consulting projects will not ruin a client, however poorly they are executed. After all, if things don't work out as planned, most largish companies or government departments can easily shrug off the few million dollars, pounds or euros that the average consulting project costs. And only very seldom do clients have the time and energy to sue their consultants. The only time consultants can cause real problems for their clients are when the clients' organisations really are in trouble and their management consultants give them the wrong answer. This has caused several bankruptcies. But out of almost a hundred client engagements, I have only ever been involved in one case, where I believe we made a major and lucrative (for us consultants) contribution to our client's eventual bankruptcy (Chapter 2 *The unsubtle art of cost-cutting*)

However, consultancy can really get dangerous for clients when it is linked to a major implementation of an IT system. In these cases, the costs can start heading up over a hundred million dollars or pounds rather than just a few million and the disruption to the organisation can be massive. For example, an oil company that can't deliver oil because the new computer system won't process any orders or deliveries can have problems. Then, when the new computer system also hasn't kept records of sales and so can't issue accurate invoices, management can start to get slightly concerned about whether their new system is helping or hindering their business.

During my consulting career, I was exposed to several situations, where consulting and IT projects went ludicrously out of control. Several were in oil and pharmaceutical companies, who had so much money that they could easily laugh off a hundred million or so wasted on fruitless IT systems. Others were government departments, who saw massive waste of taxpayers' money as a normal part of life. For example, on six huge IT system implementation projects done for the British government with a total budget of £1.1 billion, such companies as Accenture, EDS, Siemens and Capita managed to go £400 million over their initial budgets.[1] The budget for a project to provide computers for magistrates courts in Britain ended up costing almost £400 million compared to a planned budget of only £184 million, making it according to The Public Accounts Committee *"one of the worst they had ever seen"*.[1] And a £200 million system to enable doctors in the British National Health service to book hospital appointments for their patients managed to make 63 appointments in 2004 against a plan of 205,000. But not all our clients were fortunate enough to have bottomless bank accounts like oil companies and the government and so the failure of their IT systems consultants could threaten their very survival.

WHY IT SO OFTEN GOES WRONG

I had always assumed that about 30% of IT systems projects were successful – about the same percent as most of the initiatives started by our clients (BPR projects, consulting projects, mergers etc.) But some recent research suggests the success rate may be much lower,

"An Oxford University/Computer Weekly survey of IT projects in Britain found that only 16% were considered successful".[2] Another survey gave even more worrying results, *"A British Computer Society study of projects judged only three out of 500 a success."*[2]

There are obviously many reasons why IT systems projects spin so hopelessly out of control. Inadequate project management, continual changes in specification and poor communication between designers and users must take some of the blame. But my experiences have led me to believe that there are often two more fundamental and serious causes of IT systems fiascos – contract structure and reinventing the wheel. And these two reasons have a lot to do with the dubious ethics of the consultancies supplying the systems.

Contract structure: many IT systems are still developed based on what we call "Time & Materials" contracts. On Time & Materials contracts, the supplier is paid on the basis of how much time and resources they use – so the more time and resources they use, the more money they get. Thus they have no incentive to finish any systems project within a tight timeframe or with carefully controlled use of resources. If they were on contracts with a fixed price and penalties for cost and time over-runs, then many more IT systems might see the light of day faster and at much lower cost than is the case now.

Reinventing the wheel: Although their products or services may be very different, most organisations do fundamentally similar things. They make/buy something, put it in a box and sell it. Or they make/buy something put it in a shop or website and sell it. Or they take some skill/knowledge (cancer surgery, accountancy, law) provide it to customers/patients and manage their costs and budgets. Or they transport passengers. Or they handle their money. So most organisations need similar things from their systems – acquiring products or skills, inducting customers, managing information about customers, cost control/billing, HR management, financial accounting and so on. So whatever the system you require, the basic elements probably already exist somewhere in the world and could be easily adapted to your needs. However your systems supplier will usually try and convince you that your system is unique and requires them to build a new system from scratch. For example, the £200 million system to enable doctors in the British National Health service to book hospital appointments for their patients is probably not greatly different from the systems that have existed for years for booking flights, holidays or hotel rooms. But rather than trying to adapt one of these existing systems, the systems provider probably convinced the health service officials that they needed to build a completely new system – hence the £200 million price tag. It is simply not in the IT systems consultancies' interests to provide you with a fast, cheap adaptation of an existing system for a couple of million, when they can earn tens or even hundreds of millions reinventing the wheel by building you a completely new system. Yet this reinventing the wheel both massively increases your costs and also your risks – adapting an existing system is low risk, building a totally new one will inevitably bring technical problems and extra costs and delays. A journalist described how many of the large systems suppliers seemed able to milk their British public sector customers, *"Mandarins were easily baffled by computer companies, which bombarded Whitehall departments with high-pressure salesmanship and lobbying, and which had always had special scope for exploiting ignorant clients with their incomprehensible language and expertise"*.[3]

I was unfortunately deeply involved with one big systems project that had gone way off the rails. It seemed to display all the familiar features of a systems disaster – execrable project management, unclear responsibilities between supplier and customer, a poorly worded contract and a major reinvention of the wheel. In this chapter, I describe how this consultancy and systems provider tried to make the client believe things were working as planned, so we could close the project as quickly as possible and get our team out from the account without the client suing us. I was with an enormous international consultancy and IT systems provider consultancy that we'll call 'Massive Systems Inc'. Massive Systems Inc had quite a number of big systems implementations that went belly-up. Most of these disasters were quickly swept under the carpet and nobody outside the company ever heard about them. However, a few were so bad that our clients hired lawyers and the press started to sniff around. One large U.S. charity found *"four hundred serious problems"* with a system we had developed. They eventually scrapped the project after spending $12 million.[4] This was money, which might have been better used for charitable purposes rather than being given to us for a failed project. Another large non-profit group, the U.S. Chamber of Commerce, decided to cancel a $75 million contract with us because Massive Systems Inc *"consistently and systematically has been unable to deliver what the contract required"*.[4] Our client here was not very complimentary about our capabilities: *"We had an antiquated computer information system built by Rube Goldberg,"* said Frank Coleman, a spokesman for the Chamber. *"Unfortunately, we hired Rube Goldberg's nephew to fix it."*[4] We also did a 62 million euro project to develop research and tracking software for the French national library, Bibliotheque Nationale de France, with apparently similar disastrous results. A reporter wrote, *"The library administration and the union representing the library workers said that the work done by Massive Systems Inc was the main issue in a strike by library workers. The French Government has since removed Massive Systems Inc from the project."*[4]

Whenever our projects went crashing down into disaster, we fortunately had some tough lawyers, who ensured our clients didn't go about broadcasting our incompetence. For example, in one of the above cases, it was reported that rather than the client suing us for our failure to deliver, our lawyers sued our client, *"Mrs. Beene (from the charity United Way) said the lawyer (representing Massive Systems Inc) complained that the charity should have kept the matter confidential and threatened litigation, which she said she wanted to avoid"*.[4] So not only did we take $12 million from the charity for a system that they judged to be useless, but we also threatened to sue them for damages if they told anybody about their experiences of working with us. Likewise, when sued by the U.S. Chamber of Commerce for failure to deliver, we counter-sued them for breaking off our contract as we claimed that we had *"met all contractual requirements"*. The above three disasters were probably only the tip of the iceberg – they were the ones that saw the light of day. Most of our failed projects were covered up either by clients wishing to draw a cover over the failure or by our lawyers gagging clients to prevent them revealing what they knew about our incompetence.

IN DEEP S...

In consultancy, you should always be very suspicious when someone, who earns five to ten times what you could ever imagine earning, suddenly shows extraordinary interest in your life. When the sun-tanned, silver-haired business development executive (BDE) – that's what we called our salesmen – stopped by my desk and inquired after my health, my family and, most importantly, my availability, the alarm bells should have started ringing – in stereo. When his boss did the same, I should have found a deep hole, jumped in it covered myself with earth and waited a couple of thousand years. But flattery works wonders. Especially on congenitally naive individuals like myself. So when both these extremely highly paid executives told me that they had an assignment that required someone with my experience and creativity, I was foolish enough to feel some pride, that they had chosen a humble $150,000 per year middle-ranking worker bee like myself.

Massive Systems Inc prided itself on being one of the world leaders in providing both management consultancy and supporting IT systems and with over fifty thousand systems people and consultants and a revenue of billions, we were certainly one of the largest four or five in the world. Following a number of fairly hairy engagements, I had developed a bit of a reputation for what was optimistically called 'creativity' within that particular consultancy. Creativity really meant the ability to dig the consultancy out of enormous great f...-ups which people, usually over-greedy vice presidents, had got us into. However, up till then my interventions or salvage operations had usually only been worth from hundreds of thousands of pounds, euros and dollars to a couple of million each. The scale of the disaster I was about to stumble into – possibly over thirty five million dollars effortlessly removed from a client's bank account over the preceding four years – was way beyond any wit or charm I could possibly sum up, way beyond my well-known 'creativity'

In short, nothing I had previously experienced, had prepared me for the ordeal, to which I was about to be subjected. This situation truly was a monumental f...-up on a world-class scale and if the client had ever found out the truth about the work we had done and had ever got hold of the documentation that magically and unintentionally came into my possession and the tape-recordings that I made of some highly sensitive internal meetings, he could have given Massive Systems Inc's lawyers a well-deserved hiding.

The client's company was a huge multi-national household name with about seventy thousand employees in two hundred and twenty countries and a turnover of around $6.5 billion. Their margins were under pressure due to the success of a fast-moving competitor. Someone in the management team had come up with the idea that the company could make more money if it harmonised its business processes across Europe, rather than allowing all the country managers to do things their way. It was my job to lead an eight person team of consultants to do a couple of months work that would see which processes should be harmonised, how this should be done and what financial benefits this would bring. The intention of my management was that this brief study would lead to a much longer and much more expensive project, where we would help the client implement the new harmonised business processes and earn several million doing it. All in all, a pretty run-of-the-mill consulting sales project – or so I innocently thought as I prepared my team for the assignment.

The first few days of the study went quite well. We did lots of interviews, crunched the numbers and analysed the business' value chain to see what could be done better. Towards the end of the first week, I flew over to the Brussels H.Q. to talk to the newly appointed European Change Manager. Let's call him Mad Mike. 'Mike', because that's a common name and 'Mad' because he really was fuming with fury. If we were to be successful in selling a project, Mad Mike as European Change Manager was the key person who would have to buy it. So I was eager to see him early on, to work out what pressure points we could use to get him to sign on the dotted line in eight to ten weeks' time.

From the first moment I entered his office, it was rather clear that Mad Mike was not pleased to see me. In fact, as I soon discovered, Mad Mike would probably have rather had a meeting with the Grim Reaper than a member of Massive Systems Inc. As I walked into his office, he stood up towering over me. Mad Mike was tall. But then he was Dutch and Dutch people are often quite tall. Though usually they are not quite as angry as Mad Mike. Mad Mike didn't shake my hand and luckily didn't shake my throat either. "How dare you? How dare you come to see me?" he started, even before I had a chance to introduce myself, his voice shaking with undisguised fury. "You're criminals. We should be suing you not talking to you. You've taken over thirty million dollars from us – and you've given us nothing. We've wasted five years with you. Now we're years behind X………. (name of their major competitor). If I had my way we'd have you in court…" And so it went on. For some time. Though not a particularly insightful individual, I could see that I was going to have some difficulty selling a nice couple of million dollars of consulting to this particular person.

Eventually Mad Mike started to run out of steam and became a little less mad, especially when he realised that I had absolutely no idea what he was talking about. That then gave me the chance to explain about our wonderful ideas for doing a consulting project for him, all the tremendous benefits it would bring and how we looked forward to working closely with him. A very slightly less mad Mike, made it clear to me that he had absolutely no intention of working with us and didn't want to see me again, ever!

It was clear that there was something very wrong with this whole assignment. Over the next few weeks, while eagerly trying to coax this client into buying a meaty piece of work from us, I did some investigations, spoke to people who refused to be quoted and accidentally got hold of some very very confidential internal reports which never should have been seen by either man or beast. This allowed me to piece together a picture that for reasons, which became more than obvious, everyone involved had tried to brush under the carpet in the hope that it would just go away – it didn't. In fact, like a festering sore, it just got worse and worse and ever more untreatable till finally major surgery was required.

The situation I had been dropped into by my ever-ethical caring management was so indescribably awful that it's difficult to know where to start. So let me do two things. I'll first give an overview of why Mad Mike was so, probably rightly, furious with us. Then I'll describe the machinations Massive Systems Inc's management went through during the next ten weeks to try to avoid appearing in the witness box and having to pay anything from thirty five to a hundred million dollars or more in damages to this client.

THE BACKGROUND

About four to five years earlier, Massive Systems Inc's IT division had sold a huge systems development and consulting project to this client. Due to many factors including a poorly worded contract, incomparably bad project management on our part, insufficient support from the client's side and the wrong project organisation structure, the work wandered along for four years or so earning us millions, but delivering few, if any, visible results. In all this time, though system modules were apparently developed, nothing at all was implemented. So when I wandered into the picture, the client had received next to nothing from the last four plus years' work, for which they had paid us handsomely. In the meantime, their major rival had articles written about how brilliantly they had used their new IT systems to increase their customer service and competitiveness.

At a certain point our client, understandably, started to get impatient and apparently mentioned the possibility of my bosses returning the fees they had received and possibly even paying damages. This could have knocked over thirty five million dollars from our bottom line. When faced with this looming fiasco, our managing director took out the project manager and sent in two replacement project managers to sort things out. Meanwhile, a senior executive from our company was sent in to pacify the client and keep the lawyers at bay long enough for us to figure some way out of the mess.

It didn't take long for the two new project managers to understand that the whole thing stank to high heaven and that we could be in deep trouble. Carefully worded, highly confidential e-mails using euphemisms like 'risky' and 'volatile' and 'defensive' sped backwards and forwards within our company and numerous panicky conference calls were hastily organised. When the full extent of the potential catastrophe was realised by our very top management, they took the decision that the two new project managers should ensure that just a part of the new system was implemented in what they called 'a pilot country' and that if we could then get the client to sign off that it worked there, we would be legally in a much stronger position and could close off the account and get out without a court case. This became known internally as our "defend and exit" strategy. Only a few years earlier, our largest competitor had been involved in a major lawsuit over IT systems that were promised but, according to the client, not delivered. The defence our competitor used was that as two prototypes (or pilots) were completed, the client's suit was "*completely without merit*".[5] It looked like we were about to try going down the same route to extricate ourselves from this unpleasant situation. Our managing director made it very clear in messages to us (always by phone and never in writing) that he absolutely did not want to hand back any money at all to this client. Our company wanted out – and fast! I quote one of our directors from a recording I made from a key conference call, "*we mustn't get our neck stuck in a noose. We want the partnership contractually to come to an end.*"[6]

Apart from our management's obvious desire to keep as much of the client's money as possible, I later learnt that there were other reasons why our leadership demanded that we should exit from this client engagement without either negative publicity or cost. At the time, we were in the first phase of negotiations to buy another consultancy and any bad publicity or reduction in our profitability would have hurt our share price and thus our ability to complete the planned takeover, which would be mainly funded by giving the partners in the targeted consultancy a huge heap of our shares each. Anyway, the bottom line was that there should be no controversy and no money should be returned – whether the system actually ever worked or not was by now irrelevant.

I firmly believe that this strategy was extremely cynical and ethically dubious for at least three reasons:

1. Just showing the system worked in one country was no real proof that it could be successfully scaled up to fifty or a hundred countries. I have seen numerous cases where computer systems worked in small, carefully controlled test environments, but then collapsed totally when subjected to real life operating volumes and conditions

2. As our client's business was based on international activity, the system was almost useless if it was only running in isolated countries and not throughout their world-wide network

3. Our client's main competitor had apparently already achieved the functionality that our system would not give our client for several more years

But perhaps the worst problem here was that, because of all our delays, the system would probably be obsolete long before it was in use. One of our most recent internal audits uncovered many failings with our work. Amongst them was the fact that, the way the system was constructed, meant it would take from five to nine years to roll it out across the client's full operations. That would have given the system a development and implementation time of ten to fifteen years, making it effectively obsolete and needing to be replaced long before it was even up and running properly. As one of the replacement project directors said on a conference call, *"because of all the delays we've had, potentially the system will be out-of-date by the time we do get to deploy it"*. Or as a vice president concluded *"the commercially dangerous conclusion for us is that they have missed the bus for implementing because of our delays. That is commercially dangerous territory"*.[6] Not an ideal situation!

One of the people who knew something about the whole project's unfortunate history was someone, who was my coach in the management consultancy division. He had previously worked in the IT systems division after being unseated by a long-standing rival in one of many entertaining internal power struggles between the two. One day, meeting him in the office, I asked him if he knew anything about this ill-fated systems project. He laughingly admitted that he knew an awful lot. He then proceeded to tell me that:

- He had been head of the business sector that had sold the project.

- He had attended the first couple of project steering committee meetings.

- He had seen back then right at the beginning that the project was being badly run and that the project manager was impossible to deal with.

- He had decided then to keep well away from the project as he could see it was going to be "a f.....g disaster" (as he so eloquently described the situation into which I had now blindly stumbled).

Of course, his account was probably coloured by what subsequently happened and by his general contempt for his erstwhile colleagues in our IT systems division. However, it does show that for a long time people had been aware there were problems with the project, but that for internal political reasons these had not been addressed until it was far too late.

Anyway, now we were in deep – over thirty five million dollars deep, according to a tape-recording I made of a discussion between our managing director and myself. So now our most senior executives had decided the only course left to us was to deliver the absolutely minimum necessary to enable us to avoid a court case, to keep all the client's money and to get our arses out of the bear-trap. Major promotions were promised (and later delivered) to the two replacement project managers if they managed to extricate us without us having to refund any money to the client. Both are now very senior and very highly paid executives at Massive Systems Inc.

So, although Mad Mike did not have access to the same information that I managed to dig up and would probably never have seen the highly confidential report that I had got hold of, all indications were that Mad Mike's instincts were generally right – **we** had failed to deliver, **we** were mainly responsible for the system being largely useless if it ever got to be up and running, **we** didn't have a leg to stand on and dragging us to court would probably have been in our client's best interests. Fortunately for us, in spite of Mad Mike's well-grounded suspicions and fury, the client's managing director didn't know what I knew and seemed willing to accept that the executive put in charge of the relationship and the two new project managers were genuinely working in the client's interest – which, in my humble and inexperienced opinion, they most certainly weren't.

FOOLS RUSH IN, WHERE ANGELS FEAR TO TREAD

Given this critical and potentially explosive situation, you might be forgiven for wondering why on earth our management consultancy barged in hoping to sell a large multi-country, multi-million dollar project to this client – a client who could potentially sue us for the return of tens of millions of dollars for systems that didn't work plus many millions more for commercial damage to their business.

I think this is what happened. A few months earlier, our consultancy division had done a study aimed at improving operations at a few of our client's depots in one of his major countries – a project completely unconnected with the unfortunate IT systems work. The client for this study, the local country manager, had been pleased with the work and interested in buying a project to develop best operating practices and spread these to improve depot efficiency throughout that country. However, for various reasons – mainly a clampdown on consulting expenses – the project had not got the go-ahead.

A few months after this consultancy work, the CEO announced, at a world-wide management meeting, that he wished to launch a 'business process harmonisation project' to have countries working in a more uniform way reducing duplicated effort and thus improving profitability. The country manager, for whom our consultancy had already worked, questioned the CEO's decision and asked whether this business process harmonisation could actually deliver the improvements in profitability the company needed. The CEO agreed to delay the project and gave this particular country manager the task of assessing whether it was worth harmonising business processes and how such a programme should be run. As he didn't have the resources locally to conduct the study, the country manager contacted our salesman to see if we could help. Naturally, our salesman was delighted to generate more business and quickly signed a contract with the client.

This little project had a slightly difficult start, when I arrived to discover that we were expected to conduct the assessment for only about a hundred thousand dollars and working only in one location. It's difficult to do a pan-European study without travelling more than half a kilometre from your office. I voiced my concerns. But what did the salesman care? He had successfully sold a project. If I was too stupid or too useless to manage it, then that was my problem, not his.

Fortunately, our client was quite reasonable and after discussions with them, I expanded the team, the scope and the budget to enable us to visit five or six countries. So it was agreed we were to spend about ten weeks analysing the client's main business processes, initially throughout Europe, and propose how they should be improved and to what extent they should be harmonised between countries.

Possibly, the salesman didn't fully know of the difficulties with the IT systems work. Maybe he didn't consider the problems that might occur, if the client had already paid our systems company tens of millions of dollars developing systems based on the client's current business processes and then we consultants came along and suggested there might be better and different ways of working, so they could chuck away much of what they'd done and start again. As one of our vice presidents said on yet another hastily convened conference call, *"the danger we are all worried about is that criticisms might well be justified but could be contractually risky. Having our own group doing it (criticising the work already done) has the potential for a much more devastating impact."*[6]

I never managed to find out how much our BDE really knew – every time I asked him, I seemed to receive different, fairly evasive and ambiguous answers. Though, in the salesman's defence, I should say that as the scale of the potential disaster our systems people faced with this client was for obvious reasons not widely known, he probably didn't realise the massive risk we ran by launching this new project.

WALKING THROUGH THE MINEFIELD

The next ten weeks soon became like trying to walk through a minefield balancing several dozen nuclear bombs in each hand. Somehow, my team and I had to both heap unbounded praise on everything connected with our systems work and yet at the same time show the client the huge improvements that could be made by giving us consultants a few million. One of my directors suggested that every time we analysed a business process touched by the IT people we should give it a clean bill of health and every time we reviewed a process not covered by our IT project we should rip it apart. Given that our IT project covered most of this client's main business processes, this suggestion (like so many others coming from my management) was worthless.

My project went something like this:

WEEK 1

We did some interviews and studies and I had my stimulating one-to-one meeting with Mad Mike in Brussels.

When our systems people heard that we had suddenly appeared and were conducting an analysis of the client's business processes they were, so I heard, both incredulous and furious. There they were trying to extricate Massive Systems Inc from an extremely explosive situation and now we risked destabilising the careful retreat, which had been ordered by our CEO. I heard that the first reaction from our great and honourable leaders was that we should stop my piece of work immediately. But then our management realised that suddenly walking away from the contract, which our salesman had already agreed, could risk arousing the client's suspicions. So, it was decided we management consultants would have to continue our work – but under very tight management control.

A meeting between the two project leadership teams was hastily arranged. There were four people present – myself and the two replacement project managers from our systems division (let's call them Clint and Arnie). Clint was calm, collected and cool under pressure. Arnie was much bigger, spoke with a gruff mid-european accent and was highly volatile. There was also a middle-ranking executive (whom we'll call Brian) from our corporate HQ, who was quickly assigned to work with me (spy on me?) as people above started to fully appreciate the mess we had just got ourselves into.

It was a brief and emotional meeting. Clint and Arnie were under so much pressure that they had difficulty remaining calm. At the time, I wasn't fully aware of what was happening and was still pretty laid back in spite of my brush with Mad Mike. A few minutes into the meeting, I made what I thought was a rather humorous remark about the capabilities of Clint and Arnie's IT systems. Arnie exploded, stamped out of the meeting in fury and had to be coaxed back in by Clint. Brian kept very quiet. Eventually some calm was restored. We did exchange some information – but not a lot, Clint and Arnie were very cagey about revealing too much about what exactly they were up to.

I later heard that, immediately after our meeting, Clint and Arnie went belting off to their masters to sound the alarm – they claimed that we consultants were completely out of control and risked spoiling our company's whole exit strategy because we:

- Didn't understand the seriousness of the situation.

- Weren't cooperating with them.

- Weren't communicating with them.

- Were putting our whole organisation at risk.

Our leaders quickly decided that they needed to meet to work out how we could both fulfil our consulting contract and yet get the hell out of the systems project unscathed.

WEEK 2

A meeting was arranged between the CEO of our consulting business and some very senior executives in our systems company, who would probably prefer that their names were never connected with this unhappy affair. However, I have copies of the meeting minutes, so I can prove who was there. I also have tape-recordings of some quite colourful telephone conference calls made at that time. So if anybody wishes to sue me for anything I've written, please be careful, you might look quite silly claiming your ignorance and innocence, if I happen to have a recording of you, which proves your complicity and guilt.

For some reason, I wasn't invited to this great meeting. However, as I knew the meeting was taking place, Brian and I just turned up anyway. It then became a bit difficult for the Great and the Good to refuse Brian and I permission to attend a meeting to discuss my project. Thank heavens we were there, as it turned out that Clint and Arnie had intended to use the meeting to assassinate me and, if necessary Brian, but especially me. I think Clint and Arnie saw my team and I as rather useful scapegoats, if they were unable to extricate us from the IT systems disaster. So they were very keen to prepare the ground for whitewashing themselves by suitably slandering my team and I.

The meeting started with Clint and Arnie being asked by their boss to explain what the problem was. Arnie took centre stage and there followed much incoherent beating about the bush. After all, Clint and Arnie hadn't expected Brian and I to be at the meeting and they dared not repeat some of their more monstrous and slanderous allegations in front of us, as they knew we would contradict them. After some minutes, Arnie's directionless discourse stopped. Our consulting managing director then said, *"I can't understand what the problem is. Why are we here?"*[6] It should be remembered that at the beginning, we in management consultancy were not well-informed about how serious the IT systems problems actually were.

There was an embarrassed silence for a while. Then one senior executive from the systems company said some words I'll remember to my dying day. *"There is a small problem,"* he coughed slightly to clear his throat, *"you're going around turning over stones and looking under them, while we're trying to cover them with sand."*[6] He was, of course, referring to the unfortunate fact that while the aim of the consultancy work was to demonstrate that the client needed to improve his business processes and should buy a big consulting project to help him, our systems people were trying to claim that the processes and the coming IT systems supporting the processes were absolutely and incredibly wonderful and that they had delivered everything they had promised. All slightly problematic.

The discussion went back and forward. Clint and Arnie asked to be given overall responsibility for all the work with this client including the consulting project. My CEO resisted that. He could sense that the IT systems people were in a horrible hole and didn't want us dragged down there with them. Eventually a compromise was reached. It was agreed that our overall strategy would be to try and exit from this account without the client suing us for the IT systems problems. Thus my consulting team should complete our assignment but should not try to sell any more work to this client. Moreover, I was instructed to keep Clint and Arnie informed of everything we were doing and to let them review (and alter if necessary) any presentation material we developed before the client saw it.

While my attention was being distracted by all the shenanigans at the top, my project team, under the leadership of an extremely able team manager, who left us shortly afterwards, actually started making quite respectable progress. In the second week we had an irrational burst of optimism and started to seriously consider whether, in spite of being told to finish our work and get out, we could use our consulting work to rebuild our relationship with the client and really continue working for them. As I said, it was only gradually that the true awfulness of our situation became apparent to us.

WEEK 3

Meanwhile waves of fear and apprehension started to sweep through our company as more people got an inkling of what was going on. Our group CEO heard that we crazy consultants were actually seriously considering selling in a consulting project and once again sent us a clear message that the aim was damage limitation and getting out with our bank balance intact – not, repeat not, selling any more work to this client. At the same time the CEO of our worldwide consulting business, Patrick J. was in constant contact with the client's CEO. His task was to create a smoke screen to cover our disorderly retreat by discussing the long-term relationship between our two companies and all the great work we would do together in future. As Clint explained to us, the client and Patrick J. were 'close personal friends' and so the client CEO trusted Patrick J. – though, as they say, with friends like that, who needs enemies? I just watched in amazement as all the lies and trickery and double-dealing went on around me.

So, reality eventually dawned on us consultants that there could be no positive outcome for the consulting team. In spite of the hopeful messages we sent out to our management about our progress, we were clearly informed that we weren't allowed to sell a consulting project and yet we had to present work that was of sufficient quality to satisfy the client – a difficult balance to maintain.

During this week, Brian and I went over the situation again and again. Despite many years working for our systems division, Brian told me that this was probably the worst cock-up he had ever seen. Frequently, he would shake his head and say, *"I just can't believe how we got into such a mess."*[6] For me, Brian was a lifesaver. He had worked at our Group Headquarters, knew the politics and main players and so could advise me on how to handle the situation. He could also see the games Clint and Arnie were playing and help me present a balanced view of the situation to our worried leadership.

WEEKS 4 – 10

These were confusing and depressing for my team and myself. We couldn't walk away from the project as that would have aroused the client's suspicions that there was something fishy going on. So, on the one hand we had to do enough to satisfy our client that he was getting value for money. But on the other hand we had to be extremely careful about everything we said and presented and had to not push too hard for a follow-on project, which would have prolonged our company's agony at that particular client.

Clint and Arnie meanwhile were desperately looking for some way to get a signed statement from the client confirming that at least part of the systems we had developed worked. Originally, if I remember correctly, they had intended to pilot the system in Germany, one of the client's major countries of operation. However, Clint and Arnie started to get cold feet about whether our IT system could handle a business the size of that in Germany. So, through some nifty footwork, they managed to convince the client that Denmark and other parts of Scandinavia would make a much better pilot area. I don't know what they told the client, but Clint explained to me that as the client's business in Denmark was infintessimally small – less than five percent of the size of their business in Germany – it should be possible to get the basic parts of the system up and running there quite quickly, get signed confirmation from some local middle level manager (who didn't know better) that the system worked and then exit, fast! When I asked about scalability and whether the system could ever work in one of the client's larger operations, Clint just smiled and said that if we played our cards right, that would not be his problem.

Round about week seven or eight, Clint called me. He had some great news, he said. He had just returned from a meeting with the client's CEO in Brussels and they had agreed to implement a bare minimum of the system as a pilot, wind down the project and end our involvement. The relief within Massive Systems Inc was more than tremendous and Clint and Arnie got most handsomely rewarded for extracting us so elegantly from the mess. Now all that remained was for my team and I to finish off our part of the contract and get out without selling any follow-on implementation project. In a way the situation was a bit like fighting the bull at Baby Butchers – we had to do enough to stay alive, but winning was out of the question.

Finally I suppose the whole thing was a bit of an anti-climax. We did the last two weeks' work, produced the presentation that our client was to give at a worldwide management meeting, packed up and left. We did not, unsurprisingly, sell a follow-on project.

CONCLUSION

So why didn't the client pursue us more aggressively when we had so clearly failed to deliver? After all, although the client didn't have access to our confidential internal documentation, there was a lot of evidence that we had not provided any real value for the many tens of millions we were paid. I met the client CEO and members of his management team a couple of times and suspect that the client's management just got tired of the whole IT systems debacle. They had a business to run and didn't want to get involved in endless resource-consuming legal fights with us. Moreover, one can suspect that if they had tried suing us for non-delivery of the system, we would probably have counter-sued them for failure to meet their contractual obligations. So they just wrote off the money they had wasted with us and got on with their lives – saving us from a potentially horrific and costly scandal.

As I was to experience, time and time again, clients almost never sue their management consultants or IT systems providers, however badly they serve their clients. And when they do sue, they are seldom successful – most large consultancies have very good lawyers, who have considerable experience in frightening off dissatisfied clients.

(1) The Times 14 August 2002
(2) The Times 9 February 2005
(3) *Who runs this place?* Anthony Sampson, John Murray Publishers 2005
(4) International Herald Tribune (contact author for date)
(5) UOP, plaintiff, v. Andersen Consulting, defendant, Superior Court, Judicial District of Stamford/Norwalk at Stamford, CD950144480s as quoted in Dangerous Company
(6) Recordings of conference calls and meetings (contact author for further details)

CHAPTER 13

YOU CAN'T GET ANY LOWER

Sometimes in consultancy, the pressure to meet your sales target makes you do work for clients that just leaves you feeling ashamed and disgusted at yourself. This chapter briefly describes one of those cases, where we didn't have the courage to tell the client that what they were doing was both commercially misguided and morally unacceptable.

At the start of July, I received a message summoning me over to Europe to spend a month supporting a consulting sales team that was getting into a bit of difficulty. Our French office was sold out at that time and there were only two members of the eight person consulting team with any reasonable level of consulting experience. Moreover, the team had a tough assignment. They had just started a First Phase study and they had to try and complete the study and sell a follow-on project in just over three weeks before France went on its month long holiday for the whole of August. Conventional consulting sales wisdom says that if there is a holiday coming up, you have to make sure that the client buys whatever project you are trying to sell quickly, before the holiday. If your potential client has several weeks over their holiday to mull over whether they want to give a few million to your employer or keep it for themselves, the chances are that you would be out of the door. Selling consulting is all about generating a high level of enthusiasm and the appearance of action, then getting the contract signed quickly before the client has too much time to think about what he is really getting into. Given that it takes at least three or four weeks to move a client from first thoughts of a project to signing on the dotted line, there really wasn't much time to get this one nailed down.

The client was an extremely large French chemicals company with loads of plants all around the world. What they wanted to do was reduce their indirect costs – basically fire as many people as possible, who did not directly work on the production of chemicals. This meant employees working in accounts, human resources, maintenance, administration, marketing etc. However, there was a typically Gallic exception to their cost reduction plan – namely the two hundred and fifty very expensive people who worked at their Paris head office. Although the company had decided on a veritable massacre of administrative staff in the plants, they had also just taken out a lease on a shiny new head office in the centre of Paris. In this new head office there was happily enough room for the existing two hundred and fifty head office administrative staff. Moreover, all the head office staff worked for the directors, who had decided on the cost reduction plan. The directors naturally felt there could be absolutely no organisational excess fat in their areas of responsibility. Hence, there could be no talk of reducing their own staff, in spite of the fact that each of their Paris employees could cost between five and ten times as much as the average administrator out in the plants. Result – job security for the expensive Paris bureaucrats and a slaughter of the much cheaper innocents out in the plants who were not part of any of the directors' personal fiefdoms.

This was a typical 'project from hell' – a pure old-fashioned POPs (People Off the Payroll) project. No smart stuff about redesigning the supply chain, no fancy new market entry strategies, no clever acceleration of new product development, no satisfying increasing output to meet growing demand, no dramatic business turnaround, no building an 'adaptive organisation' – none of that here – only attack, rape and pillage. This was the kind of project many consultants actually tried to avoid. I was lucky that most of my consulting life was spent during a prolonged period of economic growth and so, by being careful, I mostly managed not to get caught up in too many pure POPs projects. So, although I have helped plunder many well-known organisations, I think very few people ultimately lost their livelihoods as a result of my efforts. Though, it should also be said, that there are many management consultants who relish this kind of headcount reduction project – it allows them to act tough, to swagger and swear and to make out they're the only ones with the 'balls to take the tough decisions' and 'get their hands dirty' and 'get a bit of blood on the walls'.

The approach cooked up by our salesman was very simple – do a comparison of how many people worked in the administrative functions at each of the company's chemical plants, choose a few plants with the lowest number of administrative staff as so-called 'Best Practice' and then force all the other plants to reduce down their administrative staff down to the level of the 'Best Practice' plants. In the process, we were to visit twenty to thirty plants to check out how many folks were hiding in the indirect departments and just get the other hundred or so factories to fill in questionnaires detailing how many people they employed and how much they were paid. Collecting the data, analysing it, calculating the benefits of putting hundreds of apparently unnecessary staff to the sword and getting the client to agree to pay us millions to help chuck the people out was planned to take four weeks.

In the first week, I helped the team set up and send out the questionnaires. In the second week, I spent a couple of days in Britain and another couple in Switzerland visiting various plants and local offices to make sure the local management disclosed all the information we needed to wreak havoc on their operations. We also needed to ensure that they weren't hiding any people we could pop – a typical trick local management play in these situations is to reclassify their administrative staff as direct production personnel to make their administrative costs look low.

The whole aim of the project, the process used and the hypocrisy of protecting the head office while punishing the plants was bad enough in itself. Many times, you were tempted to contact a newspaper and blow the whistle on the whole miserable affair. But the awareness of your nice big salary and personal need for a job did much to counterbalance the pangs of conscience. You did not go to bed each evening feeling you had been particularly good to your fellow human beings that day. In fact, you got drunk most evenings on extremely good wine, at the client's expense, to anaesthetise yourself against the moral pain you felt from involvement in this project. But this discomfort was nothing compared to the self-disgust I was to experience in the third week of the project.

The client was especially distrustful of the managers in his Brazilian operation and concerned they might not answer our delightful questionnaire with the appropriate level of openness and honesty. Thus he wanted someone from the project team to go down there and ensure proper compliance – to make sure they weren't hiding any people. We couldn't risk sending an inexperienced consultant. So, given that I was one of the few people on the team with any consulting experience, I was paired up with one of the client's expensive head office bureaucrats and packed off on the night flight down to Sao Paulo. As we both were to travel business class, the cost of our tickets alone would have been enough to pay some poor Brazilian's salary for a couple of years. But thoughts like that never seemed to occur to the head office staff with their large salaries, enviable job security and fine new offices in the centre of Paris.

So off we went – me and the most boring French chemical engineer that you could possibly imagine. At least, I found him boring, as I was interested in neither chemicals nor engineering. My only interest was in surviving this awful assignment and getting quickly moved on to something better. Fortunately, my travelling companion had brought some rather strong sleeping pills with him. So, after we had downed our three course business class dinners with accompanying drinks, we were soon pretty oblivious to the world and to each other for the rest of the night flight.

When I first heard that I was going to Brazil, it had briefly occurred to me that one could have a bit of innocent and even not so innocent fun down there. But I had not bargained with the admirable caution of my companion and the value he put on his own little life, while being quite prepared to devastate other people's. A company car collected us at the airport and took us to our hotel – my companion was afraid of the risks of taking a taxi. He'd heard about the crime in Sao Paulo and had no intention of going anywhere where anything unpleasant might happen. Our hotel seemed to have armed security guards hiding in every nook and cranny. My brave companion had been advised that this was one of the safest hotels in Sao Paulo. A company car collected us each day and took us to the client's office – my courageous companion felt that a taxi, even one recommended by the hotel, would be too dangerous. The company car, of course, returned us to our hotel each evening. When I suggested we hire a taxi the first evening to go out and cruise Sao Paulo's hot spots, my fearless French comrade was incredulous. No way was he venturing out of the hotel after dark. No, for him, our evenings should be spent in the safety of the hotel – a quick dinner in the hotel's restaurant sharing half a bottle of wine with him was all the fun I was to have on that trip.

Over the next few days, we assembled all the information we could on the poor unfortunates whose jobs the people at the Paris head office felt were unnecessary. I don't remember the figures any more, but imagine the average salary of administration staff at the Brazilian plants was a couple of thousand dollars a year – probably not much more. So you'd have to fire twenty or so people down there just to pay for each bureaucrat at the Paris H.Q. I did try to explain this to my client but he did not find my logic useful and so we duly collected the numbers and prepared for the slaughter of the innocents.

That in itself was fairly upsetting. But nothing compared to the little horror story we unearthed.

The chemical company had a bit of a problem at one of its plants. Unfortunately, it had poisoned a whole district and ruined the health of hundreds of workers and their families. By some miracle, the normally corrupt local authorities had taken action against the company by closing the plant and forcing the company to continue paying the wages of two to three hundred employees, who were now too ill to get any other jobs. The company's management both in Brazil and Paris were really quite keen to avoid this unwelcome and unproductive expense. Over the last few years they had apparently tried all sorts of tricks to sneak away from their responsibilities – but without success.

However, while I was there, I noticed great merriment amongst the expatriate French management team. Surprised, I enquired about the cause of such mirth. I had expected our cost-cutting programme to cause despondency. But it was not the cost-cutting that was uppermost in their thoughts – in fact, they couldn't really care – as senior management of a division of a French company, their jobs were safe. No, their upbeat humour was due to the fact that they were convinced they had finally found a solution to the sick but unproductive workers' salaries that they had been paying. The plan they hit upon went as follows. They would offer all the workers new jobs at another chemical plant hundreds of miles away. The intention was that most workers would have to refuse the job offers – some would be too sick to travel and most would not want to leave the area where they had their families and their roots. A few would go, but they'd have to pay their own expenses – no generous relocation packages for them – unlike the well-rewarded expatriate French management. Under the terms of the agreement with the authorities, if the company could prove that it had genuinely tried to provide alternative work for that plant's employees and the workers turned down the company's offer, then the company was freed from continuing to pay those workers' wages. So the sick and useless workers could now die in poverty and the company would no longer be burdened with the meagre costs of their compensation. Yes, the local management team were very happy indeed at the brilliant scheme they had dreamed up.

While one knows that large organisations are generally made up of people dedicated to the noble task protecting their own skins and at higher levels, building up their own power, ego and influence – there are, however, times when the natural results of this process do generate a certain level of revulsion and disgust and guilt at one's own involvement. I didn't feel too overjoyed about working with this lot. Fortunately, I found a way to accelerate our work, we finished early, returned to Paris with the data and the great news about management's tremendous plan and I went for an extremely costly dinner at that client's expense before escaping off the project. Later I learnt that we had botched the attempt to sell a follow-on project to fire loads of people and I was pleased.

CHAPTER 14

MAKING MONEY SHOULD BE 'E'-ASY

Maybe missing the e-bonanza

The explosion of e-business in the mid to late 1990s signalled a potential gold rush for management consultancies that could possibly equal or even surpass the feeding frenzy provided by the craze for business process reengineering about ten years earlier. After all, remember what the experts told us about the future of organisations as they hyped their own services:

> *"In the friction-free economy, new industries, products and ideas circle the globe in record time. Your company is either quick or dead"*
>
> *"Firms can't afford to ignore Web commerce. They must re-invent themselves – and quickly"*
>
> *"To succeed in the digital economy, every employee, entrepreneur and manager must embrace a new b-web strategy agenda"*
>
> *"A new order is building that obeys a different set of rules and is forcing all businesses to dance to a different tune"*
>
> *"The Internet represents such a fundamental change that organisations will have to re-invent themselves to survive"*
>
> *"In the new economics of information, industries will be deconstructed, but not destroyed; corporations will not become obsolete, but their present business definitions will"*
>
> *"Our society is changing; we are participants in and*

witnesses to a quantum leap in the way the world works and communicates"

"Hang on to your hat and smash your crystal ball. The world is changing as you read these words, and anyone who says they can understand the future – let alone predict it – should be fired"

To spare them any embarrassment, I have not assigned the above statements to the individuals who made them. These experts warned us that if you didn't get on the net, e-enable your organisation and re-invent your business model in cyber time, you were dead. Now, in the cold light of day, a few years on, after the technology collapse and the billions in shareholder value that have disappeared into thin air, some of these claims may sound a little exaggerated. However, at the time, fortunately for us in management consultancy, many clients were actually concerned enough by this new thing to come running to us for help.

But there was one problem – most of us major consultancies didn't know how to spell 'Internet', had no experience of setting up an e-business and knew little more about how to e-enable organisations than our potential clients. We had neither the skills nor the agility to grab the fantastic new opportunities presented by the growth of e-business. As one commentator wrote, *"the big management consultancies are no different from the big clients when it comes to trying to move at Internet speed. They are in the thrall of a business model built up over a long period of time, in which the control structures have rendered decision-making moribund."*[1] Another industry insider painted a similar picture of the problems facing us major consultancies, *"the point is not that the traditional consulting firms are laggards, it is that their business models are unsuited to the new e-economy that is emerging. Any company with 60,000 employees is going to struggle to be nimble; that's exactly why large bricks-and-mortar companies are struggling to catch up with dotcom start-ups."*[1]

With business process reengineering, it had been easy for

consultancies to climb aboard the bandwagon and reap the unbelievably enormous benefits. You just took a vanilla consultant or college graduate, gave them a copy of Hammer and Champy's book *Reengineering the Corporation*, put them through a one or two day training course in process analysis and, hey presto, you had a fully trained and fully chargeable business process reengineer to sell on to your clients at half a million or more per year. Using this approach, many consultancies became like factories churning out business process reengineers in the same way an industrial production line mass produces chocolate bars or washing powder. But with e-business, things were different. Most traditional consultancies made their money and bonuses by selling in as many consultants as possible for as long a time as possible. Unfortunately, to quote another commentator, *"an army of advisers doesn't cut it any more"*.[1] The new approach was almost the opposite of what we were used to. It was based more around sending in small fast-moving and highly experienced teams, who could quickly launch new business concepts in as short a time as possible, rather than a multitude of consultants staying forever lucratively tinkering with the existing organisation as many of the traditional consultancies had always done.

So there we were, mass production consultancies churning out endless dross of vanilla consultants, faced by a quite new environment. Clients were still willing to pay a fortune to their chosen advisers, but now they only wanted a few real experts rather than an army of inexperienced process reengineering clones. We leviathans of the consulting world with our many thousands of employees were in trouble – *"there is sobering reading for the traditional management consultancies in a recent survey showing that global companies prefer to take e-strategy advice from a new breed of e-consultancies. Of fifty companies interviewed, 76 per cent do not use their traditional advisers for e-business strategy. One stark conclusion of the report,* "e-business strategy needs help", *by Forrester Research, is that 'management consultants lack Internet expertise"*.[1] In summary, a massive new goldmine had been discovered and we, the traditional consultancies, had neither the people, nor the experience nor the tools to join in the gold rush and extract the gold for ourselves.

The result was that clients looked elsewhere for anything remotely to do with 'e'. This led to the few people we did have with any e-exposure jumping ship and rushing off like the Gadarene Swine to become equity holders or partners in the fast-growing new consultancies, where the work and the money were. Forrester Research described the rapid loss of skilled staff suffered by the major management consultancies; *"as a result there has been a significant drain of skills from traditional management consultancies to the e-consultancy firms with cute names, share options, flat hierarchies and avant-garde offices"*.[1] Within a couple of months our young bright e-enabled consultants seemed to have all gone, *"the people with e-business skills are picky about who they work for. They want to be in a flexible environment which the traditional consultancies cannot provide"*.[1] Some consultancies were seeing up to 20% or more of their people leaving to take part in the e-goldrush – and this 20% were those with the new e-knowledge that we needed, leaving behind those with out-of-date skills that we couldn't sell.

A second problem was that, as our major clients focused their efforts and resources on keeping up with the e-Jones, they began to lose interest in all the more conventional stuff we had always been selling them – namely reengineering, ERP, endless organisational redesigns, cleaning up supply chains and systems integration. Our conventional sources of business collapsed leaving us with thousands of classically-trained consultants, that we couldn't shift off the beach. A commentator summed up the problem, *"traditional consulting and systems integration have simply gone out of fashion"*.[1] Moreover, we repeatedly lost those new e-business opportunities that we pitched for to the fashionable new e-consultancies with the trendy names and the proven track records of success. A journalist described our difficulties adapting to the new environment, *"in the past five years, the traditional consultancies have built their core competencies around ERP. They have been slow to adapt to e-commerce because they did not have the right skills or the right mindset.*"[1] We traditional consultancies had a problem, *"it is going to be an interesting and potentially painful journey for these companies, as painful as the journey they have to consult their clients through"*.[1]

Clearly, the availability of billions in fees for anyone who could spell the letter 'e' did not escape the attention of our management and of our main competitors. Desperately we dinosaurs fought back against the aggressive new upstarts, who were stealing our best people and what we regarded as our rightful heritage – our biggest clients. *"The big firms are not taking e-competition lying down. The sector is witnessing a wave of restructuring and technology alliances – from Cap Gemini's acquisition of Ernst & Young's consulting business to PricewaterhouseCoopers separating off its consulting arm, Andersen Consulting unpicking itself from Arthur Andersen, and KPMG seeking alliances and floating off part of its consulting business – which show determination to acquire the capital and the expertise to hold the ground in e-commerce."*[1]

At the time, I worked for one of the major consultancies, which was struggling to adapt to the massive growth in e-business opportunities and equally massive collapse in sales of traditional consulting projects. Because I was working in Sales and did more international work than most of my colleagues, I had the good fortune to be exposed to our valiant efforts to disguise ourselves as e-business experts – a rather inelegant exercise, where a slow-moving, obesely overweight dinosaur tried to pretend it was a nimble-footed cheetah.

Breaking into the exploding e-business market was a bit like a collection of 'chicken and egg' or Catch 22 situations – you couldn't sell yourself to clients unless you had references proving that you knew what you were doing and yet you couldn't get the references showing a record of success until you had sold and completed a few e-business start-ups. Likewise your people couldn't learn how to do e-business start-ups till they had done some and yet your clients were now smart enough to be loath to give their projects to people, who clearly didn't have a clue about what they were doing. So there were two main challenges facing us and our traditional competitors as we watched our birthright being whisked away before our very eyes by the new breed of e-consultancies:

1. How to get a **track record of success,** when you'd never been within a thousand miles of any e-commerce whatsoever

2. How to **have trained, experienced personnel** ready to go to the service of your clients, when most of your staff were so technically incompetent that they would have trouble even working a domestic VCR

1. BUILDING A TRACK RECORD

Like our competitors, we quickly found a way past the fact that we had no e-commerce experience. In our case, we resprayed a traditional 'kick-ass' consulting project to make it look like we had been doing leading edge e-commerce stuff for the last thousand years. We then tried to use this to quickly sell some real e-commerce so we could, at our clients' expense, find out what you really had to do in this exciting new e-enabled world of opportunity and then sell this on to other clients.

We were fortunate that, at the time, we were engaged to help one of the first major European Internet bank start-ups. Now, as far as I know, all the work our consultants were doing was traditional 'Plan-Do-Review' project management to help the client's teams meet their milestones on time. So whether this had been the launch of a leading-edge e-business or a not so leading-edge fish farm, our tasks would have been pretty much the same – get client staff organised, help them with their planning, push them to do what they had planned and bash down whatever organisational or political barriers were getting in their way. I believe that other more niche consultancies were responsible for supporting the client with the real sexy leading-edge stuff like designing the overall business concept, constructing the web sites and building the technical infrastructure. But that didn't matter to us. This bank was making headlines and our name was attached to something that was perceived to be right at the front of the e-commerce wave. Through our involvement in this Internet bank, we felt that we could now present ourselves as qualified e-business experts and we aggressively went out to sell more work based on our supposed 'track record'. There was one unfortunate small detail, there were tens of thousands of us in the company and only five to ten people had actually worked on the Internet bank launch. Moreover, most of these e-people were fully occupied assisting the Internet bank add other services like insurance, shares trading and constructing an investment funds supermarket. So I can confidently say that those individuals now cruising round clients extolling our e-commerce knowledge probably couldn't tell the difference between an e-business and a sack of potatoes.

2. PROVIDING EXPERIENCED PEOPLE

We needed two kinds of people to offer full e-business launch capability to our clients:

- Business consultants who could advise on the feasibility of the clients' ideas and who could help identify new market opportunities for our clients

- Technical wizards who could create snazzy, customer-friendly websites

Finding the business consultants who supposedly had e-commerce experience was easy. Our management just chose a few people from the First Phase group, for which I worked, within our Strategic Consulting division. After all, we in the Strategic Consulting First Phase group were used to going out to clients and spinning a convincing sales story before we had gathered any real knowledge of their organisations and their business sectors. So we were the natural choices to send out with our new message about our unrivalled depth of e-expertise.

As for the technical part – our leaders set up a new division with an exciting new name to sound just like one of our pushy new e-consultancy competitors. From our thirty thousand plus IT people, they picked somewhere between fifty and a hundred people and assigned them to this new operation. Overnight, by placing so many staff in this division, we became one of the major players in website design and build. Though, unfortunately we were only one of the major players in terms of numbers of staff and not in numbers of real paying client contracts – however hard we tried, the client contracts did not come our way.

Less than two years later we had to close down the whole thing and write off considerable losses. In a rare admission of failure, our Chief Operating Officer pretty much said that our whole venture into e-commerce had been a fiasco:

"The consulting company's decision to build a stand-alone unit devoted entirely to e-business was a mistake", says X.X. the international consulting giant's chief operating officer. At the height of the dot-com craze, the ......-based company launched an e-business unit for customers looking to bring their services and products online. But as the e-business unit grew, so did the internal conflicts between it and other divisions. "We made a mistake," Mr. X. said yesterday. "It triggered some internal resentment and as the Internet hype was fading we had to reorganise. We neglected the dot-come market at the end of 1999 and at the time we were a little bit ashamed of that. We were not interested in taking equity stakes in dot-coms and we were starting to look a little more conservative than our competitors." [2]

The story of the confusion and conflict that shook our company as we tried to adapt to the internet-enabled world is probably interesting, as it illustrates how at least one of the world's largest consulting powerhouses was wrong-footed by market developments and how for the first time in more than thirty years its growth and that of its main competitors faltered. Our competitors were probably as relieved as we were, when the e-bubble so spectacularly burst, many of the trendy new e-consultancies went belly up and clients came rushing back to the safety of their traditional providers of consulting and IT services.

BLUNDERING INTO E-BUSINESS

Probably our first major opportunity to move into e-business came when a monstrous French industrial company decided that they were going to become leaders in e-commerce. A couple of our most imaginative sales people spun the client such a convincing line about how we were the perfect partner for them given our huge experience with the internet bank, that they decided to use us to help them launch their e-business ambitions. The brief for the first phase of the project was vague. The client knew they wanted to move into e-business – we were to help them decide what to do and how to do it.

Quickly a team was pulled together from France, Britain and the U.S. As the client was French, a French project director was put in charge of the consulting team. Within two days of the off-site start-up, war had broken out between the French project director, whom one could not accuse of being lacking in pomposity and arrogance, and two of the British consultants, who had difficulty working with a team that communicated mostly in French and took evident pleasure in ignoring everything the UK people said. Acrimoniously, the two Brits walked out and went back to London never to be seen on this project again. Given that I spoke French and had worked with the French office for a number of years, I was asked to move in as team manager. But I was running a really ugly, highly political project in Holland at the time and so had to decline the offer. However, I still tried to help out a bit from the sidelines and so was able to observe with interest and amusement some aspects of the chaos that followed.

Things didn't get much better after the Brits had gone. The French office only had people who knew about traditional consultancy and none of them seemed to want to get involved in something as challenging as an e-business launch. So the only consultants we could get hold of to work on the project were completely new to the company – one was two weeks with us, another three weeks with us and another joined our company during the project's start-up week. So, being fresh out of college, they knew little to nothing about business or consulting, never mind not being the e-business experts we had promised the client that we had in such abundance. Fortunately, there was one other consultant on the team, who had just joined us from Accenture, where he had actually been involved in a couple of e-business launches. But all in all, this was not a dream team. The project manager and the three vice presidents who flitted in and out as it suited them, by the way, had also never worked on an e-business launch in their lives.

In a gesture of goodwill to their U.S. subsidiary, the French client decided that the project launch would take place in New York. The plan was that our joint team of client people and consultants would fly out to the U.S. and spend a week working together with the client's American team members launching this important project. This transatlantic excursion caused us some slight problems as none of the vice presidents involved was available for the whole week, so they came and left when it fitted in with their other commitments. This meant that they never did any proper hand-overs to each other, missed some key work sessions with the client and never provided proper coverage for the consulting team for the five days. Add to this, an arrogant project manager plus an inexperienced consulting team and a disaster was pretty much inevitable.

The brief feedback that I got, when the team returned, suggested that the thing fell apart right from the start. Not knowing much about e-business, our team tried what we called a 'process-based' approach rather than a 'content-based' approach. They tried to focus the client on the *process* of how we would work together over the next couple of months, attempted to build a detailed project work-plan and tried to involve the client in a few initial brainstorming sessions around what potential e-business areas this company should go after. The client team, on the other hand, believing that they had bought the services of a leading edge e-business practitioner, expected a *content-based* approach. They wanted us to tell them what e-businesses they should be starting and how to get going – something of which we were clearly incapable given that we knew little about the client's business and that our team actually had negligible experience of e-business. With three vice presidents acting like visiting royalty and only briefly appearing when it suited them, there was nobody permanently on hand to take responsibility for sorting things out. I believe we struggled on with this client for another month or so and then our involvement in this e-business opportunity fizzled out as the client became aware we had little practical added value and considerable added cost.

The next attempt was in Holland. This was a bit more successful. One of our Dutch consultants had left us to start up his own e-business. With great foresight, our Dutch consulting operation offered him the services of a few consultants so that we could both help him out and get some of our people exposed to launching an e-start-up. So, six months later when a leading Dutch department store chain invited bids to help it set up its e-gift-shop, we were able to field a team that knew its way around websites, marketplaces, incubators, portals, B2B, B2C and all the other e-stuff. In a competitive pitch, we actually won the work. Over a period of a couple of months our team pushed and chivvied the client so successfully that the site got launched on time and to budget. This was seen as a first step towards making a name for ourselves within e-business. Unfortunately, soon after the site launch, an industry review of websites rated this one very poorly in terms of look and performance. So that pretty much wiped out our e-business satisfied client reference base. Although I spent another six months or so visiting Holland after that, I didn't hear anything more about e-business projects there.

Soon after, I came in contact with a small but growing

American/European company, with operations worldwide, which wanted to expand its sales over the Internet. Now you can, if you want, get a fully functioning web business up and running for about five to six hundred dollars from a service provider with a ready-made web-builder toolkit. Obviously, such a site would be too small scale for an international company, but it does illustrate that dipping one's toe into the e-business pool need not be terrifically expensive. After some discussions with this client about their requirements, I went to our IT people for a quote on building a simple web shop for the client to test out customer reaction. Our IT people swore blind that it would be quite impossible to produce anything at all for this client for less than two hundred and fifty thousand dollars. I suspect that the large amount they wanted had more to do with their unfamiliarity with the area than with the real level of design and programming resources required. I went to the client with our bid and he laughed me out of his office. Once again, inexperience was causing us to lose the business that we needed in order for us to learn how to operate in the new e-enabled world.

There were certainly other cases of e-business work, which I did not know about. But I think it is fair to say that if we had achieved any major successes in the e-business area, we would have all heard about it from either the company magazine, the regular e-mails detailing our major market wins or from management briefings. But there was just a deafening silence. Some consultancies obviously made a packet in the e-business market while others went spectacularly bust – we were just too big and too slow to react. Making money in the e-commerce boom should have been e-asy – but we, like some other consulting giants, missed the boat. However, in retrospect, although we may regret missing out on the potential gains, on the other hand, our inability to move quickly enough insulated us from the substantial losses incurred by some competitors who ended up with huge unpaid bills or totally worthless stock options in failed e-businesses that they had helped launch.

LIFE AFTER THE E-EXPLOSION

When the e-commerce balloon exploded with such an impressive bang leaving millions of shareholders with nothing and thousands of stock-option millionaires bankrupt, unfortunately things did not go back to 'business as usual' for the major consultancies. The consulting services market was changing:

- Major organisations were reducing their consulting budgets

- Our clients tended to be more qualified than a few years before, with MBAs now more common

- Clients were also becoming more choosy about what particular consulting services they wished to buy and so the hugely profitable multi-million, 'armies of consultants' projects which had been our cash cows for so long became rarer

- The services offered by the major consultancies were becoming more and more indistinguishable, so that price rather than brand name became the criteria of choice for many clients

Many consultancies had been patently unable to seize the opportunities offered by e-business because of their huge size, enormously bureaucratic decision-making and conservative lack of entrepreneurship. Luckily for these consultancies e-business came and went quickly before they sustained permanent commercial damage. However, the weaknesses, which had prevented us traditional consultancies reacting to the Internet opportunities, were to have a far more serious effect – many of the major consultancies also proved unable to adjust to the deeper changes in the overall consulting and IT services market. And this time, thousands of us employees would be victims as the great mastodons, for which we worked, unknowingly faced possible extinction as the climate, in which they had thrived, underwent a fundamental change.

(1) Financial Times IT Review
(2) FT.com (contact author for date)

CHAPTER 15

THE END – DIS-INTEGRATION

For thirty years up till the year 2000, management consultancy had only known growth – mostly double-digit growth. And it's not that difficult to make money in a rapidly expanding market. The bursting of the technology bubble, stock market crash and subsequent quasi-recession hit consulting badly. There were suddenly major changes in the consulting business. In the words of one commentator, *"The game is up for the old model because clients can't afford it any more. The days are gone when a client could afford to bring in his golfing chum, outline a problem and then wait for it to be solved at any cost"*.[1] Several well-known consultancies went to the wall.[2] Many thousands of consultants were thrown out of work – over eighteen months, for example, one consultancy fired over ten thousand people.

Then a series of massive scandals, including the Enron collapse and WorldCom fraud, caused U.S. regulators to demand that auditors should not offer both audits and consulting services to their clients. There were a series of huge mergers as thousands of consultants, owned by auditors, were sold off. Cap Gemini, a French-owned IT services company bought around ten thousand consultants from Ernst & Young paying around $11 billion ($3 billion in cash and the rest in shares), valuing each consultant at around a million dollars. Incidentally, by the time the Ernst & Young partners could start selling off their shares, the share price had fallen from close to two hundred euros per share to below thirty. So there were some quite disappointed Ernst & Young partners, who saw a potential fortune evaporate before their eyes.

A year later, just after firing fifteen thousand of its own staff, IBM bought thirty thousand consultants from PWC for $3.5 billion (including $2.7 billion in cash)[3], now valuing each consultant at around a hundred thousand dollars each – a tenth of the price offered by Cap Gemini when it bought ten thousand Ernst & Young consultants.

Now, with a downturn in the market and massive mergers to implement, consulting management was really put under pressure to demonstrate themselves some of the managerial qualities they had always criticised their clients for not having. However, one of the most disastrous episodes of complete mind-boggling management incompetence that I have experienced in my long career with many organisations was not in a client organisation at all – it was in the executive team of a management consultancy. In just over twelve months of bungling and botching, they successfully wiped out a several thousand person management consultancy that had been a power in the consultancy industry for over twenty years.

Looking back at the destruction of this one particular consultancy, to which I dedicated some years of my life, I have the impression of watching a huge traffic accident in slow motion. It feels like I am standing at a crossroads, while a wedding procession and three lorries are all hurtling towards each other, oblivious of each other's presence. Then they all arrive at the crossroads at the same time. The result – an almighty smash-up causing loads of damage and injury. And, of course, not a particularly auspicious start to the marriage.

In this case, the marriage was between the group that owned us pursuing its ambition to be one of the world's leading suppliers of consultancy services and IT systems and a bunch of consultants being hastily off-loaded by a firm of auditors under pressure from America's financial watch-dog, the Securities and Exchange Commission (SEC), to separate their audit work from selling consulting to their audit clients. The three lorries converging on the crossroads, where they would all pile into the wedding procession, were:

1. The collapse of the technology boom in 2000 and subsequent economic slowdown.

2. The fact that major mergers and acquisitions are notoriously difficult to manage and that most destroy shareholder value.

3. The brutal avarice and greed of the partners and senior officers of the group.

First let me describe the background to the marriage, then we'll look at the three lorries, which were to wreak such havoc on what should have been such a joyful occasion.

THE MARRIAGE PARTNERS:

THE BRIDEGROOM – TRYING TO TAKE OVER THE WORLD

The consultancy had been owned for many years by a monstrous IT systems group with tens of thousands of employees unevenly spread throughout the world. For many years the employees had been fortunate that group executives and mutual contempt had kept the consultancy and systems people mostly apart, bringing them together only when there were clients who needed a mix of consulting and systems. So, as long as the consultancy delivered sufficient levels of GOP (Gross Operating Profit) to the group, there was only limited interference from the chateau generals at the centre. And when there was interference, this had generally helped the consultancy's growth – group executives, lacking the skills to grow the company organically, kept expanding its size by buying other management consultancies. On the consultancy side, staff would regularly receive e-mails informing them that their masters had just bought them a hundred or so consultants in Germany, then another fifty in Scandinavia, then some in South Africa, then another five hundred in France, then a bunch in South America, then some in Britain and so on.

However, although this consultancy did churn out a pile of profits, I would be lying if I claimed that all was well. The market was probably tiring of its offer, its competitors had copied many of its tricks and it hadn't thought of any innovative offering for quite a few years even though it still tried to keep its fee rates at the top of the range for management consultancies. Moreover, three or four years earlier its U.S. business had crashed from several hundred consultants to less than a hundred and it had struggled to grow in Asia. And you couldn't claim to be a worldwide operation with a couple of thousand people in Europe and just a few stragglers everywhere else. So something needed to be done.

The group was big – forty thousand or so techies and a few thousand consultants. But, for the senior executives, it wasn't big enough. They wanted to be in the very top league worldwide and compete with Accenture, EDS/A.T. Kearney and IBM – the real giants of the business. And they couldn't do this without being big in The States and Europe and having a reasonable presence in the Far East. In the U.S., the consultancy had failed to grow its business in spite of repeated, widely publicised but futile U.S. recovery plans. One of these recovery plans failed, it was rumoured by vicious tongues, partly because the CEO didn't give it the management attention required. At the time, he was having a sexual relationship with a female project director many years his junior, who had gone to work in South Africa. This meant that the gentleman spent as much (if not more) time down in the South African office, where the consultancy had less than thirty consultants, as he did in The States supporting the U.S. operation's recovery plan, where the consultancy should have had a couple of thousand consultants.

Anyway, after years of failing to make it into the ranks of the world's three or four largest consultancies and IT services providers, the decision was taken at the very top of the stock market boom to buy the kind of market share that would put this company up with the leaders.

THE BRIDE – AUDITORS GORGING THEMSELVES IN THE CONSULTANCY TROUGH

At the time, the SEC in the U.S. was becoming increasingly concerned at the trend of the big accountancies towards selling consulting services to their audit clients. For many years, auditors have had a problem – how to grow their business. There are only a limited number of companies they can audit. So they can only grow their auditing by stealing market share off each other. This they do. But it means that intensive competition has forced auditing fees downwards and the service has become almost a commodity. So while auditing was still profitable, it wasn't making the kind of fortunes that many partners in the big audit practices felt they deserved.

So, if auditors really wanted to make a mint, they had to do more than just audit. What else could they do? The answer, of course, was obvious. Sell consulting – loads and loads of it. Their privileged role as auditors gave the big accountancy firms unique access to their clients' accounts and organisations. Thus they knew all about their clients' strengths and weaknesses. This put them in a wonderful position to target exactly what consulting they could sell, to whom they could sell it and how much they could charge for it. So while we at pure management consultancies had to fight quite hard to get in to see potential clients to flog them our wares, the lucky auditors had by law the access that we so desperately wanted. This allowed the auditors to grow massive consulting practices. One study suggested that many of the world's largest companies were spending five to ten times as much on consulting as they did on auditing just with their auditors.[4] A leading businessman described this rush into consulting, *"In the past 20 years most big accountants have moved into consultancy. They must have become fed up competing for audits, where clients can check the bill by judging the time the beancounters had spent. By contrast they saw how easy it is to charge for some black-hole masterpiece of advice. After all, try checking a bill for gems of wisdom – no chance."*[4]

Now, unfortunately for the auditors, there could be a small but not totally trivial problem with the source of their new-found wealth – although an auditor is paid by their clients, their duty is first and foremost to shareholders, financial institutions and other outside groups as an audit is meant to confirm that clients' accounts provide a *"true and fair view"* of the financial status of audited companies. However, when an accountancy is actually making most of its profits from selling consultancy work to their audit clients, their so-called objectivity might be questioned. How willing would the accountancy be to tell a client that their accounts smell more like a fish market on a hot summer's day than a reliable set of financial figures, if that accountancy is earning say thirty million from all kinds of interesting lucrative consultancy work from that client and only three million from the much less profitable drudge of doing the accounts? For example, in the U.S. Andersen, once one of the world's largest auditors was destroyed in just a couple of months. One of their major clients, Enron, became one of the largest bankruptcies in corporate history and several other massive Andersen clients also came crashing down as their accounts were shown to have been largely works of fiction. A senior Enron executive, who had been summoned to give evidence about the company's collapse, apparently committed suicide and top management were sued in a class action by employees many of whom lost their savings and pensions after being encouraged by top management to buy shares in the company just prior to the collapse. In 2000, Andersen was paid $25m in audit fees by Enron and another $27m in non-audit fees[6] and had up to one hundred staffers working on the Enron account.[7] Several top Enron executives, including its chief accounting officer, had come from Andersen. It was even reported that Andersen handled some of the internal auditing work for Enron along with vetting its public reports for the firm's audit committee.[7] As one commentator said describing the potential conflicts of interest between auditing and consulting work, *"in effect, the firm was working on the accounting systems and controls with one hand and attesting to the numbers they produced with the other"*.[8] Meanwhile, in Europe, some rather embarrassing questions were asked about how the auditors at the massive Italian conglomerate Parmalat happened not to notice at least $6 billion missing from the accounts.

So some auditors, sensing the way the wind was starting to blow, made the decision to flog off their consulting arms while the going was good and prices were high instead of waiting till it was too late and being forced by the regulator into a low price fire-sale. This provided the group, where I worked at the time, the opportunity to become one of the Big Five in consulting and IT services by taking thousands of consultants off the hands of one of the world's largest auditors.

So the marriage took place, vows were exchanged, several billion dollars and a heap of shares exchanged hands and the happy couple set off for the wedding feast and honeymoon. Our group's top executives could now boast to the financial press that we had now moved from the second league to being near the top of the first division. This, no doubt, left our senior management feeling pretty tough and gung-ho and swanky. However, as a financial journalist suggested when reviewing the union one year on, *"just another reminder that a merger made in the boardroom isn't necessarily a marriage made in heaven."*[9] Moreover, while our group execs could now swagger round the world surveying their vastly expanded empire, some of us at the coalface groaned with dismay. Our great leaders had chosen to hand over billions of dollars for the newly acquired thousands of consultants – where I worked, we could sort of begin to guess whose bonuses would be needed to pay for this little corporate extravagance.

Now this where the three lorries come rushing in to the picture.

1. The collapse of the technology boom in 2000 and subsequent economic slowdown

Of course, marriage is not always easy. And the test of a strong marriage and the partners' ability to form a constructive relationship is whether they can survive bad times as well as good. Our group executives were a little unfortunate. In their case, the bad times started immediately after the church service and before they had the pleasure of consummating the happy union in the conjugal bed. No sooner had the vows been exchanged and the first part of the dowry been handed over (billions of dollars in cash and shares), than the economy, which had been booming so gloriously for the last ten to fifteen years, suddenly fell over. Dotcom stocks crashed, the Nasdaq sunk through the floor and even blue chips saw their value plummet by thirty percent or more. But, more importantly for the happy bridegroom and his radiant bride, the market demand for their services dried up. As one commentator remarked, *"the timing was impeccably wrong"*.[10]

A further problem was that before the thousands consultants were bought by our executives, the good people in the audit division, which had previously owned the thousands of consultants, were bonused on the amount of management consultancy work they could generate and push over to their thousands of brothers and sisters in consulting. However, the day that the consultants joined us, this fruitful source of consulting work dried up completely. Now, freed from their links with the management consultants, the auditors started offering to do their clients' consulting work themselves. According to the terms of the sale they weren't allowed to call what they did 'consulting'. Instead they just called it 'professional services'. Anyway, for them, there was now so much to do that the chairman of the professional services firm reported that the year following our acquisition of their thousands of consultants was *"one of the busiest we ever experienced"*.[11] For them, profit per partner increased dramatically much to the delight of the partners who got two Christmas presents that year – a share of the billions of dollars cash that we paid them for taking their consultants off their hands and a surge in their work as they took on the projects, which previously they had passed over to the consultants. In fact, things were now going so well for the auditors, that many hundreds of the consultants, for which we had paid so much money, left us and went back to join their former employer to offer professional services in competition with us.

However, this acquisition had an immediate catastrophic effect on our business situation. While the auditors partied all the way to the bank, we had suddenly inherited thousands of expensive bodies to be paid. Yet it was not obvious that anybody had fully thought through how we were going to sell their services now that they weren't getting work pushed through to them from the auditors. If the economy had continued expanding, this wouldn't have been such a major problem. There would have been increasing client demand at which we could have profitably channelled the newly acquired resources. But with economic growth becoming a distant memory, thousands well-paid mouths to feed, amongst which the many partners were earning salaries of at least $600,000 per year, suddenly became somewhat of an expensive embarrassment for us. The situation was worst in the U.S. Utilisation of our U.S. consultants, which should ideally be somewhere between sixty to seventy percent, dropped down to thirty percent. After all, until then, we'd had very few people in the U.S. and so we had insufficient infrastructure to sell the time of the thousands of new additions to our payroll. In many European countries, where we had much more substantial business, utilisation sunk down to hover only around forty percent – that meant that well over half of our people were not bringing in any fee income, a disaster for a company like ours. And I believe that the Far East was no great shakes either.

If we had a couple of thousand of our people in the U.S. getting paid their salaries, but not earning any fees, that was draining millions every week in salaries from our profits and losing us tens of millions a week in lost revenue. Just in the little sub-section of the British consulting practice, where I worked at the time, about one hundred and fifty out of three hundred people were 'on the beach' (not doing any paid client work) – that was at least £150,000 a week in salaries and over £1m a week in lost revenue.

As the enormity of their error – picking up many thousands of expensive consultants without having anywhere useful to put them – began to sink in, our senior management started to flap around in panic like fish on a hook. Gasping for money like the fish gasping for oxygen, they twisted and turned as they tried to get off the hook of their own making.

They reorganised us. Then they reorganised again and then they reorganised just one more time. But that didn't do much good. Our utilisation stayed stubbornly well below fifty percent. We were haemorrhaging money – many millions every week – that should have gone into their pockets. Meanwhile, our share price lost ninety percent of its value. Our bosses were not at all happy.

Then the big chiefs started exhorting us to sell more and we received bags of e-mails about how we weren't trying hard enough and about how we were just using tougher market conditions as an excuse. We never saw any of our executives come out to sell anything. They were always too busy in internal meetings working on the next reorganisation to have time to generate some business to pay their massive salaries and generous expenses.

When the reorganisations didn't work and the exhortations didn't work, the threats began. 'If we didn't achieve our profit targets, then,' they warned ominously, 'we wouldn't get any bonuses'. We just laughed. With a collapsing market and a stale service offering, we couldn't sell even the people we already had, never mind the additional thousands. And as for our bonuses, having already paid many thousand people to do nothing for several months, any possibility of making anything like our annual profit targets was well and truly shot. By threatening our profit-related bonuses, our executives just demonstrated once again how little they understood of what was actually happening out in the market.

When that strategy failed to deliver any results, the group's executives had a true stroke of, what must have seemed to them as, genius. They realised that they could push our utilisation levels up by firing people. So now, having bought many thousands of consultants in order to be bigger, we started paying hordes of them severance money in order to leave us. I think that in all about six thousand people were laid off from our group in the twelve months following the acquisition – the lay-offs alone cost hundreds of millions of dollars and pounds and most other currencies imaginable.

Thus the first lorry that hit the wedding party – the economic slowdown – caused an impressive amount of damage to our group's hopes for their marriage. This change in the commercial environment alone would probably have been sufficient to wreck the chances of the marriage ever becoming a success. However, there were two other lorries involved in the horrible accident and their involvement in the pile-up well and truly put paid to the great marriage and to my not so great consulting career.

So, on to lorry number two.

2. The fact that major mergers and acquisitions are notoriously difficult to manage and that most destroy shareholder value

Most studies of mergers and acquisitions show that about twenty percent create value for shareholders, another twenty percent have a neutral effect and about sixty percent of all mergers and acquisitions actually destroy shareholder value. Though you have to be a little careful reading these studies – consultants trying to worry clients and frighten them into buying the consultants' services do most of them. And if you look at other studies done by consultants – for example, BPR consultants on the success rates of BPR projects[12], or Total Quality consultants on the success of Total Quality programmes or Six Sigma consultants on the success of Six Sigma programmes, or enterprise resource planning (ERP) systems consultants on the success rates of ERP implementations, or materials requirements planning systems (MRP) consultants on the success rates of MRP projects – well, all of these studies usually come up with similar figures. The message for clients is clear – unless you buy our services, your pet project has a sixty to eighty percent chance of either giving no added value to your organisation or even of destroying shareholder value. What these studies, of course, omit to mention is that many of the failed projects in these surveys were actually supported and even managed by armies of exceedingly expensive consultants.

However, even taking the consultants' figures with a pinch of well-deserved salt, it is true that most mergers and acquisitions do fail to live up to the original expectations. And the reasons for failure are usually to do with two things:

- How the acquiring company manages the people in the acquired company

- Employees focusing inwards on organisational issues rather than outwards on clients.

How the acquiring company manages the people in the acquired company

When you acquire a company with a heap of physical assets like factories, land, natural resources, new product patents or whatever, you at least get hold of things that have a value. If the merger goes well, you can make one and one equal three as you get various synergies and savings – synergies from integrating the operations of the two entities and savings from firing people doing any activities that are duplicated in the new merged organisation

Yet, if the merger goes badly and lots of people in the acquired company leave, well you've still got the physical assets you bought, so you'll have something to show for your investment. However, if you acquire a company like a law firm, an advertising agency or a management consultancy, there may be a few physical assets like office buildings, but the real assets are the people – their knowledge, their experience and their clients. If you manage the people badly, they just walk. And you are left with an expensive but empty space, which has no value whatsoever – all the acquired assets have just disappeared, with their knowledge and usually their clients, out the door.

So, the lesson is blindingly obvious – if, like this group's management, you buy a company whose only asset is its people, and you pay billions of dollars for those people, you'd better treat them with kid gloves if you want them, their knowledge and their clients to stay.

Employees focusing inwards on organisational issues rather than outwards on clients.

After any acquisition, you must focus everybody's efforts outwards to serving their customers. Employees from both the acquiring and the acquired companies will feel nervous about their positions and prospects in the new larger entity. A few joint successes out in the market will work wonders for convincing all your employees that you can build a great future for them in the organisation you want to develop. But one thing you must at all costs avoid, following an acquisition, is allowing people to become inwardly focused and spend their time obsessed with things like:

- Will my job function be different?

- Will my salary change?

- Will my future career be altered?

- Will the appraisal and promotion process be different?

- Where will I be located?

- Who will be my boss?

- What will be my new job title?

- And so on

Because, once people spend their working days trying to sort out all their personal issues instead of doing their business, your customer service will go down the pan, your sales will suffer and the result of the acquisition will be a loss of momentum rather than a gain.

Helping clients make their mergers and acquisitions work is the bread and butter of consulting. It's something that every consultant, however lowly, should know how to do. So, of all organisations, you would have hoped that we, being consultants, were well placed to make our merger work.

The first great decision taken by group executives was that they would redesign our organisation to fully integrate all the thousands of IT systems people, the tens of thousands of newly acquired consultants and our own thousands of consultants into one wonderful seamless company. Thus our management's first major decision was not outward-facing – focused on what we would do for our clients. It was inward-looking – all about how we would be organised – who would report to whom, what would job titles be, who would have the biggest empire and so on. Unfortunately, nothing here about maybe setting up a few pilot joint teams to go after certain clients and clock up a few sales successes. Here was a ginormous, totally avoidable mistake – get these thousands and thousands of people facing inwards using their time and energy worrying over their position in the new organisation, their job titles and their salaries, rather than turning their attention outwards to what new things we could do for our clients. And by some perverse logic, internal integration meetings always seemed to take priority over such unimportant trivialities like client-facing work. Meanwhile, our competitors were delighted to be able to take away our major clients from us as we failed one competitive bid after another, because the people we needed to work on the bid teams were all flying around the world attending 'internal integration meetings'.

3. The brutal avarice and greed of the partners and senior officers of the group

The third lorry that crashed into the wedding cortege was the grasping, self-centred behaviour of the management level that consisted of our vice presidents and the partners of the consultancy that we bought.

When the company was a couple of thousand-person management consultancy, one of its strongest competitive weapons was a culture of teamwork, sharing knowledge and mutual support. Each time it had a new opportunity with a client, it could pull together a well-functioning team of people from different divisions and even different countries in a couple of hours and also build a support network of experts with relevant knowledge and experience to help the team. All the consultants knew that any team's success would help the whole company, so even if we were working on another project, we would all make the time and effort to assist any consultant anywhere in the world who needed support.

But once we became an enormous monster with tens of thousands of employees, many senior managers seemed to work to just one objective – ensuring that their people were billing their time to clients so that they could hit their personal bonus targets – and sod the rest of the company! A culture of sharing and support was replaced by a culture of 'I'm all right, Jack and bugger the rest of you'.

Then when it quickly became clear that we were not going to hit our overall group profit targets, the shift towards 'every man for himself' became worse. Vice presidents, knowing that they would not get the overall company profit-related part of their bonuses, focused even more on ensuring that their particular unit hit its individual profit targets, so that they personally would at least get some bonus.

The effect on our sales was catastrophic. As soon as we merged, there was what one vice president called 'a land grab' as each unit vice president tried to claim the most lucrative clients for themselves. Furthermore, every time a client showed any interest in working with us, the manager, who heard of the opportunity, would try and keep it to themselves and make sure they sold only something that their own people could deliver. So instead of listening to clients and offering them tailor-made solutions to their organisational issues, we became a company where people were pushed to sell what our vice presidents wanted sold, rather than what the client wanted to buy. In a rapidly growing market, where clients would buy anything that sounded at all fashionable, we might have got away with this – in a rapidly shrinking market, our refusal to listen to our clients' wishes was a disaster. And the more sales declined and the more people ended up on the beach, the more each area vice president struggled to protect their individual patch at the expense of the company as a whole. You would repeatedly see cases where a vice president would sell in a couple of hundred thousand dollars, pounds or euros or whatever of their people's time rather than bringing in another unit who could have sold a project worth millions to that client.

Internally, we could see that this new self-centred culture of greed was destroying the company. In fact, things were so bad that within six months of the start of the 'integration' even people on the outside were beginning to sense that we were hopelessly in trouble. As a financial journalist wrote, *"yesterday's audited interims confirm the dramatic loss of momentum following the merger. Growth was probably negative: among the worst performances in the sector. Staff turnover rose to an annualised rate of 25%... That implies not just disruption but lasting damage."*[13]

When 'Integration' became 'Dis-integration'

The logic behind the acquisition of the many thousands of consultants looked OK on paper. There was a certain synergy between their geographical strength in the U.S. and ours in Europe. Moreover, the new company could now honestly claim to offer a full service to clients ranging from high end strategy through operational improvement consulting to all kinds of IT stuff. However, what looks splendid in a press release to the financial world isn't worth a toss if management don't have the capability to make it work in reality.

Although we now had thousands of consultants, we also had about three times as many IT people. So numerically the IT vice presidents took the majority of the key management positions. It soon became clear that, although they may have been adequate systems specialists, most of them didn't have a clue about how to make a major merger work. They seemed to approach the whole matter as if they were building a computer system with tens of thousands of easily replaceable components rather than if they were constructing an enterprise with thousands of human beings, whose loyalty and co-operation had to be earned by the leadership. To us in consulting, who were used to advising clients on mergers and acquisitions, it appeared that our management was intent on making every mistake in the book.

There were probably three major mistakes:

A. An unworkable organisation structure

B. Micro-managing many thousands of bodies

C. A disorganised sales process

A. ORGANISATION STRUCTURE – THE BEAST FROM A THOUSAND FATHOMS

On paper, constructing the new organisation probably looked easy – after all, you just draw a big organisation chart and stick many thousands of people's names on it. And if you make a few hundred mistakes, like getting people on the wrong continent or putting new recruits in as senior managers because you got their names mixed up with someone else with a similar name or you completely forgot to find a place for hundreds of staff who just got overlooked – well, you could always sort that out later. A few such mistakes could be expected when you had so many faceless people, rather than individual human beings with personal ambitions and feelings, with which to deal.

This rather mechanical process didn't make us feel particularly happy with our senior management – especially when you were one of the hundreds who got forgotten completely. However, although the process for designing the new organisation was badly timed and poorly executed, it was not as disastrous as the actual structure dreamt up at the centre. Admittedly the whole thing was pretty complex. The only answer that I have is that I would have done the whole thing differently. But 20/20 vision in hindsight is easy to have.

Within our thousands and thousands of people, we now had hundreds of things we could do for our clients and therefore loads of different ways of constructing the new organisation. There were, for example, thousands of us with in-depth industry knowledge of something like Telecommunications, Life Sciences, Manufacturing, Transport, Public Services and, in fact, any activity sector you could think of. So we could have organised the many thousands of employees according to the industry or activity sector in which they would work.

But this would ignore the fact that there were thousands more, who had worked across lots of industries but were experts in specific services like Customer Relationship Management (CRM), E-Procurement, Supply Chain, New Product Development (NPD), Sales Effectiveness, Adaptive Organisations and so on. So the question was asked whether we should base the organisation on these services and not on the industry sectors.

But again, there were thousands more who had both worked across a number of activity sectors and delivered several services – their expertise lay in what we called 'professions' – Strategic Consulting, Operations Improvement, Systems Architecture, Outsourcing, Package Solutions and other useful things like that. Perhaps, our leaders pondered, we should construct the new organisation based on these professions.

So we could organise either around industry sectors or services or professions. Then you had to add in geography – should we be organised in country units, regional units or global teams? Did we need country management at all or should we ignore geography?

And then finally, we had a bunch of people who knew how to manage client relationships and sell whatever they were told to sell, although they often had no real experience of doing anything. This raised another question – who should sell our services? – People who knew how to do things, but didn't know how to sell: or people who knew how to sell things, but had no idea how to actually do what it was that they were selling? So we also had to decide who would sell for us – traditional salesmen or doers.

All in all, a pretty complicated conundrum. And certainly one that our senior management had some difficulty in solving. However, our major competitor, Accenture, had successfully managed to create a profitable, market-leading organisation with tens of thousands of people world-wide and they even explain their organisation structure on their website for anybody to see. So it shouldn't have been so difficult for our management to have developed something equally workable. For example, given the complexity, we could even have just copied Accenture's structure for the first year or so and then gradually improved on that

Eventually after much deliberation and many expensive internal integration meetings, our management came up with an answer, of sorts. I attended four presentations of the new structure, before I started to get my mind round the thing. I think some people never understood it. Though maybe some understood it too well, because as soon as it was announced, there was a flood of people leaving the company to avoid working in the abomination that our leaders had designed for us.

One thing I've learnt over the last twenty years of consulting is that in organisations and business, if you come across something that is so complicated that you can't explain it to another reasonably sensible human being, then that thing is probably wrong. And so it was with our incredible organisation structure – it was too complex to be comprehended and was thus unworkable – our business results proved that.

Moreover, what made everything even worse was that, when top management started to see that the Frankenstein they had created couldn't walk in a straight line for three steps without falling over, they refused to lose face by admitting that the thing was ugly and inappropriate. So they fruitlessly dragged it back on to the operating table time and again as they conducted a series of what they called 'organisational simplifications'.

B. MICRO-MANAGING THE SIXTY THOUSAND

Having blessed us with an organisation structure that would

handicap our ability to compete in a shrinking market, our top executives then turned their attention to what kind of management control systems they needed to direct the mis-shapen and ungainly creature they had created.

We in consulting had been used to working in a very loosely controlled environment, where the ability to react to changing client needs, was much more important than internal procedures and controls. Of course, we had an organisation structure and several levels of management. But what was key was that teams could form quickly, work effectively together and disband after an assignment so that different teams could form around the next client project. This was close to what business books called an 'adhocracy' – because we were able to flexibly create ad hoc teams to work on any problem anywhere in the world without people worrying about whether the revenue for their work would show up on their particular unit's end of month figures. We would have become rapidly extinct, if we'd had rigid people who refused to help out some project or other because the revenue earned for their time wasn't attributed to their department. The thousands of consultants that we had just bought were also used to operating in this sort of rapid reaction environment. To be successful in consulting you needed this kind of organisational fluidity.

However, the IT folks had a quite different culture. They had always worked within a heavy bureaucracy with a mountain of formal bureaucratic processes and procedures. For example:

- They all had numbers rather than names.

- They all had to fill in time-sheets each day specifying how many hours and minutes they had worked and for which clients.

- Every client assignment had a job code. You were not allowed to work on any assignment unless a job code had been issued – even if the client was begging you to start. Job codes could take several weeks to be issued.

- Managers would refuse to allow their people to work on projects until a formal written internal agreement had been signed specifying how much of the fees an employee earned would go to the unit that sold the project and how much would go to the unit to which the person belonged. Negotiating these agreements could take weeks.

- People were not allowed to work on international assignments until an Inter-Company Agreement had been signed by the manager from the country who paid the employee and the manager of the country where the work was, agreeing how the fees for that person would be split between the two countries. Again, negotiating these agreements could take weeks.

- People were not allowed to do any international travel unless specifically signed off by their country manager.

- All expenses had to be signed by one of a handful of senior managers…

The IT company was a bureaucracy gone mad. Our consultancies had been managed based mainly on trust and mutual support. The IT company had been used to micro-managing its people and units only helped each other after a huge amount of internal wrangling about money and signing of formal agreements – a culture of mistrust and control.

Six months into the integration of the three organisations, our great leaders considered that the ungainly organisation structure was fully and successfully implemented. They then announced that all the consultants would be moved on to the administrative systems used so successfully to control the IT people. There were howls of protest from the thousands of consultants. These were ignored. But slowly and surely the place began to grind to a halt. Some of the bureaucratic problems were actually trivial and not worth the heat and energy used fighting them. But others were fundamental to how a successful consultancy worked and quite simply prevented us from competing in an increasingly competitive market:

- People couldn't get to client meetings because they couldn't get their travel expenses authorised.

- Units immediately stopped sharing resources and managers got more and more caught up in internal meetings negotiating transfer pricing of their people rather than thinking about how best to serve clients. Some people's utilisation fell as low as fifteen percent because they had so many internal meetings to attend.

- Our Strategic Consulting director suddenly found that he had to sign over three hundred 'time and expenses' sheets every two weeks – that kept him busy doing an essentially useless activity.

- We couldn't get people on to projects that we sold because of several week delays in issuing internal charge codes.

- We couldn't put good bid teams together as many unit managers seeing that the sale was being led by, and therefore would be credited to, another unit decided to hold their best people in reserve for the projects they were hoping to sell themselves – bid conversion rates collapsed as did utilisation and many of our best people were continually being prevented by their own line managers from working on assignments, where they could have added huge value.

I found myself going to the office each day but being unable to do any work, because I was ordered to no longer go and work on projects in Europe as my manager couldn't reach agreement with several other country managers on how much they were willing to pay for my services. We became a company at war with itself – so what chance did we have defending our market share against our aggressive and hungry competitors?

C. A DISORGANISED SALES PROCESS

An unworkable organisation structure, a crippling bureaucracy – these alone would have been sufficient to kill most companies. But there was one more critical error made in the integration process – nobody had really thought through how we were going to sell our greatly expanded range of services. And if your key people spend much of their time on internal integration projects, your vice presidents refuse to co-operate with each other, morale is devastated by a culture of selfishness, your speed of reaction is slowed by unnecessary red tape, plus you can't sell – well you're on your way out of business.

There were many problems in our sales process, for example:

- Many people, who were made client account managers, had never managed a client account before in their lives – they were technical IT systems project managers. Moreover, in addition to not knowing how to manage a client decision network, they also understood little to nothing about the huge range of services they now were supposed to sell. Result, they were unable to tell clients a convincing story and so didn't sell.

- Because many of our so-called sales people had never sold before, they had no experience of 'prospecting' – nosing about a client's organisation looking for opportunities to sell something. Moreover, they had little background in 'networking' – going around pressing the flesh to establish useful contacts within major client organisations. A major McKinsey client at Siemens once described the networking that led to McKinsey getting business from them, *"you have lunch. You have dinner. And then projects evolve. Very often competitive bidding doesn't happen.*"[14] But our people simply didn't know how to network properly.

- As for those client account managers who were used to flogging consulting, well many of them had almost no knowledge of systems architecture, outsourcing, applications development and that kind of stuff which occupied seventy five percent of our employees, so they shied away from anything technical. This meant that in many accounts we virtually ceased to push our systems work.

In addition to these, what one might call structural problems, there were the cultural barriers that in the new 'every man for himself' environment, we failed time and again to respond to big opportunities and in many cases handed work, that we should have won, over on a plate to competitors.

As I was working on selling major projects for all of the period during which the three organisations were 'integrated', I had the pleasure of seeing a few horror stories at first hand and even of leading some of the worst sales pitches I've ever seen. I'd like to give just one war story to show just how badly broken the whole company was.

TRANSFORMING TWENTY THREE THOUSAND PEOPLE

This was probably the biggest opportunity I worked on during that first year of the fully integrated (or dis-integrated) organisation. I will describe the events and people's behaviour.

On 10 August our telecommunications business unit received an invitation to tender for a Strategic Partnership Project with TB Retail a major national telecoms organisation in the country where it operated. The project was due to last for a minimum of 30 months with the client having the option of extending it after that. The aim was a complete transformation of their operations and the way their 23,000 employees worked. At a time when we had well over 50% of our staff unassigned (on the beach), this huge potential opportunity was absolutely vital to the future of our consulting business. This project alone could have fed our consultancy till the economy turned round.

Luckily, we were well-positioned to win the work because:

- *We had done a successful transformation programme for this client about 10 years earlier*

- *The change model and project approach proposed by this client was based on the way we had worked with them on our previous £20m+ project.*

Our reply had to be with the client in a town about three hours away from our office by 11.00 am on 24 August. Between receiving the request for proposal from the client and the late afternoon of Thursday 23 August, our Telecoms Business Unit kept the details of the opportunity to themselves and did not inform any other parts of our company even though this represented a huge profitable opportunity for the company as a whole. In particular, this project would have been bread and butter business for our Strategic Consulting unit, which had done the previous project for this important client. The problem was that the Telecoms Business Unit had its own P&L and by keeping this project for itself, it could make sure it could assign its own consultants and maximise its own profitability and therefore the bonuses of its own vice presidents.

On late afternoon Thursday 23 August, the evening before the final bid document had to be with the client, the Telecoms Vice President, who had been responsible for putting together our proposal, got into a bit of a panic. We'll call him Mr. Canada, as at the time he was arranging his return to Canada and so spent less time in the office than would have been advisable in the circumstances. On a rare visit to his work, he apparently found out that his people hadn't got themselves organised to produce a quality answer and that after two weeks' work only about four pages of a proposal document had been written. Moreover, these four pages were actually just cut and pasted in from a previous failed bid to another company. Mr. Canada realised he could no longer keep the bid within his own division and that he would have to involve Strategic Consulting (where I worked) as corporate transformation programmes were precisely what the Strategic Consulting people had over twenty years experience of implementing. And, of course, they had previously worked with this client. So the Strategic Consulting division had the credibility and had the experience – but they were kept out of the whole bid process till the very last hours as our friends in Telecoms tried to keep this one for themselves.

However, as the reply had to be in by 11.00 am the next morning, it was now too late for Strategic Consulting to achieve the client's deadline. It should be noted that most of our competitors would have had teams of five to ten people working on this bid for the last several weeks. Whereas, because one of our units, Telecoms, tried to run with this alone instead of involving the people who should have been involved, now an hour or two before the closing time, we had not yet made any progress. As the levels of panic began to rise within Telecoms, the client relationship manager was instructed to phone the client and get permission for us to extend the deadline till the morning of Wednesday 29 August.

Friday 24 August – we organised a conference call between Strategic Consulting and Telecoms to try to work out what to do. However, as everyone was leaving early for the three day holiday weekend, nobody was prepared to do any work till the following Tuesday – just a day before the extended deadline expired. I volunteered to work on writing the bid presentation over the weekend; nobody offered to help me. Moreover, most of the people on the call would be not available on the following Monday (due to the holiday) and would be coming in late on Tuesday morning as they returned from the country or from abroad (in many cases, their holiday homes in Tuscany and Provence).

Saturday 25 August to Monday 27 August I wrote a first draft proposal letter and back-up presentation for this client without knowing anything about the telecommunications industry nor what the 23,000 client staff did. Moreover, as I lived in another country from that in which the client was based, I was fairly unfamiliar with that country's Telecoms sector. Though from the name of the client TB Retail, I assumed that TB Retail must have had a lot of retail shops and that most of the 23,000 employees worked in these shops selling phones and Internet connections and that kind of stuff. I wrote the proposal and presentation on the basis of these assumptions.

Tuesday 28 August, I worked with a colleague (who also knew nothing about telecoms) to do a second draft of the proposal. Desperately, I kept phoning any names I had from the Telecoms Business Unit to try and find someone who knew something about telecoms in general and TB Retail in particular to help us.

On Tuesday morning, our Telecoms Business Unit management consulting Vice President, whom we'll call Mr. Smooth, returned from his holiday home in the South of France and came by to see if we had finished the proposal. I explained that we had just started work on it, that I knew nothing about telecoms or TB Retail, that I had nobody to help me and that we had to make a dramatic change in the way we were working together if we were to have a chance of winning this bid. He claimed he could not understand why there was a problem as he had told Mr. Canada his direct report, before he went on holiday, that this was a 'must win' account and therefore this should have been Mr. Canada's top priority while Mr. Smooth was away. Mr. Smooth said he would try to find someone from Telecoms to help us and that he would come back at 17.00 that evening to read what we had done. I asked him to stay and help us. Given his experience of the telecoms industry, his help would have been invaluable. He said he was far too busy and so unfortunately didn't have time.

At around midday, the TB Retail account manager returned from his extended holiday weekend and offered to have a look at our work. Our first surprise came when he told us that TB Retail had nothing to do with shops at all, but in fact consisted of about 20,000 people in call centres and service centres and about 3,000 people doing various kinds of administration – there were no shops! This was not exactly the basis on which we had written the proposal. We spent the rest of the afternoon trying to rewrite the proposal letter and back-up presentation to make them relevant to what we had just learnt, but it was a fairly hopeless task given the incredibly limited time and limited resources we had.

I also had three junior consultants come to help on Tuesday. Knowing nothing about the client nor the industry, there was not much they could do. So I got them searching our companies' databases for references as to where we had successfully done similar work. Although we had once been a world leader in telecoms consulting, the junior consultants had great trouble finding relevant references as our databases had been neglected since the merger and material that should have been easily available was impossible to find.

By midnight on Tuesday 28 August, we completed an attempt at a proposal and hired a car to deliver it to the by 11.00 the next day. We later learnt that our proposal was so poor that, in spite of our successful previous work with this client, we were not even considered for the shortlist. On 18 September we received an E-mail from the account manager, "Gentlemen, I have just heard from TB Retail that we are not short-listed for the transformation opportunity."

I have all the relevant documentation from this fiasco and a tape recording of the vice president for sales in Strategic Consulting describing what a "f—k up" the whole proposal work was due to the failure of the Telecoms Business Unit to start working with us till the night before the deadline.

So, people not listening to the client, not putting the right resources on the job as they tried to look after their own skins, bungling, incompetence, lack of management, leaders avoiding responsibility – our future was at risk.

THE END

During this first year of operation of the big new integrated organisation, the chief executive made many fine pronouncements about the new consulting and IT services powerhouse that he had created:

"It is my strong prediction that the new Group will be famous for innovation and leadership. We will be as flexible as we are global, as insight-based as we are technology-based. We will have a total obsession with delivery and a passion for ensuring this is a great place to work and learn. It will be an organisation filled with real opportunity for those who choose to partner with us as colleagues, clients and stakeholders"[15]

However, in reality the great new group wasn't working, we were losing business hand over fist and the waves of downsizing, all in all up to fifteen thousand people, which followed the merger had as much to do with leadership inadequacy as anything happening in the market. So, rather than integrating three organisations into one, we were dis-integrating.

As the vicious spiral of poor results, lost business and job losses accelerated, many of my colleagues in Strategic Consulting left in despair. An e-mail from one highly respected project manager gives a sense of the feeling of hopelessness that pervaded the company

"It will come as no surprise to those that know me that I resigned today and I will be leaving at the end of August. So this is a goodbye message to a number of people that I have had the privilege of getting to know over the last 5 years. It's a goodbye message in 2 ways.

Firstly I need to say goodbye to AAAA Consulting, with whom I had a highly enjoyable, challenging and fulfilling 4+ years and secondly it's goodbye to the new group.

So firstly it's a sad goodbye to

- *Working with some of the most talented, passionate, team-oriented people that I have ever worked with*

- *Caring about what we do and really making a difference*
- *The most politics-free and rules-free environment I've worked in*
- *Living the values you espouse*
- *Doing things with flair, passion and enjoyment*

Secondly, it's a glad goodbye to what has replaced those things:

- *Working with pompous partners and toadying juniors*
- *Bodyshopping rather than projects*
- *More rules and regulations than 1960s East Germany*
- *Politics rather than passion*
- *Being known as 448684643537*
- *Not feeling like you belong to a team at all.*

The 'merger' has destroyed AAAAA Consulting and all it stood for. It really is time for me to move on. Thank you for giving me a great 4+ years; it was a privilege and a pleasure."

Many colleagues asked me why I stayed on as the company headed ever more rapidly down the pan. The reason was simple – I suspected that at some point the company would initiate a voluntary redundancy programme. It would be foolish to leave with nothing if I could just hold on for a few more months and get paid for going. Sure enough, in November of that year, the country manager where I was based sent out a voice mail and supporting e-mail announcing a redundancy programme:

> *"Since the early part of the year our profitability is not at an acceptable level. Margins are down to 1% in some areas of the business and that, as we all know, is totally unacceptable.*

*Improving our profitability means reducing our cost base. And that means reducing our headcount. **The bottom line is we have to take 750 people out of the business.***"

The intention was to first ask for volunteers, but if there weren't enough volunteers to make up the required 750, then there would be compulsory sackings to reach the numbers needed. To try and encourage volunteers to go, our HR department put together a financial leaving package reasonably above the legal minimum required. What hadn't occurred to our leaders was that so many people were fed up with the company and had no confidence in top management, that there was a rush towards the exit – there were almost a thousand volunteers – rather more than the number required. Suddenly the mishandling of the redundancy process had created a new problem – too many people wanted out. And as always is the case in these situations, it's the good people, who can easily get new jobs, who run for the door leaving the dross behind. A desperate e-mail from one manager in the U.S. summed up his difficulties:

"Here we currently have a voluntary redundancy programme underway. I head up a team and can confirm that it is the best people who are applying to leave. Of my team, 16 out of 21 are applying. The ones that are left are the ones I would choose to lose."[16]

Panic at the top. Although our leaders had promised to let people know within two weeks whether their offers to leave had been accepted, they now realised they were about to lose many of their key people. Loads of frantic meetings to decide what to do. All those above certain level (earning more than $100,000 per year), who wanted out, were told that their applications would be put on hold. Hundreds of us, itching to get our money and run, instead got a letter telling us that our leaders had a small problem – a loss of key management strength:

"As you know, we have been undertaking a review of the applications for Early Retirement and Voluntary redundancy. The review process was designed to make sure that all applications were considered fairly and that the skills and capacity requirements of the business going forward are met. In order to ensure that we have the strength we need at the top of our business, we need to conduct a further review as to whether or not we can accept your application. I regret any inconvenience this delayed decision may cause you."

I believe that about three hundred people actually had their applications to leave turned down. Some I knew had even found jobs to go to and looked quite pissed off when they found that they wouldn't get a pay-off to leave. My application was accepted and my employment terminated with about a $200,000 transfer into my bank account – OK not enough to live on for very long – but I was just pleased to get a little cash from the whole sorry affair and delighted to see the back of this great new global group.

Most of the people I ever worked with are gone, the offices we worked from are gone, the name of the company we worked for is gone, the type of work we did is gone. Over the years, this consultancy had earned hundreds and hundreds of millions for its leaders. A little over a year after the great acquisition and integration, they had effectively slaughtered the goose that had for so many years laid so many golden eggs. Meeting an erstwhile colleague recently, I heard that management have now abandoned the idea of integrating everybody into one huge organisation and are now trying to split the organisation up again into three quite separate units – consulting, IT systems development and IT systems outsourcing – soon the group would be right back where it had started, with exactly the same number of people it had before the acquisition, but billions of dollars poorer than before and with a share price languishing at around 10% of its value before the merger.

By the way, at about this time, the chief executive of the group resigned. Though apparently this departure had nothing at all to do with the abysmal results of the merger. There was no connection, our PR department claimed. He had, the company declared to the financial press, always intended to retire and spend more time with his family when he reached sixty.

As for our competitors, they also went through some difficult times and some were also shedding staff – though nowhere close to the numbers we canned. However, now the consulting market has started to grow again, our competitors are no doubt thriving at our expense as the management consultancy gravy train roars on without us into an undoubtedly extremely lucrative future for all of those involved.

(1) Top-Consultant.com 5 July 2002

(2) Top-Consultant.com 30 April 2002

(3) Top-Consultant.com 1 August 2002

(4) Sunday Times 27 January 2002

(5) The Sunday Times 31 may 1998

(6) Sunday Times 6 January 2002

(7) Business Week Online 28 January 2002

(8) 'Accounting in Crisis' – Business Week Online 28 January 2002

(9) 'Wrong mate at the wrong time' – Business Week Online (contact author for date)

(10) Daily Telegraph (contact author for date)

(11) Business Week Online (contact author for date)

(12) Financial Times' Management 5 October 1994

(13) Financial Times (contact author for date)

(14) Business Week Online 8 July 2002

(15) E Mail to all employees May 2000

(16) E-mail 3 December 2001